Anywhere But India

by Nancy Orr Ramer
with Jan Shaw-Flamm

all good wishes

Nancy Ramer

D1571164

roundtuit publishing

ISBN 1-904499-04-X

First published in United Kingdom of Great Britain in 2004 by
Roundtuit Publishing, 32 Cookes Wood, Broompark, Durham

Printed in the United Kingdom of Great Britain by Prontaprint Durham
Cover design by Carole Moffatt,cover photo of author & writer by Andy Flamm, layout by Stuart Pugh & Nancy Radford

Bob and I dedicate this book to
our Beloved Grandchildren

Jessica, Kelly, Anil
Rob's Children

Sandy, Frances
Nancy Lyn's Children

David, Jonathan, Matthew
Jody's Children

Hannah, Nalini, Jeffrey
Tim's Children

Table of Contents

Foreword i
On Language iii
Note on Photographs iii
Chapter 1: Dirty Wee Protestant 1
Chapter 2: Angel Unaware? 15
Chapter 3: Never Alone 25
Chapter 4: The White Cap 43
Chapter 5: A Declaration of War..55
Chapter 6: Babies, Babies, Babies 75
Chapter 7: The Tooting Nurse...89
Chapter 8: Mr. Dunachie's Bequest...101
Chapter 9: Good Brakes and a Very Good Horn.................................121
Chapter 10: Bob's Backstory 139
Chapter 11: Jasmine and Jacaranda 151
Chapter 12: Mangl Sutra...163
Chapter 13: Buffalo Milk and High-Class Marathi 177
Chapter 14: Long Nose, Short Hair 189
Chapter 15: Repaid a Hundredfold 197
Chapter 16: Diamonds 215
Chapter 17: Lizard in the Curry Pot..231
Chapter 18: Rajamata in a Chevy Pickup...245
Chapter 19: Signs and Wonders...261
Chapter 20: A Garden of Children...279
Chapter 21: Eve Teasing 293
Chapter 22: The Joy of Four Latrines..307
Chapter 23: Farewells 321
Chapter 24: One Chicken, to Go..327
Epilogue..333
Nancy Orr Ramer...334
Jan Shaw-Flamm...334
Author's Acknowledgments 335
Writer's Acknowledgments..336

Foreword

Nancy Ramer has one of the most colourful personalities we have ever encountered. Her passage to India, as a young nurse from Edinburgh Royal Infirmary and St. Colm's Women's Missionary College, was the first step in an extraordinary life and career as a medical missionary, first with the Church of Scotland in Pune, and then after her marriage to Rev. Bob Ramer, with the Presbyterian Church USA in Sangli, Western Maharashtra. We are happy that Nancy has chronicled her life, as her account will inspire and charm readers as much as her presence captivated us.

Nancy came to India just after independence, when the country was struggling to find its own course and the "tryst of destiny" that Jawaharlal Nehru so eloquently alluded to in his midnight speech on August 15, 1947. After a century of medical missions, India had nearly 800 mission hospitals and clinics in 1947, but the number was already falling by the time Nancy took up her post at St. Margaret's, Pune in 1949. Nancy felt her calling was in community health, and soon after she moved to Sangli, after her marriage, she became involved with programs in the urban slums of Sangli. She also supported the community health work of Wanless Hospital, Miraj, and enabled the hospital to hold a weekly clinic at the Sangli mission compound. Nancy was a member of the Board of Wanless Hospital for more than 30 years and a strong champion of nursing.

The Ramers were friends of Kalindi's parents and knew her since she was a little girl. Bob and Nancy had a wide social circle, and soon after we joined Wanless Hospital in 1971, we were privileged to be counted as friends and colleagues. The Ramers kept an open house, and sharing a table there was always an experience. Nancy is a captivating storyteller, and an evening at the Ramers was never complete till she had regaled us with stories of the formidable Scotswomen who reigned supreme in the wards of the Edinburgh Royal Infirmary. With her slight Scottish brogue and uncanny gift of mimicry, Nancy kept us spellbound, and the reader of this book will enjoy the stories as much as we did when we heard them in the Ramers' drawing room after a satisfying dinner of chicken curry, pulav and chappatis.

Bob's passing away in 1984 under tragic circumstances was a blow to Nancy, but she continued her mission for several more years before moving to the U.S. to be with her children. She returned to India a number of times, and we were fortunate to host her when she visited New Delhi. She brought fresh stories and insights into mission work that were informative and inspirational. She remains optimistic and cheerful, and is a source of encouragement to many. Her most endearing qualities are her honesty, her strong Christian faith, and her infinite capacity to forgive. You always know where you stand with Nancy.

So sit back, sip your chai, and enjoy!

Cherian and Kalindi Thomas

Both Drs. Thomas are with the Health and Relief Unit of the General Board of Global Ministries of the United Methodist Church. Cherian is executive secretary, and Kalindi is a community-based health care consultant.

On Language

In a book that deals with events spanning three continents and more than a century, one must make decisions about what language conventions to observe. Nancy lived in Scotland, England, the United States, and India. Each culture has its own flavour of English, and you will find some spellings and conventions of each, as we deemed appropriate. We have attempted to define words that may be unfamiliar to some English-speaking readers.

We have chosen to use the geographical names of the times, e.g., Bombay, rather than Mumbai, in the text. Medical terminology has also changed. Here, too, we have held to the language of the times, even though other terms may be in favour now. It is our hope that readers will understand that "leprosy people" and "epileptic fit" are language of that time, used by people who were devoting their lives to a respectful and compassionate response to the needs of the people.

Note on Photographs

All of the photographs in the book are from Nancy's private collection; most of those taken after 1950 are by Bob, a keen photographer. Except for the cover photograph of the author and writer (kind permission Andy Flamm), one of Bob by son Tim, and the photograph of Nancy and Bob on the day of his death (kind permission Leroy Dillener) it has not been possible to attribute the photographs to any particular photographer.

Nancy's Small World

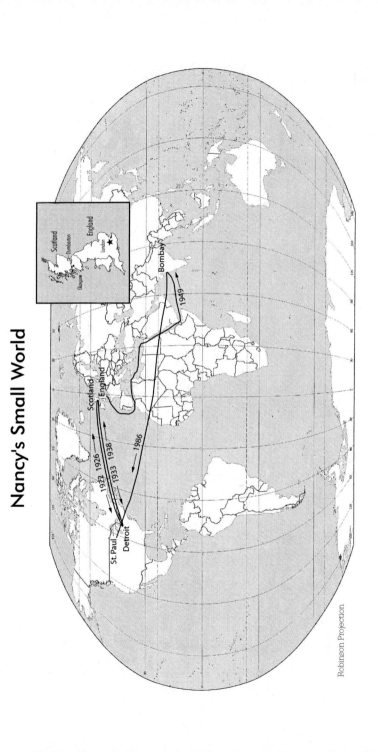

Robinson Projection

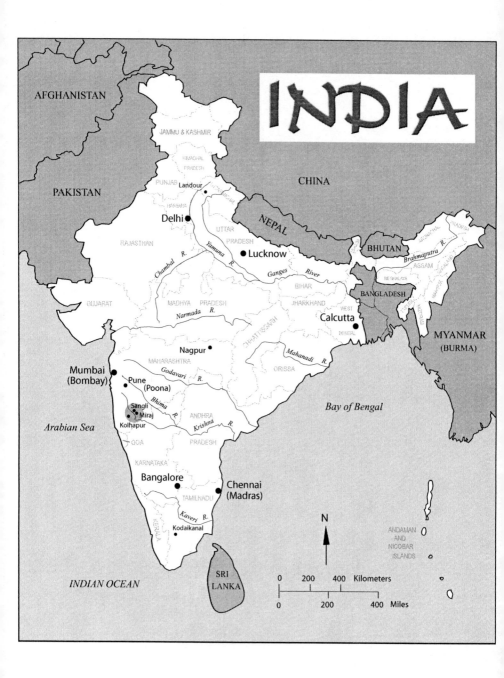

Sangli Mission Compound as Nancy Remembers It

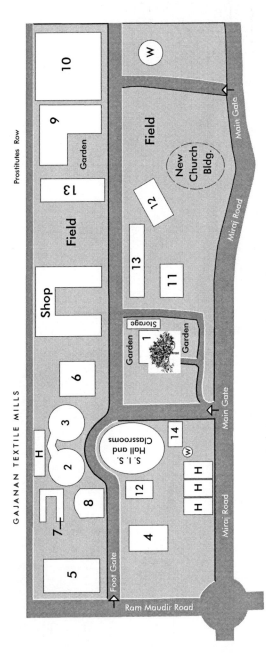

GAJANAN TEXTILE MILLS

Prostitutes Row

Ram Maudir Road

Miraj Road

Main Gate

Foot Gate

Field

Field

Shop

Garden

Garden

Storage

New Church Bldg.

S.I.S. Hall and Classrooms

1 Ramer's Bungalow
2 Creche Nurses Training School
3 S.A.P. Creche (daycare)
4 Lay Leader's Training Center

5 Primary School
6 Priti Jyot Hostel
7 Old Creche Building
8 Dilleners' House

9 S.I.S. Brown Hostel
10 Emmanuel English School
11 Seiberts' Bungalow
12 Staff Quarters

13 Servants' Quarters
14 Car Wash
H House
W Well

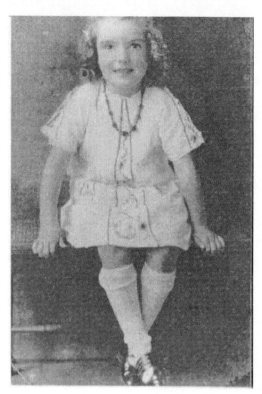

*Proud of myself in a
new dress made by Mother*

Elizabeth Blair Orr, my mother

Chapter 1: Dirty Wee Protestant

"Sixpence for your blessing, dear one, sixpence for your blessing!"

They were often a wee bit worse for the drink, the workingmen on the train from Glasgow at day's end. But to a six-year-old, their offer seemed like a good one. In Scotland in the 1920s, a little girl with blonde hair and brown eyes, an unusual combination, was believed to have special influence with God. The other circumstances of my life gave me few enough advantages, so why shouldn't I take this opportunity to make a few pence? But my mother would pull me close to the window side of the train car, and scold the tipsy men.

"Och," they said, "she has golden hair and brown eyes. She looks like an angel, so God would listen to her!"

"Superstitious nonsense!" my mother objected. "If you think she looks like an angel, I can tell you she doesn't act like one!"

Income was low, but expectations were high in our Scottish household in Dumbarton. Everyone in the family worked in the famous shipyards or for the church, or both. Hard work characterized our lives. It might sound like a dull, pinched sort of life, but for me, it was the beginning of a life of adventure and blessing.

***

My mother was Elizabeth Blair, Lizzie, born and brought up in Dumbarton, Scotland. Dumbarton is an ancient town on the banks of the River Clyde. Its dominant feature is a large volcanic rock hill on the shores of the river, on which stands Dumbarton Castle. In Roman times, this castle was a fortress, the capital of the ancient Kingdom of Strathclyde.

Dumbarton was well known for its shipyards, the most famous of which was Denny's Shipyard. The celebrated clipper ship *Cutty Sark* was built at Denny's. My grandfather Blair was a foreman in Denny's, and his three sons all trained there, two to become marine engineers and one a ship's carpenter.

My mother was the oldest of the children and, at five-foot-eight, tall for a woman of her day. She had dark brown eyes and black hair that she wore long and braided into circles around her ears. Grandpa Blair was tall, too, about six-foot with longish hair and a reddish gray beard, in my earliest memories of him. Grandpa, like everyone in the family, was a born storyteller with a great sense of humour, so laughter was one thing there was always plenty of.

Lizzie was in her late teens, and had taken maybe a year of nurse's training, when her mother died. Naturally, she then stayed home to care for her father and her three brothers. All three were full of mischief, always teasing the local highland "bobby," or policeman, or running up and down the castle. It must have been hard for my mother to have the responsibility for four men, all the washing and cooking, with no gas or electric oven, only coal, a fuel that left everything in the house covered with a fine, black dust. Yet, my mother's stories were not of her burdens, but of laughter and the fun they had together.

The family was a very deeply committed Christian family. There were plenty of good books in the house, but no alcohol, no smoking, and no foul language allowed. Grandpa Blair was a well-respected elder in the Free Church, which later merged with the Church of Scotland. His church, the High Street Church, as it was known, was *the* church in Dumbarton. Lord Overton, the local Laird (the owner of a landed estate), belonged to the church, as did other town leaders, yet I have been told that they listened to my grandfather's opinions, often calling him to emergency meetings.

The church had a mission called the Railway Mission in the poorest part of Dumbarton. There in a small building in the centre of the slums, they served hot tea and buns two or three times a week and held women's meetings, youth club, and gospel meetings. My grandfather used to take responsibility for these programs and often preached there himself. My mother played the organ, having taught herself. It was a portable organ, not a classic church organ, but Mother had some talent and great fervour, and really belted out the hymns.

One night my grandfather had invited a missionary speaker named Tom Orr. Tom had been in Africa, serving on the Congo River in the Qua Iboe Mission in what is now the Democratic Republic of the Congo. Tom had trained in Denny's Shipyard, and had been a carpenter in Dumbarton. But when he heard that the mission needed people to go up the Congo River to establish mission stations and build houses, schools, and hospitals, he had volunteered to go.

The Qua Iboe Mission had a policy that missionaries were not to go upriver and camp on the banks of the Congo in certain times of the year when malaria was especially prevalent. That was a prudent policy, but it meant that Tom would go upriver to the current site, and just when the building was going well, he would have to return to the main base. At first, he agreed to this. However, he learned that, despite carefully locking up his tools before he left, when he got back, the tools would be stolen or broken, and the men and boys he had trained would be off hunting in the jungle. So, every time he had to start all over again.

Frustrated but determined, he took a load of medicine and supplies upstream to where they had decided to build a station. For six months he trained native men and boys, treating his own malaria attacks and continuing to supervise the work even when ill and flat on his back. Ultimately, the station was finished-a hospital hut, a school with a few rooms, a house for the doctor and another for the missionary. But malaria proved to be a formidable opponent, and at the end of that time, he was carried out on a stretcher. His African friends brought him back to base, and from there he was shipped home, unconscious, to Scotland. When he woke up on the ship, he had no idea where he was, or how he came to be there.

While Tom was home in Scotland on sick leave, Grandpa Blair invited him to tell his story at the Railway Mission, where Lizzie was playing the organ as usual. Tom was intrigued with her liveliness and enthusiasm, and Lizzie was fascinated by Tom's experiences, so they soon formed a friendship. By the time he recovered, Tom was prepared to go back to Africa, and Lizzie was ready to go with him.

Lizzie's brothers strongly objected to her friendship with Tom, and when they heard that Tom had asked Grandpa for permission to marry their sister, they didn't hesitate to make their objections known.

"He isn't good enough for Lizzie. He speaks with the wrong accent; he doesn't live in the right part of town."

"He comes from a large family and one of his brothers is an alcoholic. And besides, Tom is two years younger than Lizzie."

But the brothers were no longer living at home, and Lizzie wasn't about to listen to them. Both Jimmie and Bob had married and left Scotland.

Jimmie had emigrated to Canada, and Bob with his family to Detroit, USA. Nat, a marine engineer and the brother closest to Lizzie, had been killed when he fell down the hold of a ship in Spain. His death had been a terrible shock to my mother.

Many years previously, Lizzie had been going with a young policeman, who had been offered an appointment in South Africa and wanted Lizzie to marry him and go to South Africa. But the boys were still all at home then, and Lizzie felt she couldn't leave them. This time, however, she could make her own decision, and she did. Lizzie and Tom, my parents, were married in Dumbarton on March 29, 1912.

Grandpa Blair lived with the couple in Giles Avenue, Dumbarton, and all three were ready and willing to go to Africa. However, Tom was still having intermittent attacks of malaria, and the mission doctors refused to allow him to return, so the family settled down in Dumbarton. Their first child was born on April 16, 1913, and christened Nathaniel Blair Orr. Grandpa was delighted to have a grandson called after him, and it was decided to call the baby "Blair."

The following year the Great War broke out, but Tom was exempt from soldiering for two reasons. He was still subject to malaria attacks, and he was working in the shipyard on priority work for the war effort. Shipbuilding meant long, hard hours of toil, but apart from the malaria attacks, which were becoming less severe, the family kept well. In 1916, to everyone's delight, a second child was born; a little girl christened Elizabeth, and called "Betty."

When Betty was nine months old, in the days before immunization and antibiotics, there came an epidemic of measles. Little Blair got the measles, but soon recovered. Then Betty came down with the measles and, just as she was recovering, she contracted whooping cough. In spite of all the family's care, and all the medical treatment that could be given, baby Betty died.

From the time the war ended in 1918, Lizzie's two brothers had been writing, urging the family to join them in North America. My father was willing, but my mother was loath to leave Scotland, her friends, and her church. Mother had always been active in the choir and the women's association, while my father and grandfather attended Bible class and men's prayer meetings.

In 1921, after nine years of marriage, to everyone's delight, Lizzie and Tom had another little daughter, and that baby was me. I was born in 9 Giles Avenue. I was amused to see that it is recorded that my father was present at my birth. I wonder when they started to put fathers out of the delivery room?

I was named Agnes MacLachlan Orr, after Granny Orr, and called "Nancy." In Scotland, Nancy is understood to be a pet name for Agnes. It's a cherished custom there to call a little girl after the father's mother. My grandmother was called Nancy from when she was a baby, and she was named after her grandmother who was called Nancy. So that goes way back in history.

My father came from a large family, and there were several Agneses born, but none could be called Nancy until my grandmother had died. They were Aggie, Agnes, Nessie, Nanette, and Nan, but I'm the only Nancy because I was the first to be born after her death.

***

I was only six months old in 1922 when at last the family decided to go to Detroit, and Grandpa Blair, of course, went with us. The ethnic groups were very nationalistic then, and there was a large and active Scottish community in Detroit. My uncle was a cheiftan of his Scottish clan. I remember Scottish parties in our home, and two very large men, the Boag brothers, taking me on their shoulders to dance the eightsome reel. I loved it!

Grandpa Blair and I had a very loving relationship. As a wee child, I would steal his eyeglasses and hide them, though I have heard the story so often, I'm not sure whether I remember, or just picture it. Anyway, poor Grandpa couldn't see where I had hidden them, and I would laugh until he gave me a hug and a kiss, then I'd give him back his glasses!

The move wasn't easy for Grandpa Blair, who missed his open fireplace, his church, and his friends. I was three, and he was 83, when he died and was buried in Detroit. We all missed him so much. My mother was still homesick for Scotland and, after five years in America, my father decided that Mother, Blair, and I could go back to Scotland for a year. In America my father had changed from shipbuilding to house building. It was the beginning of the Depression, and my father wasn't sure whether it would be best to stay in America or return to Scotland, so we three went ahead to see what Mother thought of conditions there.

Blair was 13, but I was five years old and have no memory of the ship's journey. For the first few weeks, we lived with my father's sister, Aunt Bessie, in Shettlestone, Glasgow. She had twin daughters about my age, and lived in a tenement, three or four flights up. I thought it was so high, and I was afraid to go down the many flights of stairs.

A friend of my grandfather's in Dumbarton, Mr. Sandy Porterfield, had lost his third wife to cancer just after we came home, and he asked my mother to be his housekeeper, in return for which he would give us room and board. He must have been about 70 at the time, an active and most jolly man, who had worked in the shipyards.

So, we three moved to Dumbarton to live with "Uncle Sandy." His only daughter was married but had no children, so Uncle Sandy spoiled my brother Blair and me. I remember these years so vividly. I always called Mr. Porterfield "Uncle Sandy." He was quite important in the early years of my life, and a very nice man, very jovial, like a grandfather. He was like that with my mother, too. Uncle Sandy ate all his meals with us, and my mother did his washing and looked after the house.

Mr. Porterfield had the bedroom and we had the sitting room, with a bed for Mother and me and a box bed for my brother. Our double bed folded up to the wall, and you put your curtains or wooden shutters over it. There was always room underneath it where you stored your clothes, which were kept in boxes. In old-fashioned houses, we didn't have hangers so much as we have nowadays, so clothes were all kept in boxes under the bed.

We were eager for my dad to join us in Scotland. People kept thinking the job situation was going to get better. The shipyard people kept saying, "Oh, yes, yes, maybe in six months." My father continued to send us money for clothes and expenses and such. He was having a difficult time in Detroit, but he was frightened to come back to Scotland as long as he was still getting odd jobs in America, so one year stretched to five. It was a long time to be separated, but in those days, it wasn't so unusual; the men went wherever they could get work.

I remember in those days, sitting in front of the fire while Mother brushed my hair and then divided it into ringlets that she would roll around an old, clean cotton stocking and then tie up in a knot on the top of my head. She would tell me stories as she did my hair. The ringlets would stay in for a week if simply combed and brushed. I hated this curling ordeal. Mother took a great pride in my hair, but I always wanted it cut short like the other girls.

***

Both Blair and I attended Dumbarton Academy, but Blair was at the high school, and I was at the elementary school at the opposite end of the town. I had a very strict kindergarten teacher, Miss Henderson. No fun and games there. You had to know your alphabet, and sit still and not talk *at all* unless called upon. That proved to be my nemesis-talking! When displeased with me, Miss Henderson would call me up front and twist my cheeks until they hurt. In addition, all the other kids laughed at my American accent and called me a foreigner. We wore uniforms and had to march in and out of the school and the classrooms. I *hated* school.

In Miss Henderson's kindergarten, we were to bring "savings" every Monday. As soon as we had put in 16 shillings, we would get a certificate in our wee blue book. Something like a government bond, these certificates could be redeemed in the post office after a year.

One Monday I was supposed to bring my wee blue book because I had completed 16 shillings the previous week. But I forgot my book, and Miss Henderson was furiously angry, pinched my cheeks, and sent me home to retrieve it. I cried most of the way. When I got home, my mother was in the washhouse. Mr. Porterfield's flat was on the ground floor of a terrace of apartments, and the washhouse where we did laundry was out beyond the backyard. Each flat had its own washday, and ours was Monday.

When I opened the door to our flat and didn't see or hear my mother, I remembered that it was Monday, so I knocked at the flat across the way. You see, Chrissie Kerr lived there and, since she was a few months younger than I, she didn't yet go to school. Mrs. Kerr was not surprised to see me, for I was often home from school due to sickness, so she welcomed me in, figuring that she was helping my mother. Chrissie and I had a fine time until I heard the doorbell and my mother's worried voice, "Mrs. Kerr, have you seen Nancy?" Realizing I was in trouble, Chrissie and I hid under the bed. It was not long until I was dragged out, and given a good scolding and the promise of more when I got home. I was sent back to school with the boy who had been sent to find me, clutching my wee blue book.

I shall never forget the scolding, the twisting of my cheek, and the scorn that Miss Henderson poured on me! I dreaded going home; I had never been so bad before. But, when I walked in the door and my mother saw the black and blue marks on my face, she was furious! I was marched down to the school again, this time to the principal's office, and Miss Henderson was sent for. After that, she never again pinched me, or any other child.

It wasn't just the talking and the forgetfulness that got me into trouble. I couldn't sing, and that was another fault. Miss Henderson seemed to think I sang off-key on purpose. So I was not popular with teacher *or* pupils. My mother took a great interest in my schoolwork, and was greatly upset by Miss Henderson's cruelty. It was heaven to be comforted by my mother when I came home in tears, and she would assure me that I was *not* a "dumb Yankee," but was capable of whatever I was asked to do. Blair, on the other hand, was good at sports, and he soon settled down and enjoyed school. He was on the football team (soccer in American terms) and had started to play golf.

Uncle Sandy was very keen on golf, and he got Blair a job as a caddie. As such, Blair could play as often as he liked. He became a very good golfer and even got my mother interested in playing. She, in turn, tried to interest me and bought me a bag of small clubs, but I found it too boring to walk around a long golf course, trying to hit a wee ball. In the winter, Uncle Sandy and Blair would make their own midget golf course in the kitchen. While they putted, my mother and I would sit by the fire. It was then that she taught me to embroider, knit, mend, and darn. I enjoyed all that for, as we worked, she told me stories of when she was young, or Bible stories, or stories she made up on the spot. They all had to have a happy ending, or I would be reduced to tears.

***

I must have been about six when I became ill with a constant sore throat and swollen glands. This eventually resulted in what I now know was cervical tuberculosis. I had a large swollen gland on the left side of my neck. The doctor wanted to excise it and take out my tonsils, but my mother had a dread of operations, and would not consent. Instead, she took me to a Christian homeopathic doctor in Glasgow. We would go to the clinic, get my medicine, look through the shops, and then attend the gospel meeting in Tent Hall, where everyone was given a free cup of tea and a large bun. Then it was on to Central Station on the tram, and back home on the train, where the motion usually put me to sleep.

It was on these train trips that men sometimes wanted to chat, and asked for my blessing. My conceit was completely squashed the time my mother snorted that I certainly didn't *act* like an angel. Although my mother would humble me and punish me when needed, I knew without a doubt that she loved me deeply.

Mother was very consistent with my treatment. The swelling on my neck had to be treated every night with a poultice that she made. I can't remember if it was a bread poultice or an oats poultice, but it was as hot as I could bear and very comforting. I *had* to eat porridge, but couldn't drink *any* milk. In those days there was no tuberculin testing for cows, and no such thing as pasteurised milk, yet it was known that TB was spread through milk.

I missed a great deal of school with my tubercular glands. Eventually, the swelling came down from the back of my ear, right down to beneath my chin. I wore bandages during the day and poultices at night. Finally, after a couple of years of this treatment, the hard lump broke, and there was continuous discharge from a little round hole. My mother would clean the sore morning and evening, and for going to school I wore a ribbon around my neck to cover the bandage. Fortunately, it was quite fashionable to have a ribbon to match your dress. I also went to "sunlight classes" to have ultraviolet rays applied to my neck. It healed very slowly, and I still have a very small scar on my neck. I think the TB episode lasted for about three years, until I was nine.

∗∗∗

When I was going to school in Dumbarton, there was great animosity between the Protestants and the Catholics. Remember, this was in 1926-1930. Dumbarton Academy was a public school (private school in American terms), and I'm sure we were a lot of snobs! Our school uniform in winter was a dark blue heavy coat, navy skirt, white blouse, royal blue cardigan, and a black velour hat with a blue-, gold-, and white-striped band around it. In the summer, we had white Panama hats with the school band around them. The Wee Academy was held in a beautiful, old building downtown. The Big Academy, which my brother Blair attended, was a new building on the outskirts of Dumbarton.

We had no school buses, so I had to walk to school, about ten blocks into the centre of the city. Unless I went about half a mile out of my way, I had to go under the railway bridge. At the side of the bridge was a large tenement where a number of poor Catholic families lived. They used to yell at us, "dirty wee Protestants!" It was all right when I had the other children to walk with me, but if I was late going or coming, I was scared stiff.

One day I was heading to school, all decked out in my summer uniform— white skirt, royal blue blazer, and white Panama hat. I can just imagine what went through the Catholic children's minds to see this vision in summer array prancing down the street. Hold in mind that I was only six years old and had no idea of the devious mind of boys. When they yelled "dirty wee Protestant," I yelled back, "You're a dirty wee Catholic!" So much for my original wit. That was enough! Mud balls came flying at me— on my white hat, my skirt, in my hair, and a particularly skooshy one all over the back of my blazer!

What could I do? I couldn't go to school in such a mess. Of course, I ran when they started to pelt me, but I had run toward the town. To go back home to change, I had to walk the long way around, crying all the way. I had looked forward to Mother's sympathy, but she wasn't at home. My next-door neighbour washed off as much of the mud as she could, and then walked me halfway to school—far beyond the danger area. But I had to explain to my teacher, and everyone sympathized with me. After school the big boys walked me home, then they went back and started a *real* mud ball fight. My mother walked me part way after that, but we never saw the boys, or if we did, they ignored us. I expect their mothers had taken a hand in the peace negotiations.

***

The River Leven joined the Clyde just beyond our church. Over the Leven bridge was a lovely public park, where I remember our school had an annual wreath-laying ceremony. It was in honour of King Robert, the Bruce, who defeated the English at the Battle of Bannockburn in 1314.

This Scottish hero is famous for the oft-told tale of the spider. Bruce had had many battles with the English and, having escaped after another defeat, he was hiding in a cave, which we were told was on the banks of the Clyde near Dumbarton. Bruce was discouraged and contemplating surrender, when he noticed a spider building a web. Each time the spider got to a certain spot, the web would break, but the spider tried again and again, and after many attempts, finally wove a beautiful complete web. Bruce was challenged and decided, "I *will* try, try again," which he did, and went on to finally defeat the English and gain freedom for Scotland. That tale was told us many, many times.

When I was a first grader, I was chosen to lay the wreath. There were bagpipes and much marching about. I did not have to speak, only go forward and lay the wreath at the foot of the statue. The admonitions from my mother had been endless. "Don't get your uniform dirty. Remember to keep your hat on straight." Much to my mother's surprise, I stayed clean, kept my hat on, and laid the wreath with great aplomb, saluting the flag and then turning to salute the assembled school, as I had been taught. I even stood at attention all through the speeches, never talking. This amazed my mother and my brother Blair, who even said he was proud of his wee sister. That was high praise indeed. Incidentally, you will find caves all around Scotland where Bruce is supposed to have seen the spider. Who can prove it?

***

The Wee Academy had a half day every Wednesday, the day of Mother's meetings, when she was often asked to speak or lead the Bible study. When she did, she liked to have a suitable solo to go with her message. Sometimes she would sing the solo herself, but at some point she decided to teach me to sing. Unfortunately, I had inherited my father's voice, and my singing was beyond hope. Finally she gave up on solos in favour of "recitations." She would teach me sacred poetry appropriate to her message. I had found my talent and could recite with great feeling, reducing the dear women to tears! Together, we were often asked to go to meetings. Mother would preach, and I would recite.

We went to all the church activities—Sunday School, Women's Guild, all the various teas and parties. When I was about eight, Mother and I went on the women's annual picnic, an event that was a day's tour. We stopped in Callendar, a lovely spot, where the women had games and races. As usual, my mother was in the thick of things. She entered a relay race and was going great when she fell very hard on her face and head. When she tried to stand, her head was covered in blood. I was terrified. We were taken to a local doctor who cleaned up the wound in her head and put in seven clips. Her knees had to be cleaned up, too, and she looked like a wounded soldier by the time we got home. Her head wound soon healed, but Mother never seemed to regain her boundless energy after that.

The minister at our Church of Scotland was very well known, as he was the first moderator of the United Church of Scotland when the "Free" church came back into the fold. Dr. Inch was a real pastor at heart; he knew everyone and was a renowned preacher. The Sunday School was a particular love of his. We met every Sunday afternoon at 3 p.m. and Dr. Inch was often there, listening to us reciting our lessons. He was a very stout man and always made jokes about his girth and the irony of his name.

During communion, children sat upstairs in the balcony. Non-communicant members, those too young or for other reasons not entitled to communion, always sat in the back of the church or up in the balcony. White cloths were laid over the hymnbook ledges. To keep me from talking, my mother used to give me an "imperial." This was a hard mint candy that had to be sucked, something like a jawbreaker. It was impossible to bite it with your teeth until almost the end when the large lozenge had become tiny. Suddenly it would disintegrate, and a wonderful burst of sweet peppermint filled your mouth. One communion Sunday, sitting in the balcony, sucking my imperial, and resting my chin on the rail, I watched with fascination as the communion was given out. Suddenly my lozenge popped out of my mouth, down onto a devout baldhead! I disappeared under the seat. Fortunately, my mother never saw the episode, so there was no further investigation. I am so grateful that the poor man suffered in silence!

When I was nine, we moved to Glasgow, about 20 miles from Dumbarton, because Blair had graduated from high school and found a day job as an office boy in Glasgow while he went to night school at Glasgow University. Mr. Porterfield was growing progressively weaker, and his daughter moved into an apartment next to him, leaving us free to move.

When we first moved to Glasgow, we lived in Shawlands, and I went to Shawlands Academy. When it became too expensive, after about a year, we moved to Battlefield in Glasgow, where I attended Battlefield Academy. By my second year in Glasgow, I had found my feet and was doing well in school, but I can't claim credit for that. Every evening after supper, my mother would sit at the kitchen table with me and watch me do my lessons. Not only that, but I had to recite everything I had learned that day. Mother knew neither algebra nor Latin, but even when I recited in those subjects, she could always tell when I was bluffing. After lessons, it was always down on our knees for family prayers before we went to bed. Even when Blair was in high school, he had to be home for evening prayers by ten o'clock, and I never heard him argue the point.

Before we even left Dumbarton for Glasgow, my mother had started to have severe abdominal pain and vomiting. By the time I was ten and we were living in Glasgow, her illness had been diagnosed as gall stones, which in those days was highly serious. The doctors told her there was no effective medicine. The chances of a successful operation were very poor, but they urged her to have the surgery nonetheless.

My father was still in Detroit earning some money by repairing houses, and every month he sent what he could. The Depression was still on, and no one knew if he could get work if he returned to Scotland. So my mother never told my father of her illness, but returned to the homeopathic doctor who had treated me. He was a great Christian, and promised that he could dissolve the stones without an operation. Neither Blair nor I realized that my father had not been told.

For three years, my mother suffered intense pain that grew worse and worse, but the doctor assured her that she had to get worse before she would get better. With a gallbladder attack, you pass a stone and you feel better, and then you have it again, and every attack is worse. She would go for three months or more without any attacks, so she would think she was getting better, only to suffer another bout. The doctor said the medication was dissolving the stones, but it wasn't, it was just the natural passing of the stones. Mother's constant worry was, "If something happens to me, what will Nancy and Blair do?"

One day Uncle Sandy came to visit, and he was shocked to find my mother bedridden. He may have been the one who wrote and told my father. By this time, my mother could not keep any food down and had constant diarrhoea. Blair would wash out the sheets in the bathtub.

One morning, just before I went to school, my mother fainted as she came out of the bathroom. I was so scared and hadn't a clue what to do. Then I remembered reading stories of the Girl Guides (Girl Scouts in America are similar) that advised, "When someone feels dizzy, give them water." Crying and praying, I rushed to get a glass of water and tried to make my mother drink it. Being unconscious, the water just ran over her face, but that brought her around, and I helped her into bed. My mother explained that you should never try to give water to an unconscious patient. I said then, "When I grow up, I want to be a nurse, so I will know what to do when people are ill."

It was a commitment that would guide my entire life.

Chapter 2: Angel Unaware?

One day when I came home from school, I saw a suitcase in the hall, and the stickers showed it was from America. I thought, "My dad!" and you know, I was *scared*. I was 10 and a half. I hadn't seen my dad for five years, and I was really scared. I'd had Uncle Sandy, and then my brother Blair as acting head of the family. I had always looked up to *them* and then my father came in. So many of the children during the war had such a hard time adjusting to their fathers coming back.

I walked into the sitting room where my mother and father were hugging each other, and I was *very* jealous. I'd never seen my mother hugging a man. She was only hugging him, they weren't doing anything else, but I was just shocked!

Mother's health was growing worse and worse, and she began to realize that she wasn't going to get better. She had written to her brother and told him that she was really ill, but she still hadn't told Tom, my father, because of the unemployment situation. If you've been out of the country, you're the last to be taken on anywhere. But either Uncle Sandy or my Uncle Bob in Detroit must have told my father. My dad didn't have money to come back to Scotland, but he was able to get onto a cattle ship. That was the way to travel in those days if you had no money. You'd clean out the hold on the ship, and for that you'd get free transport and board. He didn't tell us he was coming because I guess he didn't know when he would arrive.

So, my father moved in with us. I remember there was some embarrassment the first night my father was home. I had always slept with my mother for as far back as I could remember, and I absolutely refused to sleep on the couch or in Blair's room. It was decided that "for now, 'til she gets used to you being here," my father would sleep on the couch. I am ashamed of my behaviour now, but then I did not understand, and would not even let them move me after I went to sleep.

Fortunately, my father got a job in a furniture company. In those days the furniture companies were also moving companies; they moved people from house to house. There was a lot of work in that area during the Depression because people were moving out of Glasgow to the country to live in old dilapidated cottages where they felt they could live cheaper. My dad would go along with the van loaded with their furniture. Part of his contract with the firm was that he would do what carpentry needed to be

15

done to the cottage to bring it back up to liveable condition, so he would stay there for a week or two to do that. He got the job because he could do it all—move furniture, make cottage repairs, and fix any furniture that was broken.

***

Then my mother became very seriously ill. She slept on the couch in the kitchen, and my father and brother slept together. For a while, she continued treatment with the homeopathic doctor, but my father got mad about that. My brother had a friend who was a doctor, and he came to the house, examined her, and said, "She's dying, she's got to go to hospital." In those days they took people to the hospital to die. He said, "She's got jaundice throughout her system, which has destroyed her blood," so she had pernicious anaemia, though it was all a result of the gallstones.

My dad was paid by the hour for the days that he worked. It was very irregular, but the main difficulty was that he was away for long periods. My brother Blair, though still living at home, was putting in long days. He would walk into the city, about a 45-minute walk, and he would be at work all day. Then he went to night school, and walked home after that, arriving about 10:30 at night. That was another reason my mother had to go in hospital. I was in school, and there wasn't anybody to take care of her.

So Mother went by ambulance to Southern General Hospital, Glasgow, to die.

About that time, my mother wrote to my Uncle Bob in Detroit, her younger brother, whom she had looked after when their mother died. She asked Uncle Bob and Aunt Maggie if they would take me, at least through high school, because she could see that my father couldn't support me and pay the rent for a decent house. Plus, he was away so much, who was going to look after me? My uncle wrote back and said, "Yes, we'll take Nancy." My mother made that arrangement without telling my father. I know because my father was very upset when he found out. He found it devastating to realize that he couldn't take care of his family. I realize that now, but I didn't know it then. My father still kept hoping for a miracle, so that the family need not break up.

I was slowly losing my antagonism toward my father. As I look back on it, my father had a great deal of patience. At first, my father would not agree to my going to America, but after Mother went into hospital, my father saw the need to have someone to look after me. Many nights I was alone from after school until Blair got home late at night. My father had two or three sisters, but each had her own family to take care of. His older sister Aunt Agnes came from a small town called Girvan for a while, but she hated Glasgow, and soon went home.

Three times a week after school, I would take a bus to Southern General to visit my mother. After the first hugs and kisses, it was, "Nancy, let me listen to your lessons." She was so weak, but she would nod her head if she thought I sounded sure of myself. If not, it was, "Nancy, get out your book, and read that lesson out loud. Solve the problem like the book says. Don't guess!" After my lessons were heard, she would ask me to recite Bible verses, or one of the sacred poems I used to say at the women's meetings.

The last time I visited her, it was the same routine, until at the end, she said, "I will recite the verse." She recited the 23rd Psalm, then holding my hand she repeated, "Though I walk through the valley of the shadow of death, I fear no ill, for The Lord is with me. His rod and staff comfort me." As I looked at her, she said, "Nancy, never fear the shadows, for Jesus is with you. Never forget that Jesus is with you. He will never leave you alone." I kissed her and promised to be back in two days.

✳✳✳

The next day was a happy day at school. I no longer remember why my friend and I were laughing, but we giggled all the way up the two flights of stairs to our apartment. As I opened the door, I heard weeping, and my heart froze. I knew what it meant! My friend took one look at my face, and ran back down the stairs. Reluctantly, I made my feet move, taking me into the kitchen. My father sat with his head in his hands, and looking up said, "Your mother is with the Lord."

My brother came in at that moment; I rushed to him and begged, "Tell me it isn't true." He just hugged me. In those days men never cried.

My next clear memories are of the day of the funeral. My father's sisters and brothers came. In Scotland at that time, women had no part in funerals, so the sisters gathered in our house to have tea ready for the men when they came back. All the men went to the hospital, had a service in the hospital chapel, and went from there to the cemetery in Dumbarton. I was angry at my father because he wouldn't let me go to the funeral, or even see my mother after she died. "It is not good for children to be at funerals or to see death," was all that my father would say.

While the men were gone, my Scottish aunts sat around our apartment and gossiped, and then went into my mother's bedroom. I followed and found one of my aunts taking out all my mother's dresses and coats and laying them on the bed. The aunts were all laughing and trying the clothes on, making derogatory remarks. They were saying, "Bessie, you take this, you can get it altered to fit you, and you take that." I was so shocked and upset that I ran out of the house. I felt so alone, but where could I go?

About two blocks away was a garage. In those days the garages had the pumps inside a closed building, and the cars drove through the building. Along the side they had half walls, with smooth iron bars above that. Often we children would swing on the bars, and do all kinds of tricks. I used to go there and do that just for fun.

That day I just ran out of the house and ended up at the garage. I was sitting there alone, swinging and crying, feeling absolutely miserable. I was 12 years old.

"Why are you crying?"

I stopped whirling on the bars and looked around to see who had spoken. A little girl with long, dark hair, about my own age, was sitting on top of the adjacent bar. I had never seen her before, but she was so friendly.

"My mother died a few days ago, and they have just buried her."

"Oh. And why aren't you home?"

I said, "Well, my dad is gone to Dumbarton to the cemetery." I told her what my aunts were doing, and I said, "I'm not going to stay in the house with *them!*"

We sat in silence, until she asked, "Why don't you go to your church?"

"My church is too far away, I need bus fare, and I don't have any!"

We sat for a wee while. The girl— I never did find out her name—said, "My 'church' is just across the street, come with me, and we'll pray."

I looked up, and there was the synagogue, which I had passed many times. "But I am not Jewish, they won't let me in."

"Oh, yes," she replied.

"Well, what would we do?"

"Well, we could just sit and pray."

Now prayer was a very important element of our family life. Every night before we went to bed, we knelt and prayed, and every morning we had prayer before the day started, so praying was a very natural thing to do. Again the little girl said, "Why don't you and I go over there?"

"Oh, OK." So we went over, and she put her arm around my neck. We went into the synagogue. It was very different from our church, but they had pews, and we sat in the back. The two of us just sat there and she said, "I'm praying," and I said, "So am I."

We did not pray aloud, but I certainly had a long conversation with God. I asked why He hadn't answered my prayer to make my mother better. Why no one seemed to want me. What would I do without Mother? Oh, I just poured out everything in weeping and silent petition. As I prayed, I felt relieved, and at peace. I remembered my mother saying to me the day before she died, "Nancy, remember you are never alone. God is always with you." I remembered her praying, "Even though I walk in the shadow of the valley of death I will fear no ill, for Thou art with me." I realized then that my mother was no longer in pain, she was with Jesus, and I just knew He would look after us all.

Slowly a peace came into my mind and heart. I was very aware of God's presence, and felt surrounded by love. We sat for a long time, maybe half an hour. My new friend simply knelt beside me. After a while, I grew calm and stopped crying. When I took some deep breaths, she said, "Do you want to go home now?"

"What time is it?" I asked.

"It's getting dark."

"Oh, maybe my dad and brother will be home."

"I'll walk home with you and if they're not, we'll just go for a walk."

So we began to walk, and just as we got to the block where our apartment was, I saw my father and brother coming out, my brother going in one direction and Father in the other. They had to be looking for me. When I saw my father, I said, "Oh, Dad," and I went running to him and hugged him. He called my brother back, and with all the kerfuffle of meeting him and explaining why I had run away and all that, when we turned around, the girl was gone. I never saw her again.

Some people have said, "Maybe it was an angel," and maybe she was. I don't know. I had never seen her before, so she must have moved in different circles. But she was there that day, and I felt greatly comforted.

***

One of the aunts stayed with us for a couple of weeks, but she was very difficult—not cruel, but very difficult with all of us. When she left, my father arranged for me to call in on the next-door neighbour during the day. She was an elderly widow, not warm and lovely, but nice enough. But our family was a very loving family. We always hugged each other before we left in the morning, and I missed that very much.

But one thing the neighbour taught me was, "You're now a lady; you're 12 years old, and a lady always makes her own bed. Whenever you get up, you make your bed." That has always stuck with me, so even now when I get up, I go to the bathroom, and I come back and make my bed. My husband used to laugh about it, "If I change my mind and decide to go back to bed, I can't—she's made it!"

Eventually my father accepted that I would have to go to America. So we went to the U.S. consulate in Glasgow to see what had happened to the entry visa application that my mother had sent some months previously. The application was found, my uncle's letter attached, and we were told to wait till the authorities had investigated further.

After exhausting his patience, my father returned to the consulate and told them it was a near emergency. Finally, my father, my uncle, and the immigration people agreed on an arrangement. When I was in Britain, my father was my guardian, but when I was in the United States, my guardian was Robert Blair, my Uncle Bob. That took quite a long time to get straightened out. Then came another hold-up. My aunt had goitre trouble, and was scheduled to have surgery, so we decided to wait until after the operation. Then Aunt Maggie wrote and said, "The doctor thinks he can do it an with medical treatment so send Nancy as soon as you can!"

Early in October, we received word that my visa had been approved. There were many further visits to the embassy, more physical exams, back and forth. So much legal business. Then I was told to "go as soon as possible, before the visa runs out!" But where would we get the money for my travel?

My father was desperately looking for extra work to earn money for my passage. I remember him saying to Blair, "I do not want to ask Bob Blair to pay her fare over there as well as everything else." I heard Blair say, "Your brother, Uncle Archie, is wealthy. Why don't you ask him?" My father had three brothers, one of whom had done very well for himself. Uncle Archie was a marine engineer with the Burmah Oil Company in Burma. At that time he was home on leave in Glasgow, and he owned a lovely bungalow in a posh area of Glasgow. He, though not his wife, had come to my mother's funeral.

"I am not asking Archie for *anything!*" my father declared. Neither Blair nor I had ever met Uncle Archie and his family.

One day Blair said to me, "It's just my father's pride that he won't ask Archie. Surely, Archie could pay the £100 for your travel, and when the shipyards open, my father could pay him back, or when I finish school, *I* could pay him back. A hundred pounds is nothing to Uncle Archie." So Blair and I, without telling my father, took two tramcars to the other end of Glasgow, arriving at Uncle Archie's bungalow in the early evening.

It was a Sunday, and when we arrived at the house, it was evident they had guests. We hadn't known that, of course. We were nervous and hesitated for a long time. It was getting dark when, finally, Blair said, "We've come all this way, we better just go ahead." We marched up to the door and rang the bell. A very well dressed lady answered the door.

I didn't even know what my aunt looked like because she'd never had anything to do with us. Blair told her that he was Uncle Archie's nephew, and that we just needed to have a brief talk with Uncle Archie; it was an emergency in the family. I remember my aunt saying, "Oh, I know all you Orr. You're all unemployed and your mother has died, and you'll be begging for money, and we are *not* having beggars!" Evidently, Dad had known she was like that, but we didn't.

Blair and I were stunned, and we had turned to go away. Then Uncle Archie came to the door, just as she was shutting it on us. He said to Blair, "Come to my office tomorrow," and gave him a card.

On the way home Blair cautioned me, "Don't tell Dad, he'll be livid." The next day Blair went to Uncle Archie's office, and Uncle Archie gave him a check for £150. He gave him a bit more, he said, "because Tom is needing the help."

My father had a temper, which you didn't see very often, but he was *so* angry. "You have humiliated me!" He was so angry that he would have torn up the check, but Blair held on and wouldn't give it to him. There was such an argument between them. I'd never seen them argue, we never *had* arguments, so I went running to the woman next door for help, and she came in. Then my father and brother were so embarrassed.

Going to Uncle Archie was something my father always held against my brother. He was very, very, very angry about that. Nevertheless, he did take the £100. He accepted the money that paid for my fare, but not the additional money.

Because he couldn't afford the rent, my father could go into a workmen's hostel. As for my brother, there was a widowed lady at the church, Mrs. Black, who lived in a nice house with her daughter, Nanette. She asked if Blair, and another university student who was the son of missionaries, would like to live in the nicely furnished basement in exchange for taking care of the garden and house maintenance. They could have breakfast, dinner, and a room for that. He agreed, and lived there for about three years.

***

Because Blair had gone to Uncle Archie's office for the check, Archie knew that Blair was studying accountancy, to get his CPA. It took a year, maybe two, until Blair finished, but then Uncle Archie helped him get a job with the Burmah Oil Company. While I was in America, he went to Burma, so Uncle Archie came through on that. By that time Uncle Archie had been transferred to a Burmah Oil Company job in Glasgow, but my father never knew it. He just knew Blair went to Burma.

About eight years after I had gone to America, and indeed, had returned to Scotland and was doing nursing, my father got word that Archie wanted him to come to his home. His wife was dying. All their lives my uncle and aunt had separated themselves from the church, and now Archie was distraught. My father went to visit them, prayed with them, and arranged for a minister to come and visit.

When Archie's wife died, my father made all the arrangements. Blair and I went to the funeral and met our cousins, Archie's son and daughter, for the first time. Their mother had left everything to them. They had gone to a posh boarding school and were uninterested in having any further contact with us. I often wonder what happened to my cousins. I heard they became Communists. Of course, it wasn't as bad to be a Communist in those days. It was during the war, and Russia had become our ally, so there wasn't the stigma to Communism that there was in the U.S. in the 50's.

After that, my father would sometimes meet Archie in town, and they would have a meal together. He and my father became quite friendly without the wife. I wouldn't be surprised if my father paid him back that £100, because he was determined to do so the minute he had the money. By this time, my father was back in shipbuilding, working on the *Queen Mary*.

About a year later, Uncle Archie died, and my father was to make all the arrangements. Uncle Archie had said he wanted a church service when he died, but his son absolutely refused to have a church service. He told my father, "Well, you can pray if you want to, but we will not have a funeral service in the church." My father later told me that there was hardly anybody at the cemetery. Uncle Archie had had lots of friends with the Burmah Oil Company, but they had become separated, maybe over the Communism business.

Alas, Blair and my father never became close again. Blair worked in Burma, got married, and joined the airforce. My father married again, too. If they'd continued to live close, I think they might have come around. Fortunately, Blair came to the hospital to see my father when he was ill, and they made their peace before he died.

***

Blair's son, my nephew, once asked me, "What was the real issue between them?" I don't really know, but my father's pride was so tender then, having lost my mother, and then having to turn to his wife's brother and his own brother. I only ever saw Uncle Archie twice, but I'll never forget the humiliation on that doorstep.

I was glad that Dad had the opportunity to repay his brother, if not in money, then certainly in kind.

Chapter 3: Never Alone

The fourth of November 1933, was a dismal day. A drizzle of rain obscured the otherwise beautiful view of the River Clyde. Tears poured down my face as I waved to my father and brother, who stood on the dock to see me off to America. I was 12 years old. Our home was broken up, my father and brother each on their own, and me on my way to live with my uncle's family in Detroit. It was turning out much as my mother had planned in the final months of her illness, taking care of me with her last thoughts and energy.

Now I stood at the stern of the Cunard liner *The Athenian*. As the ship sailed into the estuary of the Clyde, the mighty engines started. I stood in the misty rain and gazed at the water as the engines carved it into beautiful foaming curves radiating out from the back of the ship. White, green, blue-black curves, topped with sparkling foam.

Farewell to Scotland. Today, I was on my way! Few people crossed the Atlantic Ocean in November, so I had a cabin to myself. I leaned on the deck rail, a solitary figure wearing a tweed coat over my kilt, trying to avoid the stewardess who was so eager to comfort me. What would happen if I jumped into that churning whirlpool? Would anyone know or care? In my mind, I heard my mother's voice, "Remember, Nancy, wherever you go, Jesus is with you. You are *never* alone!" But if that was true, why hadn't He answered my desperate prayers to heal her? Yet, to the day she died, my mother's faith remained strong. She had quoted the 23rd Psalm, "Though I walk through the valley of the shadow of death, I shall not be afraid for He is with me!"

I must have stood there for over an hour, when an arm slid gently around my shoulders. "Come, it is time for the evening meal."

"I'm not hungry."

"Perhaps not hungry, but you are wet through, and tired. Come out of this cold, damp air into the cabin."

I was shivering, my teeth chattered, and it was a relief now to go with this motherly stewardess. She coaxed me to take a warm bath, and I began to feel comforted, but when I climbed into bed, my fears flooded back. What would Uncle Bob be like? And Aunt Maggie? What would I say to them when I met them? Should I hug and kiss them, or just shake hands? I knew them only from faded snapshots. The stewardess was unpacking my suitcase, so when the tears flowed again, I hid my face beneath the sheet. Kindly, the stewardess tried to persuade me to eat from the tray that had been brought to the cabin, but I refused to take my head out of the blankets. With the click of the door as she left, more tears, more sobs burst out of me.

Then I heard the door open, and a deep male voice said, "On this ship, I am as your father. I know your father and brother are very sad at your leaving." I was so surprised, not only to hear a *male* voice, but because I had never thought about how Blair and my father felt. Poking my head up out of the covers, I saw that it was the captain of the ship, a rotund man with a smiling face. "Now, tell me what your mother or father would do before you went to sleep!"

Awed, my tears ceased, and I answered, "We had prayers every night."

"Well, then," said Captain Brown, "we shall have prayers! Will you pray, or shall I?"

"At home I always prayed first, because I'd always fall asleep when my parents prayed."

"Very well, you go ahead. Remember to pray for your dad and brother, for they are also very unhappy tonight." So I prayed, and then Captain Brown prayed. When we finished, he gave me the apple he had brought. Apples were expensive. I hadn't had one in a long time, and it was irresistible. While I nibbled at the apple, Captain Brown talked of his own family. I can't remember his stories now, but I sat enthralled then. As I listened, I reached for toast from the tray, a cup of tea, and some fruit. I began to get drowsy, and when Captain Brown took his leave, at last I fell asleep.

In the morning I felt much more cheerful, finding my way to the dining room and exploring the ship. The weather was stormy, as it usually is in November on the Atlantic. I remember standing with Captain Brown on the bridge and seeing icebergs in the distance. The ship really rolled in the storm, and I was strictly forbidden to go outside on deck. If I needed anything, one of the crew would help me. I soon began to feel at home with all these friendly Scottish sailors. Every night, Captain Brown came with the stewardess to my cabin to have prayers with me and tell stories.

After ten days on the ship, the stewardess told me, "Have a good, hot bath, and wash your hair. The immigration officers will come on board early tomorrow morning to examine you."

"Who are they? Why should I wash for them?"

"They will ask you many questions before you are allowed to enter the U.S.A.!"

"Then we must be near land. Will we be in America tomorrow?"

"No, tomorrow we are due to dock in Quebec, Canada. There the immigration officers will come aboard."

Very early the next morning, the stewardess awakened me. I dressed and was taken to the purser's office to meet the immigration authorities. I had become used to smiling, friendly people, but these were men in civilian clothes, with *no* smiles about them. They frowned at me and asked, "Why are you going to the U.S.A.?"

"To live with my uncle. These are my papers."

"Hmm! Passed by the consulate in Glasgow. Tell me, what work does your uncle do?"

"Oh," I answered cheerfully, "he works in Ford Motor factory."

"How much does he earn?" I hadn't a clue!

"Does he own his house?"

"Yes."

"Is it paid for?" I hadn't the slightest idea.

"Does he own his car? Does your uncle have any loans out?" I couldn't answer any of these questions. The officers were clearly frustrated and angry. "Who will pay for your return to Scotland?" That really frightened me! How could I go back? There no longer *was* a home in Scotland. The officers ordered me off the ship, to be taken immediately to the immigration house in Quebec. I was terrified! What had I done wrong? The officers had no time for explanations or chitchat.

The stewardess called Captain Brown, who hurried to the officers. "I will take responsibility until she gets to Detroit. Our ship docks in Montreal, and I have leave. I am at present in charge of her, so I accept the responsibility to deliver her to her uncle. He is to meet her in Windsor, so he will be with her when she enters the U.S.A."

But the officers were not about to listen to Captain Brown. "You are only her guardian while she is *on* the ship. We will notify her uncle that she is now in government custody."

Quickly, I packed. I hadn't had breakfast, but the thoughtful dining room stewards brought me a basket of food and fruit. With the Captain still protesting, uniformed officers hurried me down the gangplank. I was whisked off in a blacked-out van, through locked gates in very high walls, past armed guards who inspected the van as we drove through. I was hurried into a fort-like building, through more locked gates, past more armed guards, and up in an elevator. A guard locked the elevator as we entered and unlocked the lift gates as we exited on the top floor.

A heavyset woman in uniform came smiling to meet us. I said, "Good morning," and she answered in French! I was put into a room with two cots. The other occupant was a German-speaking woman in her fifties. Before long, the warden came to take me to the cafeteria for breakfast. It was a huge room, women on one side with their children, men on the other side, with a tall wire fence separating them. The cafeteria doors were locked, and a guard stood at attention as we entered. When some of the women saw their husbands on the other side of the room, they rushed toward the fence. The guards yelled, and surrounded them, pointing their guns and pushing them back into line on the women's side.

I'd been standing in line for food, but frightened by this show of force, I was overcome with fear and nausea, and turned crying to the warden who stood at the entry door. "I'm not hungry, *please* let me go back to my room." The warden was a kindly woman and, speaking to the guard in French, she took me back to my room. I never went back to the cafeteria again. I was terrified that I would do something wrong and bring all those guards after me. Fortunately, I had the food from the ship, which I had slipped under the bed . . . but the warden didn't know that!

In this immigration "prison," there was a large common room with a huge bay window, where we detainees were allowed to sit. The windows were barred, but there was a beautiful view of the cliffs on the other side of the St. Lawrence River. There were magazines and books to read, all of them in French. I tried to ask for books in English, but nobody understood me.

The only book I had brought with me was the Bible, so I made myself comfortable in the window seat and started at the beginning, Genesis, of all places! So boring, but at least it was something I could do to distract myself and avoid getting into trouble. One of my few privileges was to go to the bathroom without the warden, and on those trips I was able to sneak into my room to eat some of the food from my basket. Our rooms had no doors on them, and lights were left on all night, so privacy was hard to come by.

Although the people there were very kind to me, they frightened me because no one spoke English. No one explained where I was, or why I was there. My roommate kept up an angry flow of German for hours as she stalked up and down our room for most of the night. I was wakened, suddenly, with her standing by my bed, patting my hair and saying in her limited English, "Poor girl, they will kill you." I was terrified, but she walked away. I was afraid to sleep, and afraid to call out!

The oppressive situation lasted all day Sunday, all day Monday, and Monday night was another disturbed night. Very early Tuesday morning, the warden came for me and said, "You go!" Where was I to go? What was happening now? My luggage, one suitcase, was picked up, and I was escorted under guard to the main hall, where a handsome, young American immigration officer waited for me. He smiled as he picked up my suitcase.

"Your uncle has sent the bond money, and I will take you to your ship to continue your journey." I was so relieved that I started to cry. He led me out to his car and said, "Was it *that* bad?" Then I told him that I hadn't known what was going on. I thought I might be sent back to Scotland, or maybe even to jail. This young man put his arm around me, gave me a hug, and explained that the U.S. government had asked my uncle to post a $500 bond. He went on to say, "Your uncle must be eager to have you, because he sent the bond by telegram. We don't often get a reply so quickly, especially over a Sunday!" The young officer felt so sorry for me that he took me out to breakfast—the first time I ever had bacon, pancakes, and syrup! Then he put me on another ship, a French liner, to take me up the St. Lawrence River to Montreal.

I was so disappointed that it wasn't *The Athenian* with Captain Brown. The captain on *The Aquitania* was all business. Very brusque, he signed my papers and gave me over to a cheeky, redheaded bellboy, who took me to my cabin and unceremoniously dumped my luggage in the middle of the room. The weather was cold but nice, so I went up on deck, where luck was with me. I began talking with a Scottish lady who turned out to be the nursing superintendent in a Detroit hospital. She knew my aunt and uncle, and told me that I could travel with her from Montreal to Detroit. I was so pleased to have a companion, especially one who spoke English! She offered to show me around Montreal, for we were to dock early in the morning, and the train for Windsor and Detroit would not leave until late that evening. I was really looking forward to that.

The next morning we docked in Montreal. Oh, the hustle and bustle, the mad panic as everyone rushed off to meet their friends. I had to go to the purser's office to meet the captain and be "signed off," as it were. My family had arranged for the Travellers Aid Society to meet me, care for me in Montreal, and put me on the train for Detroit. However, the Travellers Aid lady had not turned up! Then I couldn't find my passport. I was sure I had given it to the purser; he was sure he had given it back. I searched my handbag, but it wasn't there. I searched high and low, but, finally, the captain had to be told. He stormed into the office and shouted at me, the purser, and everyone else in the office.

Summoning a bellboy, he told him to take me back to my cabin and help me search for the passport. It was the same snooty redhead. Scornfully, he said, "I'll find it, I'll bet it's in your handbag!" I heatedly assured him that I had looked there. He marched into the cabin, demanded my bag, and dumped everything out onto my bunk. There was the passport! I was so mad at him for finding it, but so relieved that it was found and I could get off the ship. Thank goodness, my Scottish friend was waiting for me, and the captain agreed that I could go with her, snapping, "Now you have been cleared, take everything and leave the ship!"

At that moment the Travellers Aid lady arrived. She insisted that she wouldn't release me to my Scottish friend, insisting that I must go with her. So it was back to the captain. Thoroughly fed up with me at this point, he declared the Travellers Aid lady my legal guardian, and insisted that I go with her. Triumphantly, she led me off the ship, taking me directly to the railway station, where she *dumped* me in a booth and instructed me to sit there all day. She wouldn't even let me walk around the station. At least, she did bring me a hot dog, and some comics to read.

My Scottish friend had said she would see me at the train, but when the time came, the T.A. lady put me on the train and told the conductor, "Do not let that lady *near* her!" Twice the conductor sent my friend back to her berth!

I did have some money, but no idea of its worth. Feeling grownup, when a paperboy boarded the train, I asked for a paper, then asked the price. "Five dollars," the boy said. I handed it over to him, then wondered why he smiled.

The next morning the conductor wakened me saying, "We are nearing Windsor. Get your immigration papers ready!" A great fear gripped me. Would these men put me off the train? Where would I go? What would I do? I was praying hard. Indeed, prayer had been my support all these days. On came four men, three in civilian clothes, one in uniform. It was the men in civilian clothes who worried me the most! All were tall, grim-faced men. One man called out, "Agnes MacLachlan Orr, stand up!"

My heart stopped in fright! I struggled to my feet, as if in a dream, as the men approached me, and one demanded my passport. Then the man behind him said, "Nancy, I'm your Uncle Bob!" I flung myself into his arms and hugged him; I wouldn't let go. He hugged me back and said, "It's all over now; you are *home*!" I looked up, and saw two of the kindest brown eyes, just like my mother's, smiling down at me! Home at last.

As the officers checked the papers of the other travellers going into the U.S.A., my attentive uncle sat down with me in the train, and listened as I poured out all my experiences. He reminded me so much of Mother that I just didn't feel strange at all. Finally, the train pulled out, and we went on into Detroit. When we went through customs, it was such a relief to have my uncle by my side, handling all my papers and giving all the answers. The customs officer was a friendly chap, and as he looked at the battered case, he leaned forward and whispered, "What treasures are you smuggling in?"

I was startled, and quickly answered, "I don't have anything!"

"Oh, come on, you must have presents for your aunt and uncle, come on, tell me."

I was so humiliated, because none of us had thought of bringing gifts for the family. Not that we could have. We had had a hard enough time getting together money for my travel expenses. I was so embarrassed, but at once Uncle Bob sensed my confusion, and leaning down to me said,

"He's only teasing you, for you are not allowed to bring in any gifts, and I know you wouldn't break the law." I looked up in relief at his laughing brown eyes. What a cloud lifted from my life!

Taking my hand, and lifting the old suitcase, my uncle led me through the gates to where Aunt Maggie and Cousin Irv were waiting for me. Before I knew it, Aunt Maggie's arms were around me, and her soft Scots voice said, "Welcome to your new home, my lassie."

What a kind, loving face she had! All my fears evaporated, but before I could say another word, a tall, handsome young man by my aunt's side swooped me into his arms and gave me a great hug. It was my very own cousin. He grinned at me, saying, "I always wanted someone younger than me in the family. Now I can pick on my wee sister!"

"Just you try it. I'm used to a big, bossy brother!"

Uncle roared with laughter, while Irv teased me about my Scottish *r*'s.

It was so exciting to drive home in our own car! Then we arrived at what was to me a large house—hallway, kitchen, dining room, sitting room, and upstairs—three bedrooms and a large bathroom. In the basement, wonder of wonders, a washing machine! If I remember right, it was a Maytag with wringers, and it was a marvellous thing to me. There was even an icebox, with ice in it. My head whirled to see so much all at once.

Aunt Maggie was a quiet person, but she made me feel very comfortable, as if she had known me all my life. She talked about my mother, and Uncle Bob chimed in with his anecdotes. Later, Cousin Mae came home from college, Wayne State University, where she was doing her master's. My mother had talked a lot about Mae, preparing me for the joy of having a big sister. At last, I heard her coming in the door. I jumped up and rushed to hug her. Her arms full of books, she stepped back in alarm, and I stopped abruptly, feeling stupid and awkward. Slowly, Mae put down her books. "So, you've finally got here. I hope you'll be happy." Then she gave me a peck on the cheek. It was like having cold water dashed in my face. I had expected warmth and enthusiasm from her, and it wasn't there. Later, I was to find out that this was just Mae's nature. We never were to become close.

After breakfast the next morning, Aunt Maggie told me that a neighbour was coming over to make some clothes for me. Mrs. O'Neal came sailing in about ten o'clock in the morning. She was a heavy-built, jolly Irish woman. Her curly grey hair was short and bristling, but she herself was calm and energetic. Her first words were, "So, this is your Scottish daughter, Mrs. Blair! Ooh, she needs something more than a kilt to wear. Let's have a cup o' tea, and get down to business."

In just a few days, she had made a number of outfits for me. Everything she made had to be fitted and re-fitted. She made over some of Mae's old skirts for me, and she made pretty blouses out of remnants and scraps. One of my favourite outfits was a green serge jumper with a figured green blouse, which tied in a bow under the chin. Aunt Maggie was proud of that outfit, too, and she insisted that I put it on to show Uncle Bob.

"Nancy, you look so good in that! The green suits her, don't you agree, Bob?"

"Of course I do, I told you she's a bonny lass, just like her mother!" I felt so proud and happy.

Soon off I went to school, to start eighth grade in the middle of the school year. I felt very confident in my green outfit. My Scottish coat was a bit short, but I put it in my locker, and went off with Cousin Mae to my first class. Before leaving, Mae introduced me to the teacher, "As you see, Nancy had good marks in Scotland and is ahead of her age. If you ask her to speak slowly, you'll be able to understand her broad Scottish accent!"

I was horrified. I hadn't realized that my accent was *that* different, and I was immediately overcome with shyness. The teacher welcomed me warmly and introduced me to the class. Then I sat down, and no one asked me anything.

In due course, the bell rang. I was stunned. What did I do now? While everyone poured out of the classroom, I just sat there. One girl noticed me. "Do you know which is your next class?" I shook my head. How could I speak? She wouldn't understand me. The girl kindly took my schedule out of my hand and said, "You're in my class, just come with me."

She told me that she was Lois Rutter and that she would show me the class and lunchroom. Then she asked if I spoke English. I shyly replied, "Yes, but I have a Scottish accent. Maybe you can't understand me." She laughed, "My dad speaks Cornish, your English is much clearer than his! Of course, I can understand you." Wonder of wonders, I had a friend!

During the last class, I felt a desperate urge to go to the "lavie." But what do they call it in America? I turned to sign urgently to Lois, but she was a few seats behind and couldn't see me. I squirmed, I joggled, and finally held up my hand. "Can I go to the lavie?"

The teacher was nonplussed. "*Where* do you want to go?" How could I tell her? I blushed furiously and sat down. The teacher shrugged her shoulders and went on.

After ten minutes or so, the bell rang, and school was dismissed for the day. But it was too late. I hadn't been able to control it any longer, and had just let it go. I was so near to tears. All the others left, but Lois came over, looked at my red face and at the pool under me, and said, "Where is your locker? I'll go get your coat." She brought it back, and that hid my shame.

Lois walked home with me, but I was embarrassed to go back to Aunt Maggie. I slipped in the front door to find my aunt was entertaining visitors. "Nancy," she called out, "come and meet my friend, I want her to see your nice dress."

What to do? I was so embarrassed and ashamed, so I made up a story. "The boy behind me had a squirt gun, and my skirt and pants are all wet."

I don't know if Aunt Maggie believed me, but she was most sympathetic, and assured me it would not harm the skirt. "Just wash it in water and hang it up to dry. We'll iron it later." Dear, dear Aunt Maggie. Nothing seemed to faze her.

My first day at school was over, and I had a friend. Indeed, Lois and I remained friends all our lives. My prayers that night were full of gratitude to God. I had arrived, I had survived my first day of school, and I had a friend.

***

My recollections of Aunt Maggie are hazy now, but I do remember her with great affection, a slight, delicate-looking woman with a great capacity for loving. She had welcomed me with real affection, and was very sensitive to my feelings of being lost in a strange land, amongst people I hardly knew. When I arrived home from school each day, she would be waiting to hear all about my experiences, and ready to comfort me in my homesickness. So it came as a shock to me when Aunt had to go into hospital for an operation, only ten days after I had arrived.

Aunt Maggie had thyroid trouble, familiarly known as goitre. The doctors had tried medical treatment, but her condition had not responded, so she was admitted for surgery. The family didn't seem to be too worried, as the doctor had assured them that there was no danger.

We visited Aunt Maggie in hospital the day after her operation. She looked very tired and weak, so we didn't stay long. However, she was making good progress when Uncle, Mae, Irv, and I went to the hospital the night before Thanksgiving Day. Aunt Maggie was sitting up in bed, looking well and cheerful, in spite of having a tracheotomy. I remember that she got me to tell her stories of the daft things I had done in school, mostly how the teachers misunderstood my Scottish words. The whole family was amused that I already had the nickname of "Scotty," which stayed with me throughout high school.

I was wearing my latest dress, which Mrs. O'Neal had made for me for the special dinner that we were to have for Thanksgiving Day. Aunt had me twirl around, so I pretended that I was a model, and pranced about her room. I remember her saying, "Bob, we are going to have fun with this lassie!"

The doctor came in before we left, and told us that Aunt Maggie was fine. The next day they would remove the tracheotomy tube, and then she would be able to get up. He said, "I think she should be home in about ten days, all going well." We left the hospital in good spirits.

About 4 a.m. I awoke to the sound of crying. I shared a bed with Mae, but she wasn't there, and the lights were on downstairs. Immediately I knew, and my heart filled with dread. "Oh, Lord, please may it not be true. Please may Aunt Maggie be all right. I can't go through that again. Please, Lord, help me. What shall I do?"

I went downstairs and saw Uncle Bob sitting in the armchair, his head in his hands. Mae was crying in a corner, and Irv was just standing there, so shocked. When I got to the foot of the stairs, Uncle Bob said, "Oh, Nancy, we have lost Maggie." I put out my arms to him, he hugged me, and then it seemed we were all hugging together and weeping. Uncle phoned all the relatives he could. This was 1933, and not everyone had phones.

Within an hour Aunt Maggie's mother, whom we called Granny Gold, and her two sons came to the house. Then Uncle said, "We must notify those who don't have phones. Irv, you take the car, and go see the Mairs." Then he mentioned the names of a number of friends who must be notified. As Irv got his coat on and prepared to leave, Mae said, "Irv, you shouldn't go alone. Nancy will come with you." I was so glad to have something I could do to help. Irv drove very fast and furious, his face set in grim determination.

I felt I had to say something, so I said, "Irv, I believe that Aunt Maggie is alive, and knows what we are doing."

"How can you say that?"

"Irv, the Bible tells us that. Jesus himself said that."

"But what are we to do without Mother?"

Then suddenly he slowed down and looked at me. "My God, Nancy, this is the second time this year that you have lost your mother!"

"It's all right, Irv. We just have to help one another through this."

"That's it. If I can think of other people, and not just myself, maybe I can get through this."

It was such a blessing to be able to *do* something, to have people accept me as part of the grieving family. When my own mother had died in Scotland, women had no part in the funeral. Aunt Maggie's death was so different. Her body was brought to the house, and lay in state in the sitting room. My aunt was dressed in her Scottish clan white dress with the tartan sash. My uncle was a chieftain of the clan, so there was a piper each evening, piping a mournful dirge. People constantly came and went. I was kept busy making tea and washing dishes, but I felt a part of it all. The house was pervaded by the smell of many flowers, for my aunt was well loved by so many people.

We all went to the funeral, and to me that was strangely comforting. Mother's other brother, Jimmie, and his wife had come to Detroit from Canada for the funeral. After it was all over, Uncle Jimmy and Aunt Kate stayed a few days more. The evening before they left, I overheard Uncle Jimmie talking to Uncle Bob.

"Bob, things have radically changed for you. It will be hard for you to bring up Nancy. We are willing to take her back to Canada with us. What do you think?"

Uncle Bob was quick to answer, "I think God sent Nancy as a blessing to us. Lizzie asked me to care for her. Maggie's mother is coming to stay with us to help keep house, so we will manage. Nancy will be company for me. Thanks just the same, Jimmie."

What a difference that made to me, to know that Uncle Bob really wanted me!

***

Despite the love of my Uncle Bob, my cousins, and Granny Gold, I was considered a weird foreigner outside of our house, and fell into ways that did no one any credit. I was very self-conscious, with a broad Scottish accent, my curly hair flying in all directions, and a walk that was used to swinging a kilt! I yearned to be popular, to have a group of friends, to be part of the gang. All of this was 70 years ago, and the gangs weren't like they are today, but the underlying yearning to belong is just the same.

Granny Gold was an energetic Scot determined to bring me up as she had brought up her own children in "the old country." She did not approve of girls playing with boys, nor did she approve of girls riding bicycles. How we clashed on that, for I had ridden a bike since I was five, riding my brother's bike when mine got too small. Cycling was something I felt I excelled in. Uncle Bob was a kind, gentle person, ever ready to listen to me, and most often he would intervene on my behalf, but *not* on the cycle issue. Not only could I not have a cycle of my own, but I was forbidden to ride *any* cycle in the streets of Detroit!

My friend Lois was a petite brunette with friendly blue eyes and freckles on her upturned nose. She was quiet and thoughtful, with a quick sense of the ridiculous. She lived about six blocks from my home, and we often walked home together. Next door to Lois lived Bea, who was one of eight children. Bea was a tall, athletic, curly-headed tomboy. She was captain of the girls' baseball team, and a born organizer. It was she who organized the girls' football team. Although I had been warned not to play football, I would sometimes stop on my way from school to practice tackling under Bea's direction.

Sometimes, too, I would ride Bea's bike, to show off my prowess at fast riding and the special tricks I could do on the bike. Over the months, Bea's gang became friendlier, and when they began to call me "Scotty," I felt I had been accepted.

It was after a summer ballgame that someone got the idea that a watermelon would taste great. None of us had any money, so Bobby offered to get us one from the local fruit shop, where all the fruit was piled in baskets in front of the shop. The first time Bobby rode by and snitched a watermelon, he got away with it, but the next time the melon slipped. Bobby fell trying to retrieve it and was caught by the owner, who told Bobby's father, a lawyer. Bobby was severely punished by his father and threatened with more, should he ever again do such a thing. We were all about 14 or 15 years old and resented the fact that parents were so strict, and shopkeepers so mean!

Bobby was a born leader, a classic "clean-cut American boy." He was perhaps 15 at this time, sturdy, freckle-faced, with an attractive grin. His father was greatly respected in the community. His mother was a gentle, sickly soul, and his older brother a genius, so Bobby was often left to his own devices. He was full of mischief, always providing new ideas when we were bored. He could be a tease but never cruel, and he was always loyal to, and protective of, his "gang." By most standards it was a mild gang; we never even *thought* of vandalism. There was no smoking when girls were present; that was Bobby's rule. And there was no boy-girl romance amongst this group of neighbourhood children.

A week or two after Bobby got caught, we all were again hot and thirsty after the ballgame, and Bobby asked who was brave enough to go get a watermelon. We all sat scared, and Bobby began to jeer. I saw an opportunity for fame, and volunteered to ride off on Bobby's cycle to grab a watermelon.

Minutes later-*success!* Breathlessly, I jumped off the bike and handed the watermelon to Bobby, earning his smile of approval. I turned in triumph to the ten or twelve gathered in the circle. They were jubilant, slapping me on the back and saying, "Boy, Scotty, you were brave!" "Yay, Scotty!"

"Gosh, that was quick work! Did anyone see you?"

Proudly I answered, "Oh, the old man was in the shop and had his back turned. I whizzed around on the bike and grabbed the watermelon! I don't think he even knew I had been there!" I was successful, and that's when I experienced the joy of hearing, "Yay, Scotty." I had done something special! I repeated this fruit theft a number of times and never got caught.

Then one day, a school holiday, Bea and I were downtown, just looking around Woolworth's when Bea challenged me, "I bet you're scared to snitch a ring from Woolworth's!" I was quick to accept the dare. Bea drifted off, and I walked casually to the jewellery counter. Just as casually, I slipped a ring on my finger. So it started, my game of seeing how much I could get away with. Rings, pins, cosmetics, whatever caught Bea's eye, I would cheerfully pocket. It wasn't always Bea. Sometimes it would be Bobby, or others in the gang. I was admired as the best "snitcher." I never stole when I was alone; this was a game for impressing others.

Another day, Bea dared me to go into a department store and steal a dress. I accepted the challenge. Now it was impossible for me to take any of these things *home*, so I'd give them to Bea, who would pass them on to her brothers or sisters. Then Bea started to snitch things herself, as did other members of the gang, each trying to outdo the others. Lois never joined in this, and tried to warn me, but I just laughed. I had a group of friends, so why worry?

One day, while leaving Woolworth's with a handbag under my arm, I felt a hand on my shoulder, and I froze in fright. "The store is closing, please use the other exit." The floorwalker's words were such a relief! I gave a watery smile, and hurried away. But it had given me a terrific shock!

My family in Scotland had been devoted Christians. Every evening we had knelt in prayer. I had been taught of God's love for me since infancy, and prayer was as important as breathing in our lives. But in coming to the U.S.A., I had slowly forgotten about prayer. Oh, I went to church every Sunday with my uncle and family. I even taught Sunday School, for I had been nourished on Bible stories all my life. My uncle and Granny had no idea what was going on behind their backs. Once in a while I would have a spark of conscience, but it was soon submerged.

This went on for some time, shoplifting during the week, church on Sundays. Then the spring holiday came, and I suddenly realized that it was Good Friday. If I had been at home in Scotland, we would be going to a three-hour church service. The whole previous week would have been a time of soul-searching and rededication. It was also a time of joy, for Easter was coming. I felt so homesick for my mother and family. I decided to have a three-hour service by myself. I went to my room, shut the door, and read through the Good Friday story. I was on my knees, feeling Christ's presence as I had done so often at home in Scotland. I felt His nearness, and also my mother's presence. I could hear Mother's voice, "Nancy, you know God is always with you. He knows the good that you do, and he also sees the wrong things you do. How do you think he feels about your naughtiness?" And she went on to say, "It is time to turn yourself around."

As I knelt in prayer, I began to see myself as I had been these last few months, doing anything just to prove how smart and brave I was. I saw myself "snitching," and faced the truth that I had been stealing. Believe it or not, that came as a shock! I was a thief! What would my mother say? What would my father say?

I saw myself as I really was, how stupid I had been. I wanted to be popular, but where was I heading? What kind of person did I want to be? What did I want to do with my life? These friends would last a few years at the most. Would I always have to be a show-off to gain friends? I wept, and asked Christ to have pity on me. I *needed* friends; what would I do without them?

Then it seemed as though Jesus answered, "Have I not been your friend through tragedy, loneliness, and despair? Can you not trust me to give you true friends?"

I remembered Lois, from whom I had drifted away. I knew she would stand by me—but I wanted to be popular! I wanted to be admired! I went on thinking, praying, and weeping. I knew that I did not want to be a thief. I wanted to be the kind of person God wanted me to be. I had to change direction, to turn around! Weeping, I asked God to forgive me, and to help me be strong, and resist temptation. It felt as though I was again in the midst of my family circle at prayer. I knew I was forgiven, and peace flooded my heart.

It was indeed a turning point in my life. I told Bea and Bobby that I wouldn't be coming around anymore. They thought I was crazy. Lois was a loyal friend, but I never did get in with the popular crowd at high school, and that was hard. I wasn't asked to the prom, and I often envied the pretty girls, but I still had lots of fun and laughter. I knew a deeper sense of well-being, and had no regrets.

Scotty in Detroit

Chapter 4: The White Cap

"Why do you want to be a nurse?" demanded the stern director of nursing.

I could see this wasn't going to be easy. It was 1938. I had graduated from my Detroit high school at 16, determined to pursue my goal of becoming a nurse. In the U.S.A., I was too young to start nurses' training, but I had heard you could start at a younger age in Britain. So I had applied to Western General Hospital, and sailed home to Scotland.

I answered the director's question with the story about when my mother had collapsed, and how I wanted to become a nurse so I would know what to do when somebody was sick. She continued to look at me haughtily, and said, "I *do* hope you're not going into the nursing profession for the glamour of the uniform!"

While waiting for my interview, I had seen the young nurses pass through the office, and noted their uniforms with a bit of horror. Each girl wore a nurse's cap that resembled a chef's hat. Tall and white, it sat right down on the forehead, hiding the hair. The striped uniforms had long sleeves, a white apron, and starched collar, cuffs, and belt. The girls also wore thick, black stockings, which you could barely see because the uniform came to within two inches of their ankles. As for the uniforms, I had thought, "Well, if it takes that, it takes that."

So when the nursing director asked if I was motivated by the glamour of the uniforms, I said, "Those uniforms with those stockings and those hats? I don't think they're very *glamorous*."

Drawing herself to her full height, she said, "I designed those nursing caps *myself*. The unique caps of nursing schools distinguish you from one another. When you get your cap, you should wear it proudly!" I felt about the size of tuppence.

Alas, the interview was to go from bad to worse. My papers had all gone ahead to Western General from Detroit, and I'd been notified that I would be admitted. My brother Blair had accompanied me to the final admissions requirement, a personal interview.

The nursing director's next question was, "How old are you?"

"Sixteen, nearly 17," I said.

"Oh, my goodness, we can't take you until you are 21! It's the law in Scotland. No young women can start until they're 21."

Abashed that I had already been offered admittance, the nursing director combed through the files. Apparently, someone seeing that I was *born* in 1921 had confused it with my *being* 21. While it was their error, and while they would be glad to have me at 21, they couldn't take me now.

Blair and I departed, terribly discouraged. I had left America behind and was living in digs with my dad. Here I was, 16 years old, and stymied in my pursuit of a nursing school. "Let's go for coffee," suggested Blair.

While we sat at coffee, a little woman, who looked like just a wee housewife out for a cuppa, came over to Blair and asked, "Are you Blair Orr?"

"Yes."

"I knew your mother," she said, "and I wondered what happened to the sister that went to America."

"Well," he said, "she's here, sitting right here."

The woman, a Mrs McDougal, sat down with us, and soon I was telling her the whole story, moaning about not being able to get into nurses' training. Suddenly, she said to me, "Do you like children?"

"Oh, yes, I'm very fond of children." I thought she was thinking I could be a nanny instead of a nurse.

"Do you like sick children?"

"I don't know. I never had anything to do with sick children."

"Well," she said, "you don't understand, but in this country the Registry of Nurses has general nursing, but also nursing for infectious diseases, paediatrics, and psychiatric nursing. Now, you can go into one of *those* three branches when you're 17. I would suggest that you consider paediatrics, in what we call 'Sick Kids Hospital.' You do three years' training, and you get a diploma as a registered sick children's nurse. And *then* you go on to do your general nursing. But instead of having to do four years, you only do three because your first year in Sick Kids is the same as your first year of general. Would you like to do that?"

"Oh, yes, I would!"

"Well," she said, "I'll see that you get the application forms."

Within a day or two, I had received and completed all the forms. To my surprise, I was called for an interview right away with Miss Robinson, the director of nursing at Royal Hospital for Sick Children in Glasgow, also called Yorkhill, or just Sick Kids.

When I entered her office, Miss Robinson invited me to sit down. She talked a while with me before saying, "You know, you're *very* American. I do not think that you will settle in this country, and the other thing is that your father is not a professional. All the girls that I have here, you know, have gone to public schooling, *and* they're daughters of professional men. I don't know if you'll fit in with them because your father is just a carpenter."

Taken aback, I didn't reply. Nevertheless, she continued, "Now you go and get your physical, and if everything's all right, you can start the first of June." This was the middle of April, and I was going to be 17 on May 7.

While I was waiting for the physical, still feeling very much lost, in came a tall, young doctor, probably in his mid-30s, and he said, "Where have you been?"

It sounded to me like the flirting line that boys use, *"Where have you been all my life?"* So to his "Where have you been?" in my brash American way I said, "Fresh guy, huh?"

He drew himself up and said, "I am Professor Ford. I just wish to know which country you have been in because I understand you're from abroad." Oh, dear, I had done it again.

Well, I gave my history, and when he examined me he noticed the mark on my neck from the problem with my tubercular glands and my tonsils, and commented, "You had a lot of trouble when you were young."

"Yes, I did, but I've not had any trouble at all since I was about ten years of age. I have never been sick and missed school. I'm just fine."

"Nevertheless, I think you should have your tonsils out." When I protested that I never even had sore throats, he said, "That's not the problem, they could be a source of infection to other people. You have to have your tonsils out." Well, that was another blow. Where was I going to find the money to have my tonsils out?

I met Blair outside and told him what had happened. There wasn't much time to contemplate the situation because we were expected at the Dunachie house, where we were to have dinner with the family of my brother's fiancée, Muriel. Mr. Dunachie was a member of a prominent firm of architects and surveyors and was well known throughout Glasgow. As it happened, he knew a man who was an ENT—an ear, nose, and throat specialist—and an examination was quickly arranged.

"There's nothing wrong with your tonsils," the specialist pronounced. "They don't have any infection in them or any other signs of problems."

But when the ENT phoned Professor Ford, Ford said, "I do not ask your opinion, I'm just saying if she wishes to be on the nursing staff of Royal Hospital for Sick Children, she has to get her tonsils out."

"OK," I said, "take my tonsils out." Eventually, I presented myself with uniform, and without tonsils, at Royal Hospital for Sick Children.

***

I began my training at Drumchapel, a lovely little convalescent home, up on a hill, across the canal, and away from the houses. It was a beautiful place, all on one floor, with pavilions leading out. Sister Charles was in charge of the convalescent home. "Sister" didn't mean a religious sister; that's what nurses-in-charge were called.

Sister Charles, we used to say, was like a galleon in full sail. She was pretty hefty, a very well built woman, and an impressive sight with her high hat on and this massive apron over her navy blue dress. She would often stop in to review the wards, and she was exceedingly strict.

Upon my arrival, Sister Charles directed a nurse named Muriel Winters, one month ahead of me in training, to come to my room to show me how we sewed up our elaborate caps. The caps were high, starched affairs, but when they came back from the laundry they were all flattened out. So you had to fold up the broad band in front with the little frill in the bottom of the band. Then you gathered the half circle in back and made it into a high pleat that went over your head like a kind of crown. Every week you had to put these pleats in by hand, and it was a lot of work. Then Muriel showed me how to put on my uniform, and we were put into the wards.

Now, we didn't have any preliminary training classes. There was none of this doing all your classes at one time and just going to the ward for short periods—we went immediately into the wards. As a probationer I had night duty, going on at eight o'clock at night, and coming off at eight o'clock in the morning.

Every Sunday we would have a half-day off, either the morning until one o'clock, or from one o'clock on in the afternoon, but we had to report for dinner at half past twelve. There in the dining room Sister Charles would inspect our uniforms. Our hats had to be made up right, our stocking seams straight, and our shoes polished front and back. I knew then why we had thick black lisle stockings-because you could shine your shoes with them. We would pass in front of her single file, quaking until we got past her. Despite the strict regimen, it was a wonderful summer and I learned a great deal. It was 1938, and the war hadn't yet started, though the dark clouds were gathering in Europe.

At Drumchapel, we were busy with a medical ward, a surgical ward, and the baby wards. There would be about 100 children throughout the different wards, but the TB (tuberculosis) ward had the most. I remember those beautiful days. We put coconut oil on all the children and had them outside from early morning until the evening. It introduced me to nursing, and to Muriel Winters, who became a good friend.

***

After three months at Drumchapel, I was brought in to the big hospital at Yorkhill and assigned to night duty. There we had 32 beds in the main ward, plus three side wards. All new children were put in a side ward for 24 hours to make sure they didn't carry an infection in addition to the disease they had been admitted for. Infectious diseases were rampant, and we couldn't have measles or chicken pox or whooping cough spreading throughout the ward.

I was put on what was called "sitting duty" in a side ward. One time, the side ward had just one child, and I shall never forget her. A beautiful child with a head full of curls, she was only three years old and had tetanus. I was new to this and didn't know anything about tetanus. I had had no classes--but then I wasn't meant to *do* anything, I was just there to ring the bell when the child had a convulsion.

I sat there all night long. In between the child's convulsions, I would try to talk to her because I felt so sorry for the little one. You couldn't touch her because the slightest touch, the slightest noise, or just turning on the lights could send her into a fit again. Now I'm hopeless as a singer, but she seemed to like to hear me sing in a soft voice. Oh, the hours I sat there praying and praying for that child. I also prayed, "Lord, can't you find something that will cure or prevent this terrible disease?" Tetanus inoculations were still in the future.

I dreaded coming on duty only to sit there night after night, watching that little girl grow worse and worse. I wept when she finally died. Mind you, people used to say, "Oh, you have to be hard-hearted if you're a nurse in Sick Children's Hospital." Little did they know how attached we became to the children. The children would be in hospital for weeks, and their parents could only get in to see them once a week, either Saturday or Sunday, for one hour from three to four o'clock. At four, they were out the door. If they brought something for the child, it was to be left on a table outside their door. That is the way it was done then.

Of course, we nurses attended to all the children, but there are some you have more affinity for than others. All of us had our "special" children. They'd shout, "Here's my nurse, here's my nurse!" when you came on the ward at the beginning of your shift, and it was heart-warming to hear.

After the little girl with tetanus died, I was put on the wards where, as a probationer, my duty was to change the beds, empty the bedpans, and clean the bathroom and the sluice. The sluice was a sink with a built-in washboard for scrubbing out nappies, or diapers, before dropping them into the laundry pail. We also tucked the children in at night and got them up early in the morning, took their temps and pulses, washed their faces and hands, gave them their breakfast, saw that their teeth were brushed, tidied up the beds, then washed their hands and faces again, so we were done and at attention when Sister came on duty.

One night I was on duty, still very new and very, very nervous, in this big ward of 32 kids plus the side wards. As the night nurse was leaving for her midnight meal, she said to me, "There's a boy that's just been admitted, and he has 'query appendicitis.'" (Until a specialist confirmed a diagnosis, it was considered a query diagnosis and written, for example, "?appendicitis.") "His family doctor and his parents are going to be here in a little while. Just now, they're down in the outpatients department taking care of things, but the child has been admitted and is in the side ward. Now, *nobody* is to go into that side ward, neither his parents nor his family doctor, until I get back."

So I was alone on duty when down the long hallway came a tall man, very businesslike. When he turned into the side ward, I went hurrying after him. "Excuse me, sir, but staff nurse said nobody's to get in to see this boy until she comes back. She'll just be back in about ten minutes." He gave me one dirty look, and I smelled alcohol on his breath. "My goodness, who is this?" I wondered. "Maybe he's the family doctor."

He walked into the room, pulled down the child's bedclothes, and examined him. I said, "Excuse me, sir, who are you?" He threw the bedclothes back. The little boy, about nine, was crying, so I hugged him.

In lieu of answering, the tall man just glared at me and said, "Who are *you?*"

"I'm Nurse Orr, but staff nurse is coming, she'll just be here." He marched out, and I got the boy quieted down again. When the night nurse came back, I told her about the tall man with alcohol on his breath who had marched right in and examined the boy, wouldn't tell me who he was, and was so rude that he scared me.

"Aach, that was Professor McPherson! He's the chief surgeon."

"Oh, I didn't walk with him to the door, or show him any honour!" Hospital protocol required that the doctor be respectfully greeted at the door and walked to the door as he left.

Each night, Sister made two tours around the ward to make sure the children were being attended to and that we nurses were not falling asleep. When she appeared that night, the staff nurse told her what had happened. Sister called me in and asked why I had been afraid. "He was in civilian clothes, and he was very brusque. He glared at me so, and I smelled alcohol on his breath. It worried me because I was all alone in the ward."

"Of course you'd be worried," Sister said. "I'm sorry this happened, Nurse. He should have called me before he came to the ward. They're supposed to come with a sister." By the way, the little boy was operated on by Mr. McPherson and was just fine. (As a surgeon, McPherson was "Mr." in Britain, but would be called "Dr." in the U.S.)

Two nights later when I went onto the ward, the day sister said to me, "Tomorrow morning you're not to go straight to breakfast, you're to stay on the ward until the chief comes." So, at the end of my shift, I stayed behind with sister, and the chief of staff came into the ward and asked, "Are you Nurse Orr?" To my yes, he continued, "I want to apologize for the rudeness of one of my staff, Mr. McPherson. He should not have treated you the way he did. Mr. McPherson is just coming now, and he will tell you he's sorry."

When McPherson arrived, he glared at me and said, "I didn't know you were a new probationer, but now you will know who Mr. McPherson is."

I said, "Yes, sir." And that was his apology.

The chief just smiled, but he did say to McPherson, "Please remember that nurses are ladies, and you are to treat them as ladies."

Although some of the doctors were very difficult, throughout my ten years of training, it was drummed into us, and everyone else, that nurses were ladies and professionals, and were to be treated with respect. We were also taught that we were not to have any familiar friendliness with medical students; any relationship was to be on a thoroughly professional basis. If they found you were dating a medical student, you might well be dismissed.

***

After six months as a probationer, a nursing student would begin taking classes in her off-duty time, usually two hours a day, from ten to twelve or two to four, once or twice a week. If you got off at five o'clock, you might have to go to the evening class.

We all lived in what we called the nurses' home. We received two uniforms a year after buying the first two, room and board, sheets and towels, and laundering of our uniforms and linens plus the princely sum of about £2 a month for other expenses, which included replacing our stockings. All of us were in the same boat, and we gradually became very friendly.

In the beginning, however, I had a hard time at Yorkhill because of my strong American accent, and the others were not very friendly with me. In the first year, you'd be two months in one ward, then you'd move on to another ward for experience, so just as I'd get to know the nurses I was working with, I'd be moved somewhere else. There was a common dining room, but meals were highly structured. We had marks on the sleeves of our uniforms indicating our "year." The first-year nurses never sat with the second-year nurses, and the second-year nurses never sat with the third-years. There was a home sister who supervised our meals to see that we all got enough food and so on, but also to see that this discipline was strictly adhered to. It was like the military.

After the first six months as a probationer, I took an examination, and after I passed that, I was called "upper probationer" or "second probationer." As a second probationer, I was to work with first probationers to teach them what they were supposed to do. After another six months, I was moved up to second-year nurse.

In the first year, we were taught to do bathing, backrubs, enemas, injections, and so on, and we had a chart with all these things a nurse should be able to do. Every month on the day before our day off, we had to take our charts and visit Miss Robinson, who would look at the chart and see if you were proficient in the things you were expected to be able to do. This included such things as "economy in lighting," "economy in heating," and "economy in water," which meant we were to be very careful not to waste water or heat, to shut off the lights when we left a room, and so on. Very good training that I don't think many nurses would accept nowadays.

It was wonderful when you finished your first year because, as we rotated every two months, you would again work with some of the nurses you had worked with before, and it made working in the ward much more fun. The children's wards were always very cheerful anyway. There were laughing children, and record players playing music day in and day out. We had children up to the age of 12, and we developed such wonderful relationships with them. I remember so many of those children.

As I gained more experience, I was sent down to the dispensary in the centre of Glasgow, just off Graham Street. There were three of us students working there, and a sister, and we all lived right there in the heart of

Glasgow. One thing we did a lot of was changing plasters (casts). Kids who broke an arm or leg and went home with a plaster would come in to Graham Street to get the plaster broken and a new one put on. We also did circumcisions, treated burns, and provided follow-up treatment for children who had been in hospital.

At Graham Street, the sister was an older sister, and the chief doctor was my Mr. McPherson, who did all the operations. He definitely remembered me and was *not* pleased to see me there. Mr. McPherson was Sister's pet. She had known him as a little boy who came by the dispensary when his father was doctor there, so she just adored Mr. McPherson. However, he was always snapping or yelling at me. "Quickly, give me a retractor! Hurry up, count the swabs!" Do this, do that! I was all thumbs and could never do anything right at his command.

One of the resident doctors at Graham Street was Judy Orr, one of the first female doctors I ever worked with. Her father was a distinguished nutritionist, a professor at Glasgow University. Mr. McPherson was very condescending to Dr. Orr. My maiden name is Orr, so we were Nurse Orr and Doctor Orr. Judy lived in the dispensary, too, and we became quite friendly, sometimes going out in the evening for some fun. She often said to me about McPherson, "You've *got* to stand up to him."

"He just walks in, and I get gastric ulcers! I'm scared stiff of him. I just do the dumbest things when he's around."

"Still," she said, "you've got to stand up to him."

One day we were doing a lot of plasters. Using great big scissors called plaster shears, we cut down the side of the plaster to get it off, shedding plaster dust all over. On top of that, we put powder inside the plasters so they didn't stick to the arm or leg. It was a messy process, changing plasters.

Mr. McPherson had a very smart velour hat and a fancy coat, which he hung out in the hall. This day we had just gotten all the plasters done when he turned to me, handed me a brush and his hat, and said, "Brush my hat for me." Well, my hands and gown were white with dust and powder, so when I began to brush his velour hat, it only became further covered with white dust. "I can't believe it, I can't believe it," he complained. "You've even managed to put powder on my hat!" I could have died.

That night Judy came into my room and said, "Nancy, you've got to stand up to this man. You are not to let him treat you so rudely, shouting and swearing at you! He knows he's not allowed to do that, and Sister knows he's not allowed to do that, but she just smiles and laughs at him." Of course, Sister had scolded me like anything for having made a mess of his hat.

The next day he came in to perform operations, and I was assisting. If I didn't give him an instrument quickly enough, he'd pick it up and smack it against my hand. Of course, this sometimes caused me to drop things. That day Judy was giving the anaesthetic, and she looked at me and gave the sign, "Stand up, stand up," and I said a silent prayer.

McPherson turned to me and said, "Give me the suture," and I gave it to him. He shouted, "I want it quicker!"

"Sir, I wouldn't be so nervous if you didn't shout at me." He just stopped for a moment, and he looked at me, really looked at me. Sister glared. I thought, "I am going to get blown out of here."

But McPherson just mused, "I wondered when the mouse would turn."

"I'm standing up to you now, sir."

"Good for you, good for you." And after that we became good friends, though I must say I didn't really admire him. After that I always remembered Judy's advice, "Stand up to them and don't be afraid."

***

It's difficult to describe how different nursing was before antibiotics and immunizations. I was two years into my training as a paediatric nurse, and in the midst of examinations, when another nurse on the ward exclaimed, "Nancy, you have a rash all over your face!"

I laughed, because I felt fine and I knew that some soaps gave me a rash. Another nurse teased, "I'll bet you did it to get out of tomorrow's exams!"

"I'll just kiss you all, and then nobody will have to take exams!" Laughing, I kissed all seven nurses as we went off duty, talking and joking.

The next day I dressed for work, though I felt awful, but at breakfast I fainted. The chief of the medical ward examined me and pronounced that I had scarlet fever! Off I went by ambulance to the infectious disease hospital. There the doctors were shocked that the University Professor of Medicine had misdiagnosed me with scarlet fever, when all I had was German measles.

I was kept in hospital for a week. Then, just before my discharge, I developed an inflammation of the eyelids known as blepharitis. That meant two more weeks in the hospital, two *long* weeks because I could neither read nor write. I was so relieved when the inflammation finally cleared, and at last I could go back to work. Two weeks of treatment for something that now could be quickly treated by antibiotics. What a wonderful medical advance!

Chapter 5: A Declaration of War

I remember it well. Prime Minister Chamberlain had warned Hitler that a march into Poland would result in a declaration of war on Germany. We were having special prayer in church that Sunday morning, September 3, 1939, when, at 11 o'clock, they brought the radio to the pulpit. Over the airwaves came Mr. Chamberlain's voice with the message, "Hitler has marched into Poland. I announce with the cabinet of this United Kingdom, that we are at war with Germany." There was a stunned silence, and then we prayed and went out.

I was at Sick Children's when Britain joined World War II. One day I was called and told to report to the American Embassy's office in Glasgow, where they told me that my uncle had volunteered that if I wanted to come back to the U.S.A. now that there was war in Britain, he would accept responsibility for me. After all, I wasn't yet 21. The U.S. government had given permission for me to return, and agreed to pay for the passage back. The American government was bringing all of their civilians home. But I said, "Oh, no, I don't want to go back to America. I've just had my toughest year of nursing, and I'm staying here. I want to nurse during the war."

The counsellor said, "You know, if you don't go back, you will be considered a British citizen."

"Yes, I know."

"You won't get another chance to go."

"No, that's all right, I've decided I'll stay here."

Waiting to be seen at the consulate with me had been many Americans who wanted to go back, and we had talked as we waited.

In no time, the killing began. A German U-boat torpedoed a British ship called *The Athenia*. *The Athenia* was the ship I had taken to America in 1933 when Captain Brown had been so good to me. Captain Brown was on board when *The Athenia* was torpedoed, and he went down with his ship. That ship also contained more than 1000 civilians, including more than 300 Americans, some of whom had been in the waiting room with me and had decided to go back to America. That was one of the first personal tragedies of the war to hit me.

Early in the war, we received notice that we were to register for ration cards, an identity card, and a gas mask. Upon registration we were issued a small box. It contained a gas mask and had a little pocket on the side for your identity card, a pocket on the other side for your ration book, and a place to carry your flashlight. The box had a shoulder strap, and as this predated plastic, it was covered with rexine, a coated cloth that was waterproof. You were to carry your gas mask with you everywhere you went. We nurses all went to classes to learn what to do in case of an air raid, and there were practices in the hospital.

Sick Kids Hospital was on a hilltop in Yorkhill, and its great lawn spilled down to the main roads. It looked across the top of Kelvin Hall toward the art galleries and Kelvin Grove Park. The back side of the hospital was heavily fenced because there was only a short grassy patch before a cliff that went right down to the River Clyde and the wharves, where the big ships lay at anchor. During the war, many large ships came up the River Clyde and docked in Glasgow just below Yorkhill.

The hospital was three stories high, and had pavilions jutting out. The windows in the pavilions came from the roof to within a couple of feet of the ground. Because of the blackouts during the war, all those windows had to be shuttered at night. Workers came and made shutters, long, awkward panels with handles on them. Every day nurses slid the shutters up and locked them in place before it was dark. Remember, in Scotland it got dark about four in the afternoon, and stayed dark until about nine in the morning.

During the time of blackouts, when you went out, the streetlights were bathed in blue. The streetcars, the buses, the cars, all had little blue lights, no bright, white lights. It was difficult going about at night because it was so dark everywhere. People were very friendly and would help you onto the streetcar or the bus. Often I would be running along the road to get back to the hospital on time, and somebody would shout out, "Take care, Lassie, take care you dunna fall." We didn't see streetlights again until the end of the war.

It was a time when people became very, very concerned for one another, but at the beginning, they called it "the phoney war" because there were months when we saw nothing but reconnaissance planes come over.

Nevertheless, our air raid drills continued. In addition to bombs, there was a real threat of biochemical warfare. There was a great fear of mustard gas, which had been used during World War I. One little room off the entrance hall of our ward was made absolutely gas-proof. In an air raid, babies were to be brought into that room. There were little bunk beds for the babies, and a little icebox because we didn't have refrigerators in those days. There were diapers, medicine, antiseptics, bandages, formula, and water, everything to take care of babies for 24 hours in case of a gas attack.

The children's wards then weren't like hospitals now. The kids were in their medical cots (or cribs) the whole time. The cots had sides, two of which would come down for making the bed or doing something for a child, but then the sides had to go right back up because they were terrified of children falling out of bed. Even when the children went out on the veranda, they were transported in their cots, which had big wheels.

Though we didn't have bombing right away, whenever a plane, even a reconnaissance plane, came over, the sirens would sound, and everyone had to go to an air raid shelter. Everyone had been told to build an air raid shelter in their backyard, and people would bring their bedding with them and sit there until it was over.

***

Britain had not experienced a war on its shores; the '14 war had been mostly in Europe. There were many false air raids. One night, my night off, I was visiting the Dunachies, my sister-in-law's family. The Dunachies had made a home for me ever since I returned from Detroit. There were several of us there for dinner, including Muriel, my sister-in-law, and her sister Nellie. We had eaten and were just talking when the air raid siren went off. A family friend with a car, who must have been a doctor, was there, and when the sirens went off, he said, "I'll take you back to the hospital."

"Oh, it's only 8:30. I don't need to be in until 11 o'clock tonight, I've got a late pass. I'll go on the tram. It will soon be 'all clear.'"

But no. Soon bombs were exploding all around us! As required, the Dunachies had made an air raid shelter in their backyard, but Mrs. Dunachie was ill in bed, following a gall bladder operation that hadn't gone well. Because she was in bed, Mr. Dunachie wouldn't go down to the air raid shelter either, so I said, "I'll just stay with you."

Now because I had refused the man's offer of a ride, I was stuck. It was impossible to return to the hospital because you weren't allowed out on the streets during the air raids. Air raid wardens went around the neighbourhoods, walking up and down the streets, to make sure everybody was inside.

We were sitting around Mrs. Dunachie's bed around midnight, when all of a sudden there was a tremendous blast! Her windows and the wooden shutters were shattered all over the bed, and the whole house shook. I was sitting on the far side of the room, opposite the window. Still, the explosion blew me onto the bed, and the heavy wardrobe fell over on top of me. The others had been sitting in chairs and had been thrown to the floor. None of us were badly hurt, but there was glass all over the room, and all the lights were out.

I made my way to the window and stuck my head out. It was a beautiful moonlit night illuminating a scene I couldn't believe. Across the street, our dear neighbours' house was demolished. About eight houses on that block were destroyed, as were others behind them, and on up the hill. I called out the window, trying to get the attention of the air raid warden because we needed an ambulance to evacuate Mrs. Dunachie.

Mr. Dunachie decided to try the phone downstairs. He warned, "Nobody go downstairs just now," as he carefully proceeded step-by-step along the side of the stairs. Fortunately, they were still strong, and didn't collapse and pitch him onto the floor below. Reaching the phone, he called and said, "I need help to get a person to hospital."

"Where are you? … All the hospitals are full, but we'll put you in the Red Hill Nursing Home."

Red Hill was a homeopathic nursing home quite close to us, and they quickly brought their ambulance. When it arrived, the air raid warden came running to see if he could get the ambulance to help with other injured people. The air raid wardens were always local people, and this one recognized me and said, "Oh, you've got to help me!"

"Why?" I said.

"The bombing has levelled our air raid first aid station where we had two doctors and two nurses on duty, and they've all been killed. There's so many people injured, and none of us have had any kind of medical training!"

"But I've not finished my training!"

"But you know whether a person's dead or dying; you can decide who needs to go first to the hospital. We just can't get ambulances; we don't have any first aid equipment. It's all been blown up. Please go down in the bomb crater and see if you can help people get out."

Many who had gone to bomb shelters were all right, but many in the deep craters left by the bombs were dead or injured. Most of the men in the area had been called up, but the few who were around were trying to bring people up. Then two or three lorries (or trucks) came. They were from the Royal Air Force (RAF) station near us, and they had big red crosses on them, but they weren't real ambulances. They were full of off-duty Air Force men, desperate to help, and we were so glad to get them. They helped pull injured people out of the rubble of their houses, and dug out the bodies of the children and adults who had been killed. It was a horrible sight.

All night I was called from one place to another to look at this one, look at that one, to try to stop bleeding. With the first rays of daylight, we found a man who had gone to the door to see how things were, when his house collapsed on top of him. He had been a BBC announcer and had brought his family from London to Scotland to escape the bombing. He'd just bought the house and hadn't had time to put in a bomb shelter, so his wife and two children were under the table in the dining room.

We extracted him from the door where the lintel had fallen on him. His back was broken, and he couldn't move his legs. As the men worked to free him, he kept pleading, "Go get my children, go get my children!" I ran back through the rubble to look for his children, and found his wife and two children under the table and they were all gone, all had been killed. The pressure of the blast wave had caused their lungs to collapse (implosion), leaving no marks on the outside of their bodies. It's a curiously bloodless way to die. I just wept.

Then I heard the RAF guy saying, "Come help us with this man! He's so badly hurt, I think he's going to die, and I don't want to be in the truck— I've never been with anybody who's died. Come with us to the hospital!"

The air raid warden said, "I think we're getting most of them out now. The other RAF are here, and a doctor is on the way. You can go with them." So I climbed into the truck with them, and sat on the floor. It was just an ordinary truck, there were no bunks, so this patient with a fractured spine just lay on the floor on some blankets. He kept moaning, "My wife and my children."

All I could do was repeat, "It's all right, we're looking after them. We're doing our best." His pulse was very slow, and he had trouble breathing. All I could do was sit beside him and pray with him.

As we rode in the lorry to the hospital, we could see the German fighter planes above us. They would swoop down low, and shoot from machine guns, and I was filled with such hate! If I'd had a gun, I would have tried to shoot them. War does one thing. It may pull your community together, but it fills you all with a sense of terrible hate. You fiercely want to destroy those who are destroying you.

In the lorry with me were two RAF guys, and one asked, "What's your name?"

"Nancy Orr."

"I don't believe it."

"What do you mean?"

"Well, I'm Bob Orr, and the driver is Jack Orr, and we're not related to each other. Are you related to me?" Then we started asking questions and discovered that none of us were related in any way we could discern, but we were all Orrs. It's so odd how commonplace conversation mixed in with the horror.

When we arrived at Western Infirmary with our patient, there was a terribly long line. At the gate they said, "Can you take him up to Red Hill?"

"He's a fractured spine, and he has trouble breathing." So, they took us right up to the emergency door.

Our fragile patient took my hand and pleaded, "Oh, please pray for my family, please pray that my children and wife are all right."

I had got the address of his nearest relative from him and said, "I'll get in touch with your relatives immediately." I didn't, of course; you gave that kind of information to the police, and the police contacted family. I often wondered about that poor man when he heard about his family. He was far from unique, there were so many families gone.

After taking our patient to the hospital, we went back up to Kelvindale. The air raid warden said, "Now it's daylight, and we've got all kinds of people in. You're dead tired, you'd better go." So I went by the Dunachies' and found they had gone to Mr. Dunachie's sister in Mayhill, so I took the streetcar to Mayhill to check on them before heading back to the hospital.

As I prepared to return to the hospital, Mr. Dunachie protested, "But, Nancy, you are so terribly tired." He called the hospital about delaying my return, and was furious to be told, "This is war, send her back immediately." Back I went to the hospital, still in a state of shock.

The nurse in charge was Isobel MacKay. Isobel knew the Dunachies because we had visited each other's families, although we weren't supposed to. Six months senior to me, she was in charge at this time, so we weren't supposed to be friends, but we were. When I came in, Isobel said, "Nancy, what happened?" I was cold and shaking as I told her, and she said, "What you need is brandy."

"No, I'm a teetotaller."

"Nancy, I'm a teetotaller too, but you need brandy," and away she went. She came back with "a wee dram," as they call it in Scotland. Adding a bit of sugar, she said, "Now take this, it will pull you together."

I was just drinking it when in walked Sister Baird, sister-in-charge. "What is going on here? You are drinking brandy!" Well, I burst into tears. I just couldn't take any more.

Then Isobel told her what had happened, and Sister Baird said, "All right, I understand. It was good that you had the brandy. Now go ahead, take the children's temperatures, and get around the ward."

It seemed a cruel thing at the time, but it was probably the best thing because when I went into the ward and saw all the children, I was soon able to pull myself together. Nevertheless, my half-day off for the next week was cancelled, because I had not come back to the hospital when the air raid siren had gone off. Nevertheless, I was glad to have been at Kelvindale to help during what proved to be Scotland's worst experience of the war, March 13, 1941, the Clydeside Blitz.

The great flock of German airplanes that bombed the Clydeside took most people by surprise, though Glasgow, on the River Clyde, was pivotal to the war effort. A centre of heavy engineering and shipbuilding, Glasgow was also a receiving point for hundreds of thousands of Allied troops. Yet few had expected the blitz to come to Scotland. Bombing to this point had centred on London, Coventry, and Liverpool to the south, but better weather and the increasing reach of German planes put Scottish targets within range. The RAF guys were very frustrated: "You know, we didn't have enough planes up here, we all thought they'd be bombing London."

Maybe three miles away from the River Clyde was the Great Western Road. It had been a beautiful moonlit night, and the Germans bombed along the Great Western Road as well as along the Clydeside. The interesting thing is that there was no catastrophe at the shipyards, but they got so many residential areas. It was thickly populated between the Clyde and the Great Western Road near where we lived. Historians have estimated that over 1000 bombs were dropped in that blitz, which lasted more than eight hours. It is estimated that of 12,000 Clydeside homes, 4000 were destroyed and all but perhaps a dozen were damaged.

***

During the war, medical equipment was expensive and hard to come by, and part of our responsibility as nurses was to avoid waste, especially of such precious items as thermometers. In those days, thermometers were quite different than they are now. A thermometer consisted of a thin glass tube with a thinner line of mercury running down the centre of the tube. Numbers were printed on the glass, and with the patient's body heat, the mercury rose to a point indicating the body temperature. When I was in nurses' training, we took temperatures every four hours for every patient.

At Royal Hospital for Sick Children, each ward had 16 cots on each side. The sides of the cots were only to be lowered when a nurse was present. One afternoon, I was told to "hurry up and get the temps done." I picked up the thermometer jar with its six thermometers resting on cotton in a small jar with carbolic water. As usual, I put thermometers under the arms of the first six children, then returned to the first child to take the pulse, recording the pulse and temp on the chart.

Having finished the first six, I was hurrying toward the seventh child when Eric, one of the first six, called out, "Nurse, pull up the side of the cot!" I rushed back, holding the jar of thermometers in one hand, and pulled up the side of the cot. But as I pulled up the side, the rail knocked the jar out of my hand, smashing the jar and all six thermometers on the floor. Woe is me! This was a serious offence.

After wiping up the tiny glass splinters, I grimly headed toward Sister's office. Inside, Sister was giving a personal farewell party for her favourite young surgeon, who was leaving to report to the army the next day. How I hated to interrupt the potentially romantic scene! But I had to report that I couldn't take the temps, because I had no thermometers.

Hesitantly, I knocked on the door. Angrily, Sister called out, "Come in, what do you want? I told you not to interrupt me."

"I dropped the thermometer jar, and I broke all six thermometers," I blurted out. "I am so sorry, I will pay for them, but I need to have a requisition slip signed by you, please."

Sister's face went crimson. "How can you be so stupid? You are always in a hurry, you Americans are always rushing around. For your carelessness, *you* take this requisition to Matron." Oh, no, I would have to confess to the nursing superintendent, too.

Miss Robinson was a very dignified lady, who was no less awe-inspiring than she had been at my initial interview. She very firmly ruled over all the staff at Sick Children's. To be sent to Miss Robinson was tantamount to going before the Queen, so it seemed to us. In fear and trembling, I walked through the conservatory to her spacious office. My legs shook as I knocked at her door. "Come in," came the command. "Yes, nurse, what can I do for you?"

"I am very sorry, Miss Robinson. I have broken six thermometers. I will pay for them."

"My dear young woman, this is very serious. How did you manage to break *six* thermometers?" With a trembling voice, I related the details of the terrible accident. "Nurse Orr, you must always remember that nurses must *never* act in a rush. I have noticed that you always seem to be in a hurry. Nurses must always be calm and dignified. The cost of the thermometers will be deducted from your salary for this gross carelessness. Now, remember to be ladylike and walk with your head held high."

"Yes, Miss Robinson, thank you." I slipped out the door, and feeling like a great clumsy oaf, headed toward the dispensary. Half my salary would go for thermometers, but my immediate concern was to get back to the ward to finish the 30 temps still to be taken. Miss Kay, the pharmacist, was in charge of the dispensary, and I really mean "in charge." Every ward made out a list each evening, sent it down to the dispensary before 5 p.m., and lo, the next morning, a huge basket filled with all the requested items would be delivered to the ward. The strict rule was that no one was allowed to go to the dispensary without a note from Matron or a prescription from a doctor.

Everyone was scared of Miss Kay, even the doctors, for she would check their dosages, and she loved to call them to her office, point out their errors, and give severe reprimands. Miss Kay was only about five feet tall, and she had a badly repaired cleft palate and harelip, which in no way hindered her vocal outbursts.

Trying to show a brave face, but quaking in my shoes, I slid the requisition through Miss Kay's window. She picked up the paper. "Six thermometers! Why do you need six?"

I stammered out my reply, "It was an accident. I was pulling up the side of the cot ..."

"Nonsense, no accident—pure carelessness. I never heard of anyone breaking six thermometers. Don't you know there's a war on? Do you think mercury grows on trees? Our brave, wonderful, merchant marine sailors are dying at sea. Our existence depends on them, and you toss away *six thermometers!*"

"I'll pay for them, Miss Kay, I ..."

"Of course you'll pay, but you can't pay for the lives of the sailors who have to bring the mercury through enemy waters. *Six thermometers*, when our children are starving." An assistant brought the thermometers and handed them to Miss Kay while she continued to berate me. "Soldiers dying in France, bombs falling all around us in Britain, and all Nurse Orr can do is break *six thermometers*."

Finally, she handed over the thermometers with a parting shot, "Don't let me see your face for a long time!"

I returned to the ward feeling such a fool. My mind churned with the insults Miss Kay had hurled at me, and my eyes filled with tears, so that I failed to notice, just ahead of me, a woman scrubbing the corridor floor. Nice soapy water on a tiled floor met rubber heels, and *swoosh*—I was flat on my back! I sat up in the pool of soapy water, looked at the packet in my hand, and let out a yell.

The maid rushed up to help me. "What's the matter then, have you broken your leg?"

"Oh, I wish I had. I've broken six thermometers! If only I'd broken a leg!"

"Aach, dinna say that, Lassie, wit is thermometers? Ye can aye get new yins."

I let out another howl. I stood up, water dripping from my white apron, wet down my back. Tears flooded my eyes and poured down my cheeks. The maid was eager to help, and tried to mop me up with a towel.

What should I do? Should I run away? Why did I want to be a nurse anyway? Maybe I could run across the street and buy six more at the chemist's (pharmacy)? That was out of the question, I didn't have enough money. No, I would just have to face up to it, even if it meant dismissal. At that thought, fresh tears welled up. When I got to the ward, Nurse Beebe called, "Thank goodness, you're back, Orr. Help me get the teas out, then finish the temps!"

"But I fell and broke the new thermometers!"

"Oh, no! Sister will kill you! Go tell her now, she is still with Handsome Harry in Sisters' room!"

Gulping down my fears and my tears, I timidly knocked on the door. "Come in," called the angry voice. "I told you I was not to be disturbed!"

"Sorry, Sister, but on the way back I fell on the slippery corridor and broke the new thermometers! I'm so sorry, Sister," I blurted out. Sister's face went scarlet. "You stupid fool! I can't believe that anyone could break 12 thermometers in one day!" She swore at me as she handed me the new requisition, adding for good measure, "Take this to Matron, I hope she throws you out!"

These words ringing in my ears, I trudged off through the conservatory once again, praying the whole way. Once again, I timidly knocked. "Come in! Well, what is it?" Miss Robinson was on the phone. "I'm so sorry, Miss Robinson, I broke six thermometers, and ..."

"So, you forgot my signature, give me the chit." Hurriedly, I pushed the paper in front of her. Still speaking on the phone, she signed the slip, and waved me out! She didn't realize it was a *second* request. Whew! Now for Miss Kay!

At the dispensary, I avoided Miss Kay's window, going around back where the assistant saw me and listened to my sad tale. "Do *not* tell Miss Kay, she is still muttering angrily, and taking this out on us! I know she is about to go off duty, and tomorrow is her day off. You go back to the ward, and I will bring the thermometers after she leaves! Go, quick before she sees you, and don't you touch a thermometer for a month!"

I scurried back to the ward to find that Sister had gone off on a date, the relief nurses had come on, and my shift was over! I had survived.

***

With the war on, every aspect of daily life changed. Many people were called up, and others volunteered. Although he was married, my brother Blair volunteered for the Royal Air Force, and operated radar on the shores of Britain through the entire war, never going overseas. Many who wouldn't join the military because they refused to kill were sent to work the mines. They got extra rations, but believe me, it was a lot harder than being in the army, the air force, or the navy because they received no shiny uniforms, no great praise or glory, and it was a highly dangerous job. When I nursed adults, I saw the frequent and terrible results of many mining accidents.

So many kinds of food were rationed, including eggs, bacon, butter, and meat. Chicken wasn't rationed, but it was very expensive. However, we could get rabbit meat and fish. There was a black market in rationed goods, but it was considered very unpatriotic to buy from it. So most of us learned to get by on one egg a week and two slices of bacon every two weeks.

There was much discussion of recipes using foods not on the ration, and other ways of stretching what you had.

In hospital we were given two little plastic boxes with covers, about the size of an 8 oz. cup. Each month your allowances of butter and sugar were doled out into your ration cups. We took our cups along to a meal if we wanted to use the butter or wanted the sugar for our tea. When you went visiting, you took your own rations, so you didn't use up the rations of your hosts. Because children, babies, and nursing mothers were given extra rations of milk powder and orange juice, mothers started coming to our antenatal clinics, something they'd never really bothered to do before.

My father was working in the shipyards. He had married again after I was in nursing, and my stepmother had two sons and a daughter who worked in aircraft production and received extra rations. So when I visited them, I would get a lamb chop, a sausage, and a real egg instead of powdered eggs.

In a sense, it was a wonderful time. People were very generous with one another. When the parents of our sick kids came on their weekend visits, they often brought cakes to the hospital, despite the tight rationing of chocolate, flour, sugar, and eggs. Everyone was encouraged to grow a Victory Garden. People grew vegetables in every spare bit of land in the city, from vacant lots to public parks.

Clothing and shoes were rationed, too. With a year's clothing rations, you could buy a winter coat, and that was all. Most of my rations went for stockings because I kept getting holes in my lisle stockings. Good thing we didn't have silk, or it would have been even worse. Some of the nurses who weren't so hard on their stockings, or who had boyfriends in the military who gave them stockings, would give me a couple of their coupons to help me get by. Having ration coupons was only half of it; you still needed to pay for everything, just as before the war.

One of the most severely rationed products was petrol, or gasoline. Only doctors, ministers, and emergency workers were allowed to have private cars, so many people put their cars up on blocks for the war years. District nurses and mailmen went about on bicycles. The milkmen and the men bringing coal delivered with horse and cart. There were many horses and carts on the road, and very few lorries.

The air raid sirens went off frequently, and we immediately stopped whatever we were doing. The two nurses responsible for the babies would take them to the baby room, while others put two children into each cot and wheeled the cots into the long corridor, which had thick, tiled walls and no windows. We put a thick woollen blanket over the cots, so if any debris fell, the blanket could protect them. We had to shut all the doors and put the shutters up on the ward windows. If it was a very bad bombardment, the nurses were to stay in the corridor underneath the children's cots. We had plenty of practice as time went on.

There were different hospital sirens for a real air raid than for a practice. The first time the real siren sounded at the hospital, we jumped out of our beds, grabbed our uniforms, and ran to our wards for roof duty or ward duty. The frenzied medical director was on the loudspeaker saying, "Nurses, get to the children very quickly. Put two cots into one child, put two cots into one child, and cover them up!" Then someone must have told him what he was saying, because he got flustered, and said, "Oh, you know what to do, you've practiced it often enough."

Although most air raid warnings continued to be for surveillance planes, we had to swing into action every time. I can still hear those sirens, bone chilling, ear splitting whines that went on and on. Jolted from sleep, we'd grab our uniforms and gas masks, run through underground corridors, upstairs to the wards to join the night nurses frantically pushing cots into windowless corridors, putting gas masks on children, carrying our own masks to put on if the gas warning went off.

The air raid practices were hard physical work, but an actual raid warning meant pandemonium, for the kids would cry and cling to us while we breathlessly shoved six-foot cots around the ward. When the "all clear" sounded, we had to pull the cots back to their regular places, put the children back in their own beds, and soothe them to sleep. Sometimes we would return to our own rooms in the nurses' home next to the hospital, only to be summoned again by a siren an hour later. It brought us all very close to one another.

Once at Sick Kids, we were up seven times during the night. Then at 6:30, when we should have been getting up for the day, the fire alarm went off. I was struggling into my uniform when over the loudspeaker we heard our superintendent announcing urgently, "All staff to wards immediately, the entire hospital must be evacuated in 30 minutes. Run to your wards.

Urgent call! Get the children out of here!" This warning was especially chilling: We were *never* told to run.

From all directions people ran, doctors, nurses, and maintenance staff, everyone rushing to the wards. We were told nothing about the emergency, only to get the kids *out* of the wards, not into the corridor as usual. When I got to my ward, Sister calmly said, "I want two nurses to get the case papers out and tie them to each child's arm with bandages. Then write the child's name and diagnosis on adhesive tape and apply to their forehead." Other people were dressing kids in warm coats over their pyjamas, and making sure they had their gas masks. Three or four children at a time were put on gurneys, wheeled to the ward door to be identified, then pushed down the corridor at a run to waiting ambulances and cars.

Over BBC radio, a call for help had gone out to all of Glasgow. The police were everywhere, along with Red Cross staff, truck drivers, and anyone with a car. The hospital doors stood wide open. People ran to the door and grabbed up the children, rushing them to safety. The response to the BBC appeal had been instantaneous.

In the chaos, a six-year-old wailed, "I want my ma!" An American Red Cross nurse gave him a sixpence as she rushed by. That silenced him, and we had just gotten him taped with his identity and bandaged with his records when he let out an enormous howl, "ma sixpence!" He had dropped his coin. I assured him that he'd get another sixpence later; there was no time to hunt for it now.

"Ma sixpence!" he cried again.

A policeman handed him a sixpence from his pocket and said, "There ye are, laddie. Keep a good hold on it, and away you go!"

But "laddie" grabbed the door frame, protesting, "This isnae ma sixpence! Ah'm nae goin' withoot ma ain sixpence!" The police peeled his arms from the door frame and wheeled him out to the waiting ambulance, but all down the corridor we could hear him screaming, "Ma sixpence, Ah want ma sixpence!"

After what seemed hours but was only 30 minutes, we had emptied the ward. Over the public address system, we heard, "All children have been evacuated. All staff, go to the emergency exit, where transport awaits you.

Do not go to your room. Do not wait for further orders. Evacuate the hospital immediately. Run!" Again, that most terrifying word—*run!*

But as we headed for the lorries that were to take us away, I was asked to go back to leave a written message saying that our children had been taken to Ruchill, the fever hospital. I had just left the note when Professor Fleming arrived. Fleming was in charge of Sick Kids.

"Where is everybody?" he demanded, thoroughly puzzled. "You've not been bombed, there's no damage to the hospital!"

"I know, sir. I don't know what it was, but all the children had to be evacuated to Ruchill."

"I'm going to go see the children," he said. "Come with me."

As we drove away, we learned from the BBC that a German bomb had gone down the funnel of an ammunition ship, but had not exploded. The ship was docked on the River Clyde, at the bottom of the cliff on which our hospital was built. If the bomb in the ship exploded, the whole hospital would be blown to bits.

At Ruchill, the children with infectious diseases had been removed from one ward to make room for our kids. When Fleming and I walked in the door, our children yelled, "We've got kippers, we've got kippers!" Everybody in Scotland loves kippers. They're smoked herring, delicious, but very bony. In Sick Kids, the children were fed a bland diet of porridge for breakfast; minced meat, potatoes, vegetables, and milk pudding for dinner; eggs and tea at four o'clock; then cocoa before they went to sleep. *Here* they were getting kippers!

"Kippers!" the chief exclaimed. "My children are not to eat kippers! The bones will be sticking in their throats! Take the kippers away and get these children some decent food!" So the kids began stuffing kippers in their mouths as fast as they could before the kippers were hustled away.

Later, we learned that when the bomb was located, some extraordinarily brave engineers went down into a ship full of ammunition, and defused it. Then, to be sure, the ship's hatches were opened, and it was allowed to slowly sink. Miraculously, not a single life was lost.

***

The war raged on. Because of the bombing in the south and the possibility of a German invasion, the government and many individuals felt that children should be evacuated. Many people in the cities sent their children to live with relatives in the country. Others arranged to send their children to relatives or friends in Canada or the United States. Children headed overseas were to be taken to certain port cities to be shipped out. The parents left their children there and were told, "You may not hear from your children for quite some time because we will not be sending them on a ship immediately; we'll be waiting for a convoy. It may take two weeks or more before they wind their way across the Atlantic."

One Sunday I was at lunch and about to go off duty when I was called back to the hospital. The previous night, a ship carrying children to the United States had been torpedoed. One lifeboat full of children had not been rescued until daylight, when a ship headed toward Scotland had spotted them. The ship had brought them to Greenock, near us in Glasgow, and they were being admitted to one of our side wards.

The lifeboat had held five children, the youngest a six-year-old girl, the oldest a 12-year-old boy named Cecil. I was being called back to take care of them. I found the poor things not crying, but stunned to silence. They were being treated for shock. I held them on my lap, hugged them, and talked with them, and after a day or two, they began to come out of it. I asked about their families, and came up with the bright idea to write a letter to their parents. Several weren't old enough to know their home addresses, but Cecil knew his, so I had him write a letter to tell his mother, Mabel, that he was OK and had a lot of adventures to tell her about their rescue. Then I wrote an additional note to tell her about the other four children and that all were doing well.

Cecil's mother lived in the Isle of Wight, on the English Channel off south-central England, very close to France. When she received the letters, she thought, "I should never have sent him. I want him back." So she went to the government offices where they had originally brought the children, and told them she wanted Cecil back. Not only did Cecil's mother demand his return, she got in touch with the other four mothers who all decided they wanted *their* children back, too.

This was in opposition to the government plan, which was to send them out again, and it created something of an incident. The Criminal

Investigation Division, CID, came to the hospital, and I was called to Matron's office to be questioned. Why had I written those letters? Did I realize what a disturbance it caused? I was reprimanded, and told to write no more letters. Mabel, however, had written to thank me for writing, saying how much it had meant to all the mothers.

Soon Cecil was diagnosed with diphtheria, and was removed to the infectious diseases hospital. I couldn't get in, but I talked to him through the window to let him know that someone was watching out for him. The other children went back to their parents, and when Cecil recovered, he went home, too. Mabel wrote and invited me to come visit them when the war was over.

Some time later I saw an advertisement from a Scottish woman who was ill and wanted to return home to the Isle of Wight, but needed a travelling companion to help her. My annual one month's leave was coming up, so I applied. After I was accepted, and I received my permit to travel, I wrote to Mabel, who asked me to stay with them when I arrived.

Cecil's family had a lovely old English house and a little bit of a farm with two cows and some chickens. Cecil's father was too old for active duty, so he was working in the aircraft factory. I had a wonderful time on the Isle of Wight visiting with Mabel and her husband. Cecil was their only child, and they were so thankful that his life had been saved.

The second time I visited, Cecil's family had two men billeted with them. A billet is an order to lodge someone in your home. People who were on assignment for the government or with the army would be billeted into homes. The government paid for their keep, but you were required to accommodate them.

The men were brothers, Rev. Kirkland and Mr. Kirkland. One worked in the aircraft factory, and the other was chaplain to that factory and another on the Isle of Wight. Mr. Kirkland used to talk with me about my work, and one time he asked, "How do you know if a person is a state-registered nurse?"

"You just get her number and get in touch with the state registration," I said. "Ask her where she trained."

After I was back at work in Scotland, I received a letter from Mabel saying a nurse in the aircraft factory had been arrested as a German spy. Mr.

Kirkland had obtained her register number, and found it wasn't authentic. Further investigation revealed other inconsistencies, and she was arrested.

At the end of the war, we learned that the Kirklands billeted with Mabel's family were actually on home assignment with the CID to track down fifth columnists and spies. A fifth columnist is someone who works within a country to aid the enemy, a collaborator, and the phoney nurse proved to be just such an enemy.

With the Protestant bike

The Tooting Nurse

Bob Ramer while a student at
Colorado School of Mines

Chapter 6: Babies, Babies, Babies

There are always heroes of war, but I already had heroes and heroines, people I had admired since childhood. They were missionaries such as David Livingston, Mary Slessor, Hudson Taylor, and Adoniram Judson. Their stories were so vivid that in my imagination, I was right there with them. Those who most captivated me were Mildred Cable and Francesca French, missionaries with the China Inland Mission. They managed a mission station with a girls' school, a church, a dispensary, and an "opium refuge" where addicts could receive treatment. When I was about 10, I told my mother that I wanted to be a missionary. Mother had smiled and said, "You need to have some kind of training to be able to help others, not just preach. You have to be prepared."

From that moment I had dual goals—to be a nurse and to be a missionary. These goals became a covenant to God in 1939. The meeting was in Glasgow, but Dr. Sidlow Baxter of Charlotte Chapel, Edinburgh, was the preacher. Twenty graduates from Glasgow Bible College were being dedicated and sent forth to various mission fields. The war with Germany had just been declared, so we all felt the danger they faced in going abroad. A powerful preacher, Sidlow Baxter issued a call for any in the audience who were willing for God to use them as foreign missionaries. When we stood, Dr. Baxter told us that God would accept our offer, but might not send us where we wanted to go. As he prayed for us, I felt a strong assurance of God's presence.

About six months after this meeting, I had time off, so I went to Edinburgh to hear Dr. Baxter preach at the Easter morning service. That was more than 60 years ago, and I still remember the sermon. Dr. Baxter drew on the story of the two friends who met a stranger on the way to Emmaus, after Jesus was crucified. At first they just walked along, but when they invited the stranger to stay with them, they recognized him as Jesus, and rushed back to tell others in Jerusalem.

Once again, I had a very real spiritual experience of the Holy Spirit. Dr. Baxter invited any who were moved to come talk with him in the vestry. In my turn, I told him of my promise to God, at his meeting in Glasgow, to be a missionary. He asked what I was doing now. I told him that I was doing my paediatrics training. He said, "I don't mean that, I mean what are you doing for Jesus *right now?*"

Taken aback, I wondered how I could do more. As a student nurse, I was on the wards 10 hours a day, and had classes in my off time. I only had one day off a month, and a half-day on Sundays. I could barely attend church.

"Ah," Dr. Baxter replied, "you have to find a way to witness to your nursing colleagues. Start a prayer group when you come off duty!"

"But we don't get to our rooms till 9 p.m.," I explained. "Besides, I don't know another Christian nurse in the whole hospital."

"Well, you have to pray that God will send you one more Christian nurse, and you two should pray together each week, and invite other nurses." Then Dr. Baxter's eyes, one brown, one blue, looked into mine as he said, "Nancy, you must finish your paediatrics nursing, then do your general training in the very best hospital in Britain, then do your midwifery training because only the very best, most qualified people should be sent out in God's name."

As Dr. Baxter prayed for me, I realized how much study, work, and spiritual preparation lay ahead of me-at least 10 years' worth! It was a sober lass who walked out of that church, but I was even more determined to prepare myself so God could use me. I returned to the hospital, and prayed for another nurse to help me start a prayer group.

A few months later, I attended a special tea for Christian nurses, in one of the Glasgow tearooms. As I registered at the door, the receptionist said, "Oh, are you Nancy from the Royal Hospital for Sick Children in Yorkhill?"

"Yes, I don't know any *other* Christian nurses there."

"Come, you're not the only one," she said. "Let me introduce you to May Wilson, she is a senior there!"

After a few months of praying together each week, May and I started a group, which met for prayer and Bible study every Monday at 9 p.m. God had answered my prayer. After three years there were 30 regular members, and other nurses took over the leadership when I graduated.

***

After graduating in paediatric nursing, I was ready to do my general training, and had been accepted to one of the top hospitals in Britain, St. Thomas Hospital, London. Shortly before I was to go, however, St. Thomas was badly bombed, and their buildings were destroyed. They suggested that I apply to Edinburgh Royal Infirmary, also a highly regarded hospital. I was accepted at Edinburgh but told I would have to wait two years to be admitted, as they had a long waiting list. So, in the meantime, I took midwifery training at Bellshill Maternity Hospital in Lanarkshire, in the centre of the mining area. Miners had big families, so there were babies, babies, babies—plenty of opportunities for learning.

Once, during my midwifery training, I was delivering a baby when the amniotic fluid suddenly sprayed all over my face and into my eye. The baby was coming, and there was no time to waste, so I wiped my eye on my shoulder and got on with the job. After the birth, I washed my face, but forgot all about the amniotic fluid in my eye and the stern warning to put the recommended drops in the eye *immediately* in case of such contamination.

Two days later my eye was infected and swollen. The state exams were coming up in a week, and I could not see to read! If I couldn't sit the exam this time, I would have to wait another six months. My loyal friends read to me, and helped me study, and I begged to be allowed to sit the exam, but I was forbidden to do so. However, the next day when I woke up, my eye felt better, so off I went to the exam centre. I slipped off my eye shield, walked into the exam room, picked up my paper, and proceeded to write for three solid hours.

"Time is almost up—only 10 minutes left." Good, I had finished in time! I sighed, then returned to my paper to read over my answers, but I couldn't see a word! All was black! I sat there scared out of my wits! I sat quietly praying as people started to leave. The examiner collected my paper, but still I sat. One of my friends whispered, "We can leave now, let's go."

"I'm blind! I can't see anything," I almost sobbed. My friend went for a staff person, and I was taken by ambulance to the eye hospital. I was told it was eye exhaustion. Both eyes were bandaged, and I lay in bed for three or four days, just waiting to see if my sight would return. In all, I was off duty for four weeks receiving treatment. Thank God, my sight came back, but after that I needed glasses for reading.

Happily, I passed my written exam and was ready to take my practical exam a month later. After that crisis, I never again took my eyes for granted.

***

As we became more experienced in midwifery, we went out into the district to deliver babies. One day, the district midwife was out with another patient, so I took the call. The instant I got there, I could see that the poor woman was extremely ill. Immediately, I called for help. I took her blood pressure and it was dangerously high. Soon two doctors and a nurse arrived in the ambulance that was equipped for doing a caesarean section on the spot.

When the chief obstetrician examined her, he said, "It's got to be done right away!" We laid sterile sheets on the dining room table, laid the woman on them, and did an emergency caesarean. It was a heart-pounding experience for everyone involved, but it ended well with a healthy baby and mother.

***

Sometimes our runs out into the districts were adventures above and beyond the delivering of the baby. One time Alex, the maternity hospital ambulance driver, and I were sent out into a driving snowstorm to bring a patient back to the hospital. The ambulance was a huge wartime field ambulance with the basic necessities, but no modern comforts such as heating. Along the way, Alex hummed, "I'm dreaming of a white Christmas." The snow was falling all around us, and I shivered with cold in my nurse's cape and uniform.

"Oh, Alex, I'm freezing. Can't you sing something else?"

The usually dour ambulance driver laughed and answered, "Aye, Lassie, how about 'I've got my love to keep me warm?'" Since Alex was well into his 50s, and I was in my early 20s, I knew he was teasing me. We were headed for a far-off miner's cottage on a tiny farm. The roads were rough and covered in snow and ice, so the midwife couldn't get there on her bicycle. That's why we'd been called out in the ambulance.

I'd begun the journey sitting in the attendant's seat, a collapsible one in the back of the truck, but it was terribly cold back there, and I was being jostled from side to side on the icy roads. So I came up front and wrapped a patient's blanket around my legs, thereby breaking two rules: "No nurse sits in the front of the ambulance," and "Never use a patient's blanket."

Alex soon stopped singing to concentrate on driving, for the snow was falling so thick and fast that we could barely see. At every crossroads, I'd jump out, wipe the snow off the signboard to check our direction, and we'd go on. With only my nurse's shoes, not boots, my feet were soaked, but Alex didn't dare take his foot off the gasoline for fear the cranky engine would stall. I didn't trust myself to keep the engine running in a blizzard; in fact, I didn't even have a driver's license.

Despite Alex's cautious driving, we slid into a ditch. We tried to dig ourselves out, but to no avail. Seeing some lights ahead, Alex walked to the cottage and came back with a man. Luckily, we were at our destination, but the mother was "near her time. Ye'd better hurry, Nurse."

Seeing how deep the snow was on Alex's trousers, I accepted the huge Wellington boots they'd carried out for me. Taking my big white pillowcase full of sterile sheets and towels and my black instrument bag, I shuffled off toward the house.

The moment I saw the mother, I knew there was no time for the usual full prep, so I scrubbed, washed my lady well, and rescrubbed just in time to see a buttocks, or breach, presentation.

"Oh, no, Lord, what do I do now?" This was her second baby; everything was supposed to be normal!

Then I remembered the chief's teaching: "The main thing in an emergency is to stay calm, do not rush things. Be patient, work it through as you would on an examination paper. Above all, keep your patient calm and sure of your ability—even if you're scared stiff."

Scared stiff, I was. "Don't worry, Mrs. McAdam, we'll soon have the wee fellow out. Just a bit of patience, don't push too hard. Just pant, then push when I tell you."

To my amazement, all the teaching we had on breach delivery came back to me step-by-step. As I worked, I kept praying, "May she be all right. Help me to do the right thing." Finally, the baby was out, *but with the cord wound round his neck!* I quickly cut it. At first the baby didn't make a sound!

The steps came back to me: "suction tube, slap his back, breathe into his mouth," and—Praise the Lord!—he yelled his head off!

So far, so good. Remembering, again, "Give the child to the father to wrap up and keep warm. If the mother is bleeding, and the placenta is not yet released, rub the uterus. Don't panic, don't push, don't pull, keep calm."

At last, a mighty pain, and the placenta came out intact! But she was still bleeding. Silently, "Lord, stop the bleeding!"

"Administer ergometrine, hand on the fundus." Now what? No telephone, what else can I do? Pray, surely. The uterus is soft, the mother very weak. What more? The chief's words, "Keep calm, reassure the patient." Keep praying.

"Mrs. McAdam, look at your fine wee son." When she turned to look, out came a huge blood clot. "Thank you, Lord. I hope that's it." And it was. The bleeding stopped; the uterus was hard. I kept her warm and still as I cleared away the mess. After helping her drink a hot cup of tea, I covered her with all the blankets I could find, and she slept. I sat beside her all night, worried about haemorrhage, but in the morning, she was much stronger. I bathed her, and wondered about stitching up the tear. I had used all my sterile stuff, and had no local anaesthetic. Could she take the pain?

The father gave me tea and bread, and went out with Alex to see what could be done about the ambulance. Then I heard a great rattle and noise. I looked out to see a tractor coming through the snow, and on it, the local midwife with all her sterile equipment! She had spent all night trying to get to the cottage. She soon had the stitches in, and told me I could go back, and she would stay with the patient to make sure that there was no further bleeding. She was as exhausted as I was, but took over cheerfully. Meanwhile, the men used the tractor to pull the ambulance out of the ditch.

Everyone was so happy that both baby and mother were well. Donning my now dry shoes and stockings, I was lifted onto the tractor and taken to the ambulance. On the way back to hospital, Alex and I were both singing at the top of our lungs, "I'm dreaming of a white Christmas!"

***

During my midwifery training, after attaining the title "maternity nurse" at six months, I moved into the heart of Glasgow to do deliveries in the homes in the slums. At Rotten Row, the nurse was in charge of the patient. We took medical students on call with us and taught them to do deliveries.

We midwives waited in the hospital waiting rooms for calls, then took turns doing deliveries. There would be about six students and six nurses, and we would play games, talk, and write silly poetry. When Sister told us that no cases were expected, some were given permission to go out to a nearby movie, where we could be reached if we had to go to a patient. There was great camaraderie, and fun amongst us all.

***

To graduate from Bellshill, you had to observe 10 deliveries with a midwife, do 25 deliveries under a midwife's supervision, 25 more on your own in Rotten Row, the Glasgow slums, and 25 more out in the district, that is, in the country. Ten of those deliveries had to be observed by the chief obstetrician. Then there were the written and oral exams. A Mrs. McDougal was nursing superintendent at Bellshill, as well as Secretary of the Scottish Nurses Association. It turned out that *she* was the little lady in the coffee shop who had suggested paediatric nursing at Yorkhill, and cleared the path for me to enter nurses' training years before.

When I graduated from Bellshill, I stayed on for six months to work with the Flying Squad, the ambulance crew that went out for deliveries.

***

Bellshill Maternity Hospital had a Nurses Christian Fellowship in which I was involved. When I graduated and went on to Edinburgh Royal, once again there was weekly prayer and Bible study, and it was in these groups where I met most of my closest friends. In the city of Edinburgh itself, there were many Christian youth meetings and rallies with wonderful singing and good fellowship. I joined Charlotte Chapel and attended as often as I could. It may sound as if I was a goody-goody, but I was *not*.

In Edinburgh Royal, where I went for my general training in June 1943, nurses were forbidden to date students or residents, but we could go out in groups, which was a lot of fun, though war continued to touch every aspect of our lives. As soon as the medical students finished their residencies, they were off to war. We all had to take turns sitting on the roof, fire watching. At the hospital, we had the radio on all the time because we had to know where the planes were headed. Then came D-Day, when the Allied invasion crossed the English Channel to land in Normandy, France. Three wards in the Royal were cleared, as we prepared to receive soldiers flown over from France. The wards filled quickly, and the operating went on at a furious pace.

The soldiers arrived filthy and often unconscious. I remember cleaning up one soldier who was covered with dirt and oil. As I washed him up, he gazed up and asked, "Am I in Heaven?" He was really in shock.

"You're next door to it," I said. "You're in Scotland." His name was Bill Bush, and whenever he came back in to the ward, he always teased me about being this Scottish angel in Heaven. He had been a tank driver, and the Germans had thrown a hand grenade into his tank. The tank went up in flames, and he jumped out. But the captain sitting beside him had gotten caught, and Bill went back to pull him out. The captain was so badly burned that he died. Bill survived, but with terrible burns and a badly scarred face.

The townspeople were very good to the soldiers in our wards. They would use up their precious sugar to bring baked goods to the soldiers. People within walking distance of the hospital would invite them to their houses for tea. It would never have been allowed in ordinary times, but as it was wartime, we were allowed to take the soldiers out in groups of four or five. The outings were organized by the military and the ward Sister. Patients had to have a uniformed nurse with them, and alcohol was strictly forbidden. This was how I came to know Johnnie.

Johnnie was a sergeant whose leg had been blown off when his tank was blown up. A newspaper reporter before the war, he was a handsome Welshman with a great sense of humour, who treated all the nurses with respect. He also made sure that all the men in the ward respected the nurses—no swearing, no dirty jokes, and no pawing.

When we took the men out, each man could choose his nurse, and Johnnie chose me. I was thrilled to be selected, and the ward Sister was all for encouraging us. Sister McKay was in charge of Ward 34, and she doted on those she called "my boys." Nearly all our patients came to us in shellshock, so we tried to help them back to reality. The ward was full of laughter and great caring for each other.

After some months, Johnnie asked if I would be his girl. By this time, I felt I was in love with Johnnie, too, and we made plans for after Johnnie got his artificial leg, and was discharged. Johnnie said he would get his sportswriter job back, and we would live in his hometown. When he was ordered to a special rehab unit in England, we hated to part, but looked upon it as a step toward the future. At first we wrote twice a week; then it became once a week, then the letters came further and further apart. I wrote to ask Johnnie if he wanted to break it off, but his answer came quickly, insisting that we go on.

After Johnnie left, I met again a man I'll call Hamish, whom I had known in Glasgow as a divinity student who went to the rallies. At this time, Hamish was an assistant minister in a church, and he asked me to help with the youth work there. Some nursing friends and I ended up spending a good deal of our off-duty helping at the youth club, and teaching in the Sunday School. I wrote telling Johnnie of my activities, and he replied, "Don't get too religious, or expect me to go to church." That stung! Suddenly, I realized that I had not even talked with Johnnie about my faith! I prayed earnestly, and convinced myself that I would convert him.

I had some leave coming, so I wrote Johnnie to say that I could come to visit him and his parents. He replied at once saying that he would make arrangements. It was the same cheerful, handsome Johnnie who welcomed me at the station, full of plans and excitement. He took me to a hotel, saying his parents didn't have room. Then we went for a walk, and all the old attraction was there.

He took me to a pub to eat. Of course, alcohol is sold in pubs, and I had never been in a pub before. I told him I didn't want to go, but he just laughed. In the pub, he had many friends, including a number of newspaper colleagues, to whom he introduced me as "my girl, my very special girl." They teased him, and joked about weddings. Then I heard them say he was missing a football game that he was to report on. He answered, "I'm writing it up now." He sat listening to the radio, and writing the whole thing as if he had been there. I was disturbed, but rationalized that he wanted to have time with me, and it would only be this once.

After seeing a movie, we went back to the hotel for dinner. I talked about my work at the church, and the big meeting I was organizing in Edinburgh with Dr. George McLeod, founder of the Iona Community, as the speaker.

Johnnie wasn't the least interested; indeed, I think he was bored. We talked, kissed, hugged, and at the close of the evening Johnnie left, arranging to pick me up for church in the morning. After he left, I wondered if I could fit into Johnnie's life. When I asked about his family, Johnnie had said, "You wouldn't like them. They drink too much, especially on a Saturday."

That night I prayed hard, remembering my promise to God. If I married Johnnie, I certainly would never be a missionary. The next morning Johnnie picked me up at the hotel, delivered me to the church door, and said, "I will pick you up in an hour." I was shocked and asked, "What will you do after we are married and have children?"

"Oh, I have no objection to you and the children going to church, but I refuse to go, so I'll stay home and read the papers." I sat in the church, miserable, as I contemplated my future. I was about to graduate my general training, and had told the Church of Scotland that I wasn't interested in being a missionary because I planned to get married soon.

After church, Johnnie took me to lunch, and I tried to tell him how important my faith was to me, how important it was for me to have a husband who shared my interests, and I told him of my promise to be a missionary. Johnnie laughed and said, "You can be a missionary here, and convert me. It will take a lifetime, but go ahead and try."

Then it hit me; he thought my faith a whim, and my conviction a joke.

Later, at the train station, I said, "Johnnie, I am fond of you, but we have nothing in common now. You don't understand my love of God and the church, and I don't appreciate drinking and dog racing, so now, just let us break it off. No more letters, this is finished."

Johnnie looked shocked, but, collecting himself, he laughed and said, "Oh, you'll get over this. I'll write and convince you."

"No, it is over." I got on the train and wept most of the way to Edinburgh, but I knew it was the right decision. Johnnie wrote two or three times. The third time I replied and told him to date other girls with whom he had more in common, and the letters ceased.

Meantime, I was very busy organizing this big meeting in Edinburgh for nurses from all the Edinburgh hospitals. The mayor of Edinburgh and the moderator of the Church of Scotland were to be there. Hamish was a great help, getting in touch with people, and seeing to some of the details. He knew all about Johnnie, and I knew he had a girl at home, "Mary," whom he had been going with for years.

I was very involved with Hamish's church, and we were often together. One day Hamish was to meet me to go to a movie with a group from the youth club. He came to the hospital, and as I walked out I saw him and thought, "What a lucky girl is Mary!"

Taking me aside, Hamish said, "I have arranged for another minister to take the group, I want to talk to you." We sat on a bench in The Meadows, a public park behind the hospital, and Hamish said, "Nancy, maybe it is too soon, but I have to tell you I have fallen in love with you. I know you are getting over Johnnie, but I have never been so in love before!"

I was thrilled. "But what about Mary?" I asked him.

"I've known Mary for years. I love her, and I did say I would marry her someday, but I had no idea what love really is, 'til I met you." We hugged and kissed and from then on, I was out with Hamish as often as possible. He was every inch a Scot, handsome, full of fun, and he had a wonderful way of talking to everyone in the same friendly way, whether he was speaking to a Laird, or to one of the wyfies (wives) in the slums. They all could appeal to Hamish for help. A prominent minister was nurturing Hamish to be his deputy, and "the boss" was quite pleased when he heard rumours that Hamish and I were going together.

With his broad shoulders and rugged features, Hamish looked like a cheerful farmer—until he began to preach, when his sincerity and deep faith won many hearts. His forte was reaching out to the poor, the troubled youth, and the ordinary person in the street. The Presbytery, the governing body of the church, considered Hamish a radical. Being an early member of the socially conscious Iona Community, Hamish was an ardent Labour Party member, and a keen socialist. He loved having friendly arguments about "the stodgy church" of Scotland, yet he was a loyal member of the Presbytery.

It was then the rule that all ministers had to wear clerical collars when off duty but within the bounds of the Presbytery. With these "dog collars," the ministers were expected to wear black suits. Hamish rebelled, wearing a light brown Harris tweed jacket over dark pants, and whenever he could, he would whip off his clerical collar. Many times he was reprimanded, but he always charmed his way out.

By this time, I was in my last year at the Royal, and had passed all my exams, so whenever I was off duty, we were together. Hamish was the opposite of Johnnie. He was deeply involved in the church, and we shared so many interests and friends. My family was fond of him, and did all they could to encourage our relationship. Hamish was passionate and very romantic—singing songs, quoting poetry. I kept thinking of Mary, but he assured me that relationship was over. As he became more and more passionate, I stepped back with a flash of insight and asked, "Have you had intercourse with Mary?"

He laughed, "Yes, but it doesn't matter."

"It does matter, Hamish. If you have had intercourse, as far as I am concerned, you are *married*."

He was shocked. "Don't be silly! On the farm, the animals are doing it all the time; it's doing what comes naturally." Seeing my deep repulsion, he asked, "What can I do? If I break off with Mary, will you forgive me and marry me?"

I stood back and said, "I forgive you, but after you have broken off with Mary, we should not go out together for six months. Then you will know which one of us you truly love." He agreed.

After a trip home, he returned to say, "Mary is such a child, and our families are all angry at me for breaking her heart. So just wait a while, because I did tell her I was in love with you." So, we saw each other, and it was hard to control our passion, but somehow God always brought us back from the edge. Hamish would always say, "I'll never force you," and he didn't. It was a tense time. We would agree not to see each other, then be thrown together at meetings and feel drawn together again.

Finally Hamish said, "Nancy, I love you, and I love Mary. She doesn't understand that my love for you is so different. I want to marry you, and I wish I could marry you both."

After much prayer and weeping, I knew I had to break it off completely. I secretly hoped that it would cause Hamish to cut it off with Mary. He had always said, "If you ever want to break it off, don't write a letter, tell me to my face."

So, I wrote a letter, and arranged to meet Hamish in the crowded Princes Street Gardens. As we sat on a bench, I read the letter I had composed. I told him, "I could never accept being one of two loves. I want to marry a man to whom I will be the only love in his life. I would rather be single and free than continue this friendship."

For a long time, we sat quietly. I know I was praying. Finally, I told Hamish that I had accepted an appointment in London and would be leaving, and that we should never contact each other again. Finally, Hamish said, "I have sinned, and now I have to be responsible for my actions. You are a strong person. God has great plans for you, but I have to rebuild my dreams."

The ever-romantic Hamish began to sing softly, "In the gloaming, oh, my darling, think not bitterly of me. I have gone and left you lonely, left you lonely, left you free."

I got up, and walked toward the hospital, signalling him not to follow. He sat with his head bowed, quietly wiping away the tears. I walked hurriedly, surreptitiously wiping my own.

***

Then came tremendous news. The Armistice had been signed! The fighting ceased on my birthday, May 7, in 1945, and the Armistice was signed on May 8. That day all the lights in Edinburgh blazed on, celebrating the end of the blackout! We nurses no longer had to shutter the hospital windows! That night we went straight from work into the city.

Church bells rang, and people poured outside, linking arms with one another and dancing down the street, praising God and singing hymns or war songs, shouting, "Victory has come, Victory has come!" That glorious night was one of the happiest of my life.

At every street corner, we would stop and dance some reels, or the "Dashing White Sergeant." It was all Scottish dancing, all down the mound, down Princes Street, down to Lothian Road, and back around, and we never slept that night. It was so wonderful! No planes overhead! The air was filled with a sense of joy and relief.

Then when VJ Day came in August, it was also great. Despite the end of the war, rationing continued for some years in Britain. The war was over in

1945, but we still had rationing more than six years later. Gradually, however, things went off the ration. I always admired the way Britain handled the postwar years, so there wasn't panic, or a depression when people were suddenly out of work. British factories resumed the making of luxury items such as china, but only for export. The money was needed to repay our war loans. The luxury goods we couldn't yet purchase at home were displayed in store windows with the promise, *"Britain can do it. We'll be next."*

Chapter 7: The Tooting Nurse

Leaving Hamish behind, I left Scotland for a fresh start in London as a Ranyard nurse, doing public health nursing in the city slums. After six months' training, the London City Council assigned me to the Tooting Broadway District. Thus, I received the questionable title of "the Tooting nurse."

Although I was under the jurisdiction of the city, I also worked for the Ranyard Mission, a small arm of the Anglican Church. Ranyard had been started about 100 years previously by Ellen Ranyard, who was concerned about the women in the slums of London. These poor women had no health care, and little spiritual care, so Mrs. Ranyard talked with Florence Nightingale about how to help them. They determined that a midwife and a Bible woman, or deaconess, should live in the slums together and be constantly available to help the women with their deliveries, their children's health, and their spiritual needs. The Bible woman would have a thorough knowledge of the Bible and serve as a social worker-missionary.

When they put their plan before the bishop, he suggested that local churches employ the nurse and the deaconess, who would be under their care. They would be known as the church nurse and the church mission deaconess, and would be considered part of the staff, meeting weekly with the pastoral committee.

A goodly number of the Anglican churches adopted the idea, so that by the time I joined Ranyard, there were probably 75 to 100 nurses and deaconesses, scattered all over London. No longer did the pairs necessarily live together; most had their own flats.

During my months of training, I lived in Ranyard House, in the centre of London, in a quiet back street near Euston Station. There we had lectures on pastoral care and counselling of the dying, as well as Bible study classes. We also attended the Queen's Nurses' lectures in preparation for passing our district nurses government registration exams. This was just after the war, and the devastation from the bombing could be seen everywhere.

I loved Ranyard, and soon after passing my exams, I was appointed to St. Nicholas Parish as the Tooting District Nurse. Every day I got cards from hospitals, notifying me of patients who had been discharged and needed dressings or follow-up. There were a number of tuberculosis patients, who had to be visited daily. I also went to a local chemist's for my orders from the District Health doctors. I had no phone, and because of war restrictions could not get one, so the doctors left their messages with the chemist, and I picked them up every morning and evening. The chemist's was directly opposite St. Nicholas Anglican Church. The staff in the chemist's shop soon became my friends, and we had our mid-morning coffee together. Dennis, the owner of the chemist shop, was a Catholic, and he would call the priest, Father O'Reilly, over from the Catholic Church on the corner to join us for coffee.

I had a number of Catholic patients, many of whom never attended church, and I would customarily ask if they wanted to see the priest. Some who knew they were dying wanted the priest, but they often didn't know him, and many were afraid he would yell at and chastise them. They sometimes would agree when I offered to come *with* the priest. Then as soon as they saw Father and his caring ways, I could leave. The Methodist Church, which was down Broadway a bit, also helped support me, so I attended their church one Sunday a month.

Most Sunday mornings I attended St. Nicholas, and greeted people at the door. On the third Sunday of the month, in the afternoon, there were christenings, and the deaconess and I were to attend them all. I would get to know the parents, then visit the family within a month and at every anniversary of the christening for the child's first five years. The deaconess visited more frequently, and guided them into Sunday School.

Every Thursday evening the St. Nicholas church team would meet. The rector was Rev. Neil, a traditional type, maybe in his 60s, though he seemed old to me. He knew nearly everyone in the parish, for he kept an eye on all that he married, buried, or christened. Rev. Braziere was the curate. He and his family had just been released from a Japanese concentration camp in China. The deaconess was a stately, older, and very solemn lady, who worked mostly with the rector. Then there was Mr. Walker, a city missionary in his 40s and an energetic Cockney. Mr. Walker was in charge of the church's mission house at the other end of the parish. I often helped him as he visited old age pensioners, and organized and ran youth groups, Sunday School, and Sunday evening services.

Each Thursday, one-by-one, we spoke of our week's work. I would report on my patients, including whether or not they received spiritual care from any denomination. If they had no church connections, then it was the responsibility of St. Nicholas to provide it. When I asked the patients if they would like a visit, it was OK if they said no. Many would say, "My house isn't clean enough for the rector, but let the missioner come." Mr. Walker, with his London accent, fit right in.

Rev. Neil was gracious about their preference for Mr. Walker, but the rector had one major flaw. He was an Irish Anglican and vehemently opposed to Roman Catholics. About once a month, he gave a sermon criticizing Catholicism. Concerned that I had to go to a Catholic chemist's every day, he sometimes asked me, "Do you feel safe?" I assured him that Dennis, the owner, was a gentleman, and very kind. I neglected to mention that I drank coffee every day with the priest, a cheery Irishman, "full of the devil," as he described himself. Between Dennis, the priest, and the two lady attendants in the shop, I knew all the gossip in the area, which was very helpful as I went about my rounds.

In those days we district nurses got around on bicycles. Mine was a rusty old Raleigh with very high wheels, and awkward to handle. The bike was so high that when I stopped, I had to jump off because my feet didn't reach the ground. One snowy day with icy roads, the bus in front of me suddenly stopped, and I fell with the bike on top of me. I was fine, but the bike most definitely was not. Sighing, I took my bike to the repair shop, then walked to the chemist shop to pick up my orders. I was all dishevelled, and there were holes in my stockings, but my friends at the chemist's soon cleaned and bandaged me.

Later, Father O'Reilly offered to walk with me to pick up my bike at the repair shop, and he heard the man say, "This is an ancient model; it's time they got you a new one!" There was little hope of that. Bikes were rationed, and there was a waiting list. I just laughed and pedalled off.

A month later, at the chemist's, Father O'Reilly called Dennis to come outside, then they called me out. All the staff were there, and in the midst of them was a beautiful, brand new Raleigh bicycle! Father said, "There you are, take it away, and the Lord be with you!" Overwhelmed and thrilled, I gratefully accepted.

Father O'Reilly had made an announcement to his parishioners in church, and these folks had raised the money for a new bicycle in a month, all the time keeping it a secret. I have no idea how he got around the waiting list, but that was typical of Father O'Reilly. After coffee, I rode off on my rounds, leaving my old bicycle to be collected later. At the rectory that night, I cheerfully told my wonderful story. To my amazement, the rector was angry, far angrier than I had ever seen him.

"You will *not* ride a *Catholic* bicycle! Take it back to them, and tell them we will look after our own! I will not be beholden to *them*." Rev. Braziere had arrived as we were talking, and he suggested that we have an Anglican dedication of the bike, thereby making it OK, but Rev. Neil would have none of it, and I had to take the bike back. Rev. Neil did eventually get me a new bike, but nothing so grand as the Raleigh.

Later, when I left Tooting for missionary college, the rector insisted I take the bike with me, and added, "Be sure to take it to China with you." I had that bike for 40 years. I rode it daily, taught all my kids to ride on it, and when I left India, I gave it to a Scottish missionary family. It was certainly a *sturdy* bike.

When I reluctantly took the new bike back to Father O'Reilly, he just laughed and said, "Someone will use it." Thereafter, he would occasionally tease me, asking, "How's the Protestant bike behaving today?"

As a nurse, I reported weekly to the public health officers of the district, Dr. H. and Dr. C. Both were very fine general practice doctors, and well liked in the district. Every Thursday morning, for perhaps an hour, we discussed new patients, and changes in treatment for the continuing patients. I discussed my concerns, and they taught me any new procedures I needed to know.

Dr. H. was easygoing, but very professional. He was a lay reader at St. Nicholas and often preached at special services. Dr. C. was very reserved and had a sceptic's view of the church. One time when I was in the office, the phone rang. Dr. C. answered it, and after listening said, "Madam, there are two doctors in this practice. Dr. H. is the one who preaches, I am the one who practices! Dr. H. is not here at present," and he hung up. Looking at me, Dr. C. grinned, speculating, "I wonder how many people she retells that story to?"

Shortly after I arrived in the district, it had been Father O'Reilly who found me a place to live. It was a two-bedroom apartment owned by Mrs. Treadwin, who shared the apartment with me. Treddy was a barmaid in her 50s who wanted nothing to do with church. Widowed, she had two sons. One was a pilot overseas, and the other had Down syndrome and lived in an institution, where she visited him regularly. Treddy was a joy to live with, and I grew very fond of her. A very motherly woman, she welcomed my Scottish friends, and my nursing friends, and they all learned to love her. Sometimes Mr. Walker and I arranged programs for the old age pensioners, and although I'm not much of a singer, we would sing songs of the beloved Scottish entertainer Harry Lauder. Treddy enjoyed these "concerts," as she called them, and laughed hysterically when I went off key, and Mr. Walker went off key right along with me. I was very happy in London, and felt I had found my special place.

Life was good, but my conscience would never let me completely enjoy it. In my mind, I knew I had promised to be a missionary, but had settled into an easier way. So, unbeknownst to anyone in London, I wrote to the China Inland Mission (CIM), applying to go to China. Having done so much preparation, I had no doubt that they would accept me. As I put the envelope in the mailbox, I prayed silently, "Lord, everyone says I'm a missionary here, so if I don't get accepted, I will know it's your will."

The China Inland Mission replied, "Your application has been accepted. We are pleased to note all your training, but you will also need to attend two years of Bible college, for which you will be responsible for the fees. If you are willing to do this, you should come for an interview, wearing a suit that you have sewn yourself."

I was *not* a talented seamstress and had never sewn a dress in my life, let alone a suit! And after 10 years of nursing, I had no money in the bank. How would a public health nurse in the slums of London accumulate the money for missionary college? Without question, I could not afford it. Relieved, I wrote to the CIM to say that I could not pursue missionary work. Fine! Now I was off the hook. Still, there was a nagging in my soul.

One day a photographer in Tooting took a picture of me in my full dress nurse's uniform. A good photograph, it was the best I ever had, and the photographer even displayed it in his window. On the spur of the moment, I sent a copy to Hamish, adding, "Do not write back!" Did I mean it? I don't know, but he did reply, "Thank you. It tears my heart." I didn't answer.

When my two weeks' holiday came around, I went back to Scotland to stay with Blair and Muriel in Glasgow. Not knowing about his relationship with Mary, Muriel kept urging me to see Hamish, but I demurred.

Then I had a call from a minister in Glasgow, a close friend of Hamish's, asking me to come for tea, so I did. The minister and his wife were both good friends of mine. Before our tea, he took me into his study and said, "Nancy, Hamish's senior minister has asked me to talk with you. Hamish has had a breakdown, and has refused to come back to his church in Edinburgh. The boss has been to see him, and Hamish says he is going to leave the ministry. We all know he is in love with you, but you seem to reject him. Is it because you have some highfalutin idea about being a missionary? Nancy, you and Hamish are such a good match, and you would be a wonderful couple of missionaries for Scotland. I can't understand you."

In silence, I walked across the room and stared out the window for a while, then walked back to sit by the fire, having decided that I must explain. "Yes, I think Hamish is having a spiritual breakdown. I will tell you in confidence why I feel I cannot marry him. Hamish has had sex with Mary, and he can't seem to stop. He has promised if I marry him, he would have the strength to cut off Mary. But I could not marry a man who has had intercourse. Would you want me to?"

Stunned, my friend said over and over, "I couldn't imagine such a possibility. Now I see why Hamish is in his own hell. Of course, you wouldn't marry him." He and I prayed for quite a while, prayed for Hamish, for Mary, and for the church. After our tea, he delivered me to the bus. "You have made the right decision, Nancy. God will bless you."

After my two weeks' holiday, I was happy to return to London and my work with Ranyard. I felt so at home; people would stop me in the street just to talk. I lived not in a large, impersonal city, but in *my* district, Tooting Broadway. One of my regular pleasures was the regular London meeting of the Iona Community Women Associates, and I attended about once a month. There I formed a deep friendship with Rosemary Tyndale-Biscoe, who at that time was in her late 60s.

A kindly, unremarkable, grey-haired lady, Rosemary had been a British spy in Poland, and had been instrumental in the escape of many high-level Polish officials at the time of the Nazi invasion. When I knew her, she was very involved in church work and made a point of visiting with those in prison. One time she invited a friend and me for tea, and when we arrived, we were introduced to a man of about 40. Making conversation, I asked what he did for a living, to which he said, "I just got out of prison for murdering my mother."

Nearly speechless, I recovered enough to say, "Would you like more tea?"

I had amazing friends within my Ranyard colleagues, too, among them Kathy Ball and Emily Parker. Emily had served in the British army as a nurse, and had been with the first contingent to enter Bergen-Belsen prison camp, the camp where Anne Frank died. What she saw there, and the things she had to do, permanently scarred her. She had nightmares after which she would be withdrawn for days, carrying on gallantly with her work, nevertheless.

Kathy had been a nurse in London during the terrible blitz, but she maintained her cheerful outlook, despite the horror she had experienced. During the war, Kathy was engaged to marry her beloved, who was a fighter pilot. He had his leave coming, and the marriage arrangements were all in place. Then the day before the wedding, Kathy got the dreaded news. Her fiancé had been killed in his last sortie over enemy territory. At first, Kathy seemed to be all right, but suddenly she suffered a nervous breakdown. All her hair fell out, and it never grew in again. In those days, wigs were very obvious, and Kathy was so self-conscious. She and I were stationed in different districts, but tried to arrange days off together, when we would wander around London, go to shows, or visit each other's area. I was busy, and life was full of friends and challenges.

Then in about October, I received a letter from my friend Rev. Lawrence of Cockenzie, a small fishing village on the east coast of Scotland. I had spoken in his church a number of times when I was at The Royal. He had heard that I had applied to the China Inland Mission, but had not been able to accept their conditions. He knew of my longing to go to China, and wrote, "Nancy, why do you not write to the Church of Scotland, and apply to them? The Church of Scotland has missionaries in Manchuria." I had withdrawn my application with the Church of Scotland when I thought I would be marrying Johnnie.

I thought I had forgotten that idea of being a missionary abroad, but as I prayed, I felt, "Maybe I have it too easy here. Maybe God *does* want me to go overseas." I hesitated for a long time, but finally I wrote the letter, telling them that I had not married after all, and did not intend to. Was there a place for me in China? Again, I hesitated at the letterbox, envelope in hand, wondering, "Should I send it?" It would mean leaving my friends and the happy, satisfying job I now had. Then the thought came, "You will always feel you should have tried." So I took a deep breath and mailed the letter. Some days later came the reply: "Please come to Edinburgh for an interview."

Miss Burns-Brown, the Women's Overseas Secretary for the Church of Scotland, was on sick leave, so my interviewer in Edinburgh was a woman named Katherine, a young missionary on furlough. She asked the usual questions, and at the end concluded, "You appear satisfactory. I will recommend you to the board, but you know, you will have to go to St. Colm's Women's College for two years before being sent overseas." That was a blow. The same obstacle as before! I felt I had good experience in church work, having been trained by Ranyard as a church nurse. Having attended so many Bible study conferences, what did I need of St. Colm's? I asked about fees, and how I could support myself while in this residential college. Katherine replied, "Did your parents leave you any money? Would your brother be able to support you?"

"He has just been demobilized, and is trying to establish himself, and look after his own family," I answered. "I have no resources except my salary."

"Then you are in no position to be a missionary!"

Furious at this second roadblock, I was stalking out of the Church of Scotland building, when whom should I run into but Dr. George MacLeod, founder of the Iona Community!

He stopped me and asked, "What are you up to these days?"

That's all it took. Out poured my frustrations, including "It seems you have to be rich to be a missionary! But Jesus didn't choose rich people for his disciples! Why do I have to go to St. Colm's?"

MacLeod laughed, and said, "Be still, Nancy. God knows what he is doing. Just wait for him to act." Then, when I calmed down, I realized that I was off the hook! I did not need to leave my beloved Tooting, so I returned to London in a happy frame of mind. Being the person I am, however, I ended up telling everyone of my journey to Edinburgh, the whys and wherefores. All assured me that I was God's missionary for Tooting. I relaxed, and settled down again to my rounds, and my morning coffees with Father O'Reilly and Dennis.

Suddenly, out of the blue, came a letter from Miss Burns-Brown, the Women's Overseas Secretary. "I have the pleasure of announcing to you that you have been accepted as a missionary candidate. You are to start training at St. Colm's College in January 1948. All your fees and boarding charges have been covered by an anonymous donor. We trust you will accept this offer. Please reply immediately."

Again, I was thrown into turmoil. "I'll bet George MacLeod did this!" I thought, and sent off a hasty letter, saying he should not have interfered.

His answer was short and to the point. "I have nothing to do with this. Maybe the Lord has. Ask him!"

I talked to the rector, and his quiet reply was, "God will supply all your needs. We want you here, but if we go against his will, neither you nor I will know any peace. Go forward a step at a time. You will enjoy college. God has provided; accept his gift." So, I wrote and accepted the invitation to go to St. Colm's.

But I couldn't help worrying, "How will I support myself for two years?" So I wrote asking if I could work as a relief nurse on the weekends.

"No," came the answer. "You will have church duties every weekend."

Then I got a letter from Miss MacNicoll, principal of St. Colm's. It was a lovely, welcoming letter, but it also included a list of all that I needed to bring with me to St. Colm's—sheets, blankets, tablecloths, pillows, a list that would furnish a house! At least it seemed that long to me. I *owned* no sheets, no pillows, no dishtowels, and not even any towels. All those things had been provided by the hospitals, and now at Treddy's, I used hers. I boiled with frustration. One particular article on the list infuriated me. I was to bring a banquet-sized tablecloth with 12 dinner-sized napkins! What would I need with a banquet tablecloth in China?

The letter had arrived just before my stop at the chemist's. I complained fiercely over coffee, "How stupid! I can't get all those things together in two months' time!" This was after the war, and we still had clothing ration coupons. You couldn't buy anything of cloth without them. Energized by my fury, I pedalled off to my next case—a Mrs. Fishpool, who lived in a poor working-class area on Fishpond Road. Yes, those are the real names. Mrs. Fishpool was badly crippled with arthritis, so I would visit her twice a week to help her with her bath, her injections, and any other needs. She could not walk, but when I came to the door, she would crawl out of bed and down the long hallway to let me in.

Many's the time I told her, "Just give me a key. Everyone else does." It took her so long to answer the door and when I left, I had to walk behind her as she crawled to see me out. That day, as I followed her to the kitchen, where her bed was, she asked, "Have you heard from Scotland?"

Well, that started me off about the huge list and all the stupid things I was supposed to bring. As I talked, I put on the kettle, heated the water for her bath, bathed her, dressed her, sat her by the fire, and made her a cup of tea. I had just sat down to have a cuppa with her when Mrs. Fishpool said, "Would you please get something out of that trunk for me?" Such tasks were difficult for her with her arthritis, so it was not an unusual kind of request. "Down at the bottom, there is a parcel wrapped in brown paper. Bring it to me and open it." So I did. As I carefully unfolded brown paper, then tissue paper, there was revealed a huge Irish linen tablecloth. Banquet-sized!

"Where on earth did you get this?"

"At the beginning of the war, my son was stationed in North Ireland," she answered. "The British navy surrounded Ireland, to prevent them from trading with Germany, and the Irish people had nowhere to sell their beautiful Irish linen tablecloths. My son bought one cheaply, the largest size he could find, and sent it to me. I have no use for it, living here in this little place. I know now that God sent it for you, and I am thrilled to be able to help you."

"But, Mrs. Fishpool, you could sell this and get a lot of money for it!" I protested.

"I would *never* sell it. My George sent it to me, and he was killed in Burma. Now he has given me the chance to give you a gift, which pleases me greatly. Take it with you now!"

If God could produce a banquet Irish linen tablecloth, I guess he really meant me to go to St. Colm's.

Leaving Mrs. Fishpool, I pedalled on to a very notorious neighbourhood to give a young woman her penicillin shots. She was, by profession, a prostitute, and made no secret of it. She had two children, whom she loved very much, and really struggled to support. At that time women often dyed their hair blond or red or black, but she had, by mistake, dyed her hair a brilliant green. It made a startling first impression, but after my initial shock wore off, I quite enjoyed my visits with her.

Being in such a neighbourhood, I couldn't leave my brown paper package with my bike, so I brought it in. Seeing it, her children jumped up and down, "What have you brought us this time?" I was embarrassed that it wasn't for them, so to quiet them I told the story of the banquet cloth. Then I got on with my work. When I finished with my patient, she shyly asked, "May I see your tablecloth?" On a table covered with newspapers, I opened the parcel, showing the snowy white tablecloth. To my amazement, she whipped out a measuring tape. She expertly measured, wrote and scribbled on the newspaper, and then declared, "I can make 12 napkins out of this. I *thought* this was a *luxury* banquet cloth. By cutting it to the usual banquet size, I can use the remains to make 12 napkins. They will be luncheon-sized napkins, but nowadays, that's what hotels use at banquets. Leave it with me, and I will sew them."

I gaped at her!

Laughing, she said, "I trained as a seamstress. Before the war, I worked in a factory sewing Irish linen. I still repair tablecloths for the hotels, but I don't get enough to support my family. That's why I have my night job." Of course, I left it with her. I did worry as to how well she would do and how dirty it would be when I got it back. But when she returned them to me, the tablecloth and 12 napkins were all beautifully clean and starched. She apologized that she was not able to have larger hems on the napkins. By then I *knew* God was behind all this.

The next two months flew by. People gave me blankets, sheets, pillows, and by the time I went to St. Colm's, I had everything on the list. The St. Nicholas Parish gave me the bicycle for my own, and passed a motion to send me £10 sterling every month till I was again on salary! The Ranyard nurses gave me three full nurse's uniforms, all lined for chilly Manchuria. They also arranged for me to get my social security contributions returned to me for each month that I was in school. My dear old age pensioners gave me a wonderful large green aluminium suitcase. For 40 years, that suitcase went everywhere with me. So many blessings and generous farewells!

I left London soon after Christmas in order to have a few days' holiday before starting at St. Colm's. When I arrived at Blair and Muriel's, she told me that Hamish had phoned and wanted to see me. After I had left Scotland in the summer, our mutual friend had persuaded Hamish to come back to the ministry and work with him as his assistant minister. So Hamish had been working in Glasgow for six months. I told Muriel, "It is all over, tell him I think it best not to see or talk to him." But he persisted, and finally I met him in a restaurant downtown.

We settled in a secluded spot in the restaurant. Hamish looked miserable. He could barely get the words out as he asked me the signs of pregnancy. When I described them, he told me he was quite sure that Mary was pregnant, and what should he do? I just looked at him, "What do you feel you should do?"

He answered, "Oh, I know I should marry her."

"Hamish, it was your choice, and now you have the consequences of that choice."

"You are right. But my life could have been so different!"

After finishing the meal, I parted with Hamish. We agreed that he had to tell his senior minister and according to the rules of the church, he should confess before Presbytery (the church's governing body) and accept its discipline. We parted with a hug and the assurance that we would pray for each other.

Hamish did do all that in due course. His license to preach was revoked, and he was suspended for three years. He became a schoolteacher, and he and his wife had a son. Oddly, perhaps, we remained friends, and I visited with them before my departure to India, and again, years later, with my husband while home on furlough.

Chapter 8: Mr. Dunachie's Bequest

Whenever we knocked at the door, the wyfie who answered would say, "Come awa' in, Lassie. Ye'll be frae the college. Wit country are ye gonna be ganging tae?"

Such was a typical greeting when we young missionaries-to-be went on home visits in the Edinburgh slums for our first practical experience. It was January 1948, and I was newly arrived at the Women's Missionary College, St. Colm's.

Overlooking the Royal Botanic Garden in Edinburgh, St. Colm's was in a large, beautiful house, which was itself surrounded by lovely grounds. It was associated with the University of Edinburgh, but run by the Church of Scotland. Each of us students had a small, single bedroom on the third floor. Mine faced the Botanic Gardens, and I often meditated looking out over the flowers. The teaching staff had quarters on the second floor. The ground floor held our dining room, the principal's sitting room, classrooms, and at the far end, a beautiful little chapel.

There were perhaps 30 of us women in residence, some of us preparing to be church sisters (directors of Christian education, in American terms), others to be missionaries. Still others were international students who had been sent by their countries to Edinburgh for education. There were women from Norway, Ireland, Wales, Jamaica, China, and Denmark.

St. Colm's had four resident women professors. Dr. Helen MacNicoll, our principal, was a wonderful woman with a great sense of humour. Unfortunately, she suffered from a rare neuromuscular disease, which caused a gradual muscular degeneration. She had been a missionary before returning to Britain on account of her illness, which we called creeping paralysis.

Then there was Dr. Harris, "Miss" Harris. She was in charge of Bible teaching, and she counselled us as well. Miss Stewart taught us about the cultures of the countries where the Church of Scotland (C. of S.) had missions. We learned about all the countries because we didn't know until later to which country we would be appointed. The C. of S. was in the Caribbean, South America, Jamaica, with a large presence in Africa, Pakistan, India, and China. Lastly, there was Miss Danskin, the youngest teacher, and she was in charge of activities.

Those of us who were to become missionaries were taught to preach and to lead church services, Sunday Schools, youth groups, adult education classes, and the Women's Guild. In addition, we all had daily chores to do, such as dusting and starting the fires, as well as keeping our own rooms clean. There were a couple of maids who cared for some of the common areas, but we took turns cleaning the dining room and Miss MacNicoll's room, and setting Miss MacNicoll's fire. We also took turns working in the kitchen and serving meals. All this was part of being "the humble servant," an attitude we were taught to cultivate. In this small community, we all came to know one another very well and very quickly.

At St. Colm's, we had prayers every morning and chapel every night. On Thursdays Miss Danskin taught us Scottish dancing. Before her instruction, we had just danced with exuberance, but now we had to learn to dance *properly*. One Friday afternoon a month, there was an open house for which we had to be specially dressed. We took turns preparing a fancy tea, and serving with proper graces the many church officials and high society visitors who came. You might not think so, but hospitality was an integral part of mission work.

Then Friday night was fun night when the staff and students did daft things to amuse each other. We had a lot of fun at St. Colm's, especially with the Irish Presbyterians because the Irish and the Scots are very close, and we were always teasing one another. In addition to the fun and group study at St. Colm's, it was a time of much personal study and introspection, which were a tremendous help to me.

In addition to all our theory classes, we gained practical experience by going door-to-door in the poor areas. But because those we visited were so familiar with the routine of St. Colm's students—"Wit country are ye gonna be ganging tae?"—it was not especially relevant experience for us. Those we visited would chatter on comfortably because students had been calling on them for years.

In search of more realistic experience, I spoke to my minister in the Auld Kirk (Old Church), Ian Reid. He was trying to build up a congregation in a slum clearance area. I had worked there and knew it to be an area that sorely needed help. I suggested that the church invite St. Colm's students to come and do their "practical" there. Ian thought it a good idea, and approached Miss MacNicoll. She agreed to send two students, and they loved it. Eventually, Ian was organizing our church visitation, and after some years, he became a visiting professor at St. Colm's.

Several of my friends at St. Colm's became friends of many years. My first day there, I struck up a friendship with another new student, Joan Hume. A nurse and a midwife, Joan came from the Highlands. She had been married to a banker, but during the war he had taken ill and died. After that she felt a call to the mission field.

After the *insistence* that I needed two years of missionary school, I had only been at St. Colm's for about three months when I was told that between my Ranyard Bible studies and what I was doing at St. Colm's, they felt that I would be ready to go to the mission field in July. They told me I had been appointed to Mukden, Manchuria, where I was to be the nursing superintendent. Shortly before my appointment, Dr. Mary Lui, who was a doctor in China, had arrived at St. Colm's and moved into the room next to mine. She was there to do her British post-graduate work at Edinburgh University in preparation for becoming the medical superintendent at the mission hospital at Mukden. When she learned of my appointment, she was pleased and excited.

Once we knew we would both be going to Mukden, we met in her room every evening, and had prayer together. She prayed in Chinese, and I prayed in English. Her prayers seemed so passionate, and so full of humble adoration. I could not understand a word, but I felt the outpouring of her love for God. A quiet Chinese lady, she told me how she had dreaded becoming medical director because all the Scottish nursing directors she'd known had been so stiff and formal. We were both delighted that God had allowed us to get to know each other as friends before we were to work together.

Late one afternoon, I was called to Miss MacNicoll's office where I was greeted, as always, with a smile and a warm handshake. But the news wasn't good, and her words chilled me. "I have just come from a meeting of the Foreign Missions Board. We have received a telegram from China saying, 'All missionary visas have been cancelled. Send no new missionaries to China.' Nancy, the Communists have taken over the city of Mukden and the province of Manchuria. This means that your appointment to China is cancelled."

"I could go to South China!" I interrupted.

Miss MacNicoll shook her head sadly. "We cannot risk that, for it seems inevitable that China will fall to the Communists, and all missionaries will be interned. We cannot risk sending new missionaries to any part of China. However, we do want you to be a missionary. Where would you like to go?" I was stunned; I had never thought of going anywhere but China! God had put that desire in my heart; why must I change it now?

"Thailand? Tibet? Japan?" I suggested. But Miss MacNicoll just shook her head.

"The Church of Scotland has no missionaries in any of these countries. But there is a great need in India. The mission there has begged for a nurse."

My reply was prompt. "No, I could never go to India! What about Africa? I could go to Africa."

"Nancy, the need for you in India is great. The Board of Foreign Missions has appointed you to Poona, India."

"No," I objected. "The Indians want all the British out. How can I go there and talk of God's love, when the British have been so cruel to India?"

At this my principal laughed. She had spent her childhood in India and had returned as a missionary until her illness forced her return to Scotland. "Nancy, missionaries are not soldiers or businesspeople. The people of India know the difference. You are going to show God's love; you are going to share their lives, to teach the nurses. God needs you there."

But I refused to be silenced. "God has called me to China. Why would he change his mind now? I could go out with another mission or go to South China. I just can't go to India! I'll go *anywhere but India*!"

Just then the evening chapel bell rang. Miss MacNicoll said, "It is time for chapel. Take tonight to think it over. Come back at nine tomorrow morning with your answer." Then she had a quiet prayer with me, and dismissed me to chapel.

Why did this have to happen when I was all set to go to China? What about my friendship with Dr. Lui? Didn't that mean something? My thoughts were awhirl. Should I leave St. Colm's and go back to Tooting? I was determined; I would *not* go to India! At chapel that evening, the first hymn was "Praise ye the Lord, the Almighty, the King of creation! ... ." I struggled through the first verse, my voice choked with tears. Then in the middle of the second verse came the words, "Hast thou not seen how thy desires e'er have been granted in what He ordaineth?"

It was more than I could stand. I covered my face and ran out of the chapel, racing up the stairs to my room. Thinking I was ill, one of the older deaconesses ran after me, calling, "What's wrong, Nancy?" I didn't answer, but before I could escape into my room, she caught my arm and turned me around. "What is it, Nancy?"

I rudely replied, "They say I can't go to China; the Board wants me to go to India, and I *will not* go to India." I turned to go in my room, but she swung me back again.

"Are you going to go where *you* want to go, or are you going where *God* wants you to go?" Angrily, I tore my arm from her grasp and slammed the door. I flung myself down on my knees, demanding, "Lord, don't fail me now. Show them that it is your will for me to go to China."

I spent the rest of the night arguing with God. "Lord, you know that it will be better for China if the Communists are run out. Lord, make some miracle for me to go to China. I'm not afraid of the Communists. Why can't I go anyway?"

Through all my arguments there persisted a soft answer in the back of my mind: "Nancy, Nancy, it is hard for you to kick against the pricks." The expression comes from Acts 26:14, when God confronts Saul (later known as Paul) on the road to Damascus. It refers to oxen kicking the stick with a nail that was used to prod the oxen as they ploughed, and means making things worse by defying authority or change.

I searched the Bible for comforting words. I prayed and wept until many hours later when, exhausted, I said, "Lord, if this is truly your will, I will go." Only then did I have the peace to sleep.

In the morning, I appeared at the principal's office, and Miss MacNicoll calmly asked, "Well, Nancy, what is your decision?"

"I will go to India, but I don't promise to be happy," I replied in a rush of words. "I hate the heat, and will probably be sick. Anyway, I'll only go for three years!"

"Nancy, sit down. Let us pray." She prayed for God's guidance for me and for all involved in this decision. After the amen, she went on, "Now, Nancy, in only one word tell me if you are willing to go to India or not."

"Yes, but…"

"No 'buts,' only yes or no!"

I sat quietly, and I knew that I had to surrender to the Lord. The words of the hymn came to me, "I'll go where you want me to go, dear Lord. I'll do what you want me to do."

I hung my head and gave over my will in one word, "Yes."

Quietly, Miss MacNicoll talked of the hospital in Poona, where I would be going. She told amusing stories of her life in Poona, where she had been born, and described the Indian people she had worked with. Again we prayed; then I heard the bell for my next class. As I was leaving, I turned and said, "Remember, Miss MacNicoll, I am only going to stay three years in India! Start looking for someone to take my place!"

She looked up and laughed. "Nancy, I prophesy that you will not be *three* years in India, but *thirty-three* years!"

Racing down the stairs to class, I muttered, "Not me!"

When Dr. Mary Lui heard the news of the Communist takeover, she burst into tears. The Church of Scotland people called and told her that she could stay in Scotland. She didn't have to return to China, where Christians were being persecuted and imprisoned. But she refused and said, "I cannot leave my people. I must go back to my family, and my people, and my church." Mary Lui did go back, and I never heard another word from or about her.

Thereafter, when I went out to speak at churches, the minister would often introduce me by saying something like this: "Nancy, like David Livingston, wanted to go to China, but God sent David to Africa, and now He is sending Nancy to India. Everyone knows how God used Livingston, so we will be watching to see what God does with Nancy in India!"

In no time, I detested the mention of David Livingston!

***

My experiences at St. Colm's shaped my decisions many times over the years. There was one Bible study in particular that had a direct and pivotal effect on my life.

In Bible study class, we were assigned portions to read, with questions to be answered on paper for discussion in the next class. The questions were:

What is the background of this portion?

Who are the main characters?

What were the reactions of each group included in the story?

Why do you think this portion is included in the scriptures?

Look again at Jesus' words. Do these words have any meaning for you today? Is there any decision that you feel you should think about?

I had had a lot of Bible study at Ranyard in London when I was training to be a church nurse, but this was so personal, so meditative. We each spent hours in our rooms, considering these passages. We took turns leading the class, and the day before we were to lead the discussion, Miss Harris would meet with the leader to go over the passage with her.

The portion that I was to lead discussion of was Matthew 5, verses 17-30. After a discussion of many verses, Miss Harris honed in on verses 29 and 30, asking what I thought Jesus meant by these words as written in the King James Version:

"And if thy right eye offend thee, pluck it out, and cast *it* from thee: for it is profitable for thee that one of thy members should perish, and not *that* thy whole body should be cast into hell. And if thy right hand offend thee, cut it off, and cast *it* from thee: for it is profitable for thee that one of thy members should perish, and not *that* thy whole body should be cast into hell."

I said, "If I knew I was doing something wrong, even though it was very important to me, I would have to give it up."

"That's right," she said, "but what kind of things do you think of?"

I was thinking of time and money and going to the mission field on a low salary, but she said, "Oh, no, it's much more personal than that. What do you think about sex?"

Now this was 1948 in a women's college where sex was not discussed! Of course, I was a midwife, but still, I was rather taken aback. Miss Harris was single—all these women were single—and she was maybe in her 50s. Nevertheless, I spoke up quite cheerfully, "That I have to give up the idea of friendship with the opposite sex, as it may lead to sexual involvement."

Miss Harris looked at me and said, "Let's imagine a scenario of your future. You are the nursing superintendent, working closely with the missionary who is the medical superintendent. You and he are together most of the day, handling emergencies, solving hospital crises. Meanwhile, the doctor's wife is at home with the children and busy with all that goes along with housekeeping in India. During the summer, she takes the children up to the hills for two months at a time, to get away from the terrible heat. You invite the doctor to come over for a meal. You are often invited to other people's homes, and walk back to the hospital together. You find yourself looking forward to that time together. Doctor invites you to go with him to the mission annual meeting in Bombay.

"It's all perfectly harmless until you realize that you are beginning to fall in love with each other. He has given you signs that he shares more with you than he does with his wife. You are in India, thousands of miles away from home, and there are very few confidants in the field from whom you can seek advice. So, what would you do?"

I saw where she was leading me. After all, I had already said no to Hamish and Johnnie. "I would talk to him, say we had to see less of each other, and not go places together."

"By your method, you are only making him more aware of your presence. The more you absented yourself, the more you would be attracted to each other. Flee from temptation!"

She continued, "You haven't done anything wrong yet, but it's a very important part of your life. You know the culture of India—no dates, no young men and women in the Indian culture going out together. There are no concerts to go to, no movies, and you and the doctor share so much.

"This is where you cut off your right hand. You write to the women's secretary in Scotland and tell her you have gotten excessively fond of the doctor. Without it going any further, there will be a telegram that you are transferred to another hospital, and there will be no necessity for you to tell anybody anything. You just go, and have no further connection with this man by letters or any other means. You have to start all over in building a relationship with your new staff." This I understood. Hadn't I just done that when I left Hamish and went to London?

"But," she says, "there is another way in which you have to pluck out your eye. Let us picture another situation. As a nursing superintendent, you become known professionally, and in India you get ahead very fast. You have started new programs; you are well settled and respected by the Christian and non-Christian communities alike.

"However," Miss Harris went on, "along comes a single man, not a doctor, but a lay missionary in a rural area. The two of you become friendly, and he asks you to marry him. You know he needs a wife; he is alone on the mission station, and the nearest hospital is miles away. To marry him would mean leaving all you have worked for, giving up your pride as a successful professional, and going who knows where. What would you do?"

"Flee temptation!" I answered confidently.

Wrong again. "Consider this," she replied. "By marrying this man you would be establishing a Christian home in an isolated area. You would be a witness to the love a husband and wife should have for each other. Would you cut off your pride to make a home for this man and to support him in his work? Would you be willing to 'pluck out your eye,' to give up becoming renowned in the mission field and fulfilling your dreams? Which do you think Our Lord would consider more important?"

"But, there would need to be love for each other!" I protested.

"True," said Miss Harris, "but if God called, He would supply all. I do not know what God has in store for you. Just always be alert to what God is telling you."

This gave me a lot to think about—but not for long. Hadn't I shown that I could give up all to follow Jesus? Besides, I never expected to meet a single missionary man because in the Church of Scotland men had to be married before they went out. Little did I know, the *American* Presbyterians *did* send out single men who lived with other missionary families until they got married. That discussion of Matthew 5 proved to be excellent preparation for the future.

Another shattering event of my life at St. Colm's was the introduction of the dreaded Miss Lambert, a former Church of Scotland missionary in India. Now a visiting professor from The London School of Oriental Languages, Miss Lambert came to St. Colm's to teach an intensive, three-week course in phonetics, with oral exams at the end of each week. Miss Lambert was intense; she listened to your breath, noticed the movement of your lips, watched the twist of your tongue, and immediately corrected you. Even at meals, she watched how we talked. She had no sense of humour at all and never relaxed. We all found her classes excruciatingly difficult, all except Nancy Patterson, who had a degree in English and language arts. So in the evenings, Nancy P. would gather us all together and re-teach Miss Lambert's lesson of that morning. By the end of the three weeks, we were all exhausted, but we somehow passed the exams!

At the end of May came the highlight of our preparation as missionaries. One by one, we candidates were commissioned and presented to the General Assembly of the Church of Scotland in Edinburgh. General Assembly was a very dignified affair held in a beautiful old building. The moderator and vice moderator wore lace cuffs and coattails. The queen attended or sent her royal representative. There was always a packed audience on the Thursday evening when the General Assembly dedicated new missionaries, welcomed those on furlough, and honoured those who were retiring. That year 19 single women and some men were commissioned to go to various parts of the world.

We were introduced to the assemblage according to our assigned country. It appeared that if you were called Nancy, or had the last name of Orr, you were destined for India. There was Dr. Agnes (Nancy) Brash, Anne (Nancy) Patterson, and me, Agnes (Nancy) Orr, as well as Michael Orr and his wife Margaret. My first St. Colm's friend, Joan Hume, was also being sent to India.

Michael Orr was the son of Professor Orr from New College, the highly esteemed seminary of the Church of Scotland. Afterwards, many in the reception line assumed I was Professor Orr's daughter. I tried to explain, but it happened so often that Professor Orr finally whispered in my ear, "Just let it go, and accept my family for the evening." I readily agreed. Through the years, this remained a joke between Michael, Margaret, and me.

The commissioning was a most impressive and moving service, and we were all "on the mountaintop," a spiritual high point. My brother Blair came from Glasgow for the event, and James Dunachie, Muriel's brother, came with him. James was one of my heroes and mentors; he had spent more than 20 years as a missionary in China. So many people greeted us in the reception line and, suddenly, there was Hamish with his wife Mary. I was taken aback, but Hamish just beamed and said, "Mary and I are so proud of you." It was altogether a momentous evening.

The next afternoon, all the new women missionaries were introduced at the Women's Guild annual meeting in Usher Hall, one of the largest halls in Edinburgh. As we stood together on a platform to be introduced, this vast congregation sang to us, "May the Lord bless you and keep you. May His face shine upon you, and give you peace." As they sang, my heart rose in indescribable joy, and I could feel my mother's presence. I felt humbled and filled with peace and joy. It was an experience I will always remember.

***

We three Nancys and Joan Hume were all graduated and duly commissioned, but there was, just then, no ship available to take us to India, so we needed to come up with something worthwhile to do as we waited. I had been to the Iona Community before, so I asked permission to go to Iona to be a youth leader with Dr. MacLeod, and both Joan Hume and I were allowed to go.

In 563 St. Columba had come from Ireland and founded a Celtic monastery on the island of Iona. From there, his priests and laymen travelled throughout Scotland, spreading Christianity. In 1938 Rev. George MacLeod had founded the Iona Community there to rebuild the ruined monastery, and from it to once again send out people in mission all around Scotland. (George MacLeod was the man I had falsely accused of finagling my scholarship to St. Colm's.)

When Joan and I arrived, there was still much rebuilding to be done at Iona, so we were all sort of camping out there. There were divinity students who would come up for the summer to work as masons and carpenters. It was thought that they would be more effective later if they knew what it was to do manual work, not just be in college and seminary. At the same time, there were youth camps for teenagers.

The Iona day began at 9 a.m. with a service at which Dr. MacLeod spoke. After that, we broke up into groups. As a leader, I would have 10 people, and we would discuss a Bible passage and what it meant to us. In the afternoon, there were games and other activities such as swimming for the kids to do. In the evenings, we had informal discussions on different social subjects, and as this was at the end of the war, we had a whale of a lot of things to discuss. In each group of 10, there were probably a couple teenagers from a wealthy church, another couple from a poorer church, some from the remand home (juvenile court), and some from the slums, so there were a variety of perspectives. Every evening at 5:30 Dr. MacLeod would meet with the youth leaders for an hour to prepare for the next day. At the time, Dr. MacLeod was over 50, unmarried, full of energy and fun.

Near the end of our time at Iona, we received a telegram from the Church of Scotland Foreign Mission Board to say that we—Joan, Nancy Patterson, and I—were to go at once to London to stay with Miss Lambert where we would have phonetics and language classes until a ship became available. When we opened that telegram, Joan and I were furious! I had been corresponding with India, and the current nursing superintendent at Poona wrote to say that one of the things I would be doing was giving anaesthetic to patients. Although I had often assisted in surgery, I'd never had training in anaesthesia, so Joan and I sent word to the C. of S. to ask if, instead of sending us to London to learn language, which we could do after we got to India, would they please send us both to a six months' course for nurse anaesthesiology?

The word came back: No.

We continued to argue, and ended up appearing in person before the Foreign Mission Board with all these stern Church of Scotland ministers, as well as the lady I now believe anonymously paid my way to St. Colm's. Everyone looked at me, so I spoke up: "It just doesn't make sense to learn language in London when I have to do anaesthesia when I go there, and I've never *done* anaesthesia. Anaesthesia is a very tricky thing. I have seen so many people die with reactions, and I certainly don't want to be responsible for something like that!"

When I finished, they all just sat and looked at me. Finally, Dr. Black said, "You know, if you can find a place to stay in London, you don't have to *live* with Miss Lambert, but I think it would be very good if you studied with Miss Lambert for about six months." Request denied.

If we had to study with Miss Lambert, I was determined not to live with her, too. I had stayed in touch with Bill Bush, one of the soldiers I had nursed during the war. Because he had been so badly burned, he had been with us for several months, and we had become friends. So I wrote to Bill in London, and he replied, "Nancy, it's the end of the war, and it's so hard to find a place. You've only given me a couple of weeks' notice. However, if you're willing to go to a working woman's hostel until I can find you somewhere, I'll see what I can do."

In the meantime, the Mission Board told us to pack up our clothes for India because we might go there directly from London. We could leave our trunks in Scotland to be forwarded, but we were to take our suitcases with us. This was complicated because we were going to London at the end of August, knowing that we were headed into the cold winter. I wouldn't need winter clothes in India, but I'd certainly need them in London. Muriel, my sister-in-law, offered me her fur coat, worn at the sleeves but still warm, saying, "You can always send it back by mail." Joan was a widow, but she had a fur coat her late husband had given to her. Nancy Patterson's mother heard this, and not wanting her daughter to be outdone, said, "Well, she can have *my* fur coat." And so, there were the three of us missionaries with our *fur* coats.

When we departed for London, our minister and our wonderful youth group came down to the station with arms full of chrysanthemums to see us off. They were all singing in the station as we left, and I just made it onto the train as it pulled away. The minister, who knew I didn't want to go to India, called after me, "Nancy, it's going to be all right because you're doing God's will!"

I was mad, and my last words were, "It must be God's will because it isn't *mine*!"

As we settled in on the train, the conductor came by and asked, "Where are you ladies going with this luggage and your fur coats?"

"India," we replied.

"You don't need fur coats in India," he said, stating the obvious.

When we arrived in London, we engaged a taxi to take us to the hostel, but the driver kept saying, "Are you sure this is where you're going?" A hostel is the cheapest of accommodations and rarely used by the carefully dressed and well educated, but we confirmed that that was our destination.

The hostel was in the midst of a slum clearance area, so you can imagine the reaction when we arrived in our fur coats. As we walked into the office, a very garish woman wearing tons of makeup looked up and said, "Yes?"

"We have booked a place for the three of us."

"You have?"

"Yes, we've come from Scotland."

She found our reservations and said, "You are booked, but I don't think you'll like it here." Nevertheless, in we came with our suitcases, our fur coats, and our bouquets of chrysanthemums. We were in a dormitory with seven other women. There were no cupboards there, just beds and blankets, so everyone put her belongings underneath the bed. Of course, our fur coats wouldn't fit in our suitcases, and with no such things as hangers or wardrobes, we just shoved them under our beds, too.

As the other women came home around 5:30 or 6:00 and saw us, their eyes grew big. "Where are you working?"

"Oh, we're going to classes at University."

"What kind of classes?"

"We're learning another language to go to India as missionaries."

Missionaries? That was the *last* thing they expected. We heard one woman yell, "I've three *missionaries* in my dormitory!"

After settling in, we phoned Miss Lambert, who told us where to show up the next day. Later, Bill Bush came to see us, and he said, "There's a chance I could get you into a flat in one of these high-rise places if you can look after yourselves, do your own cooking and laundry and such." While visiting his wife, who had tuberculosis, at the sanatorium, Bill had met a woman who was visiting her husband there. When her husband died, she couldn't bear to go back to the apartment they had shared, but neither did she want to give it up.

Of course, we said, "Sure!" and it was arranged. Meanwhile, we'd become friendly with the other residents. When we moved out, the other women in the hostel were very sweet. They helped carry out our belongings, teasing us, "Don't forget your fur coats. You'll be needing them in *India*!"

Our new apartment was five stories up with no elevators, but it was our own place, which was wonderful. There was one bedroom, a sitting room, and a small kitchen. We tried to be quietly friendly with the neighbours, but the widow had instructed us not to be too friendly because she could lose the place if it became known that she had sublet.

As for our studies with Miss Lambert, I regret to say that she was even worse than she was in Edinburgh. She started Nancy Patterson and me on Marathi, and Joan on Nepali, which has the same script and the same language sounds. We received all too much one-on-one attention. I would arrive for an eight-hour day of language study and say, "Good morning, Miss Lambert. It's very rainy this morning, isn't it?"

"Marathi, bola!" "*Speak in Marathi!*" and I would stumble through, trying to say it in Marathi. She would put talcum powder on a mirror, then have you talk so she could see the pattern of your breath in the powder. We would struggle through this for an hour, then I'd have to go sit with earphones on for another hour, listening to a tape. On the tape, they would pronounce the same word over and over, and you were to say it in the interval. It was 60 long minutes of trying to match your accent to the speaker's.

With Miss Lambert, the work was never-ending. We had a red book for vocabulary, a blue book for grammar, and a green book for colloquialisms. At lunchtime we three would go down to Russell Square and walk around and around the square, Joan and me in tears. Thank goodness for Nancy Patterson! She devoted every evening after dinner to helping Joan and me, and we all grew very close.

It was altogether a very difficult time, and Miss Lambert finally said to me, "The trouble with you, Nancy, is that you will talk, and you'll talk *all the time* in Marathi, and people will understand you, but it will not be *pure* Marathi!"

I thought, but didn't dare say, "I don't care, as long as they understand me!"

At this time, so soon after the war, electricity wasn't continuously available. The electricity, when we had it, ran on a meter. You'd put in a shilling or two or three, and the electricity would flow for a while. One morning before dawn, Joan shook me and said, "Wake up, wake up, it's dark! We can't study, there's no light. Get up and do something! Where are the candles?" We were all fussing around about the candles when I looked out the window and noticed that the electricity was on everywhere else. So, still half asleep, I went to my handbag, found two shillings, and slipped them in the meter. When the lights blazed on, Joan and Nancy were ecstatic. "You're brilliant. How did you do that?"

To my chagrin, some years afterward when I was being taken on by the American Presbyterian Church, they required a recommendation form, and one of the questions was about my attributes. Nancy Patterson, who wrote a recommendation for me, penned, "Nancy Orr is wonderful at mechanical things. She has a mechanical brain."

When I read this, I said, "Nancy, why in the world did you say that?"

"Because," she said, "you got the electricity going in London!"

Now in the midst of all this language study, I began to suffer abdominal pain. I knew that it was my appendix, but I ignored it. Then one day Joan and I were on the train when I doubled up with pain. "Nancy," she said, "when you do that, you've *got* to go to the doctor!"

I agreed to be taken to see a doctor I had worked with in Tooting. The minute I walked in, Dr. C. said, "Oh, how nice to see you! I hear you're studying language. How are you?"

"Oh, I'm just fine."

Joan, from the outspoken Highlands, jumped in with "You're not fine! You've got appendicitis!"

Dr. C. looked at me and said, "What?" After examining me, he concluded, "You've got a chronic appendix, and you'd better get it taken care of before you go to India. Do you want to go to a London hospital, and we'll operate?"

I considered London, but at Edinburgh Royal, where I had trained, when any of the nurses got sick, you were treated like a princess with a private room up on the nurses' sick bay, so I said, "I'd like to go back to Edinburgh." In those days appendix surgery meant seven days in hospital.

"You're just getting away from Miss Lambert!" Joan accused me.

When I phoned Edinburgh, they said, "We'll phone back tomorrow," and then they immediately phoned Miss Lambert. The next morning I arrived at class and said in Marathi, "Good morning, Miss Lambert. How are you this morning?"

"I am well, but *you* have appendicitis, and you didn't tell me. I have had orders from Edinburgh that you are to go back *immediately*, in the *middle* of your studies! You could have had your appendix out here, and I could have come and visited you in hospital!"

"Oh, thank God for Edinburgh!" I thought.

"You're to go back immediately. Now, I suggest you wait two days. You can wait two days, I'm sure. They'll make the arrangements at Edinburgh Royal, but in these two days I'm going to give you all the homework you'll need to do."

That evening Joan said, "If I had known, I wouldn't have made you go to the doctor. Now *we* have to have extra classes to take up *your* time!" They all came to see me off at the train, and I can still see Miss Lambert walking along the train as it was pulling out, saying, "Don't forget to study your vocabulary, and your blue book and your green book! You have to continue to study those when you go to Edinburgh!" Thus, I escaped Miss Lambert and had my appendix out in Edinburgh Royal.

Oddly enough, when I was in the sickroom at Edinburgh Royal, I received a letter from Johnnie, the sergeant journalist I had broken off with years before. It was addressed to Edinburgh Royal Infirmary, and just happened to arrive while I was there as a patient. The letter was quickly delivered to the sickroom. It said he'd been thinking it over, and he'd joined a church. Could we start over again? Could he come to see me? I wrote back and told him he could come see me if he liked, but I was on my way to India, and I was definitely not going to change my mind.

I never heard from him again. Afterwards, I wondered, "Why would Johnnie suddenly contact me?" It was such a coincidence that I was in the hospital for one week, and that week the letter came. Though I didn't want to go to India, I was committed, and I knew I was committed. I think it was God testing me.

After I had my appendix out, I finished recuperating with my brother Blair and his wife Muriel in Glasgow. Muriel's father, Mr. Dunachie, was living with them by then. He was dying of prostate cancer and didn't want to stay in the nursing home, so I nursed him at home for the month until he died. My sister-in-law's parents had been like parents to me all through my years of nursing. We had gone through the Clydeside blitz together, and Mrs. Dunachie had died shortly thereafter.

In those days we didn't have central heating in Scotland; we used heaters we called electric fires. Mr. Dunachie, like many cancer patients in those days, had a big, open wound from treatment with radium. When I changed his dressing, I used cotton wool, or cotton batting, to cushion the wound from the bandage that held it on. Because the cotton was cold, I always put it on a chair near the electric fire to warm a bit first. Luckily, my brother paused to help me make the bed that day, for when I flipped back the blankets, the cotton wool was thrown onto the electric fire, and it instantly went up in flames! Blair saw it first. He dived over and knocked the cotton off the fire, then grabbed a blanket to smother the flames. I poured on a jug of water. It went "Ssssss," and Mr. Dunachie asked, "Do I smell smoke? Has anything happened?"

"No, no, there's nothing happened," I reassured him as Blair scooped up the ashes and scrubbed the floor.

On the day before he died, I was changing Mr. Dunachie's dressing when he said, "Nancy, how can I ever repay you?"

"Oh, Mr. Dunachie, you've done so much for me."

"I am praying," he said, "that God will send you a good husband in the mission field, and that is my bequest."

I just smiled at the time, fully expecting to spend my life as a single woman. I never gave it another thought until a couple of months after I was married, when I remembered and realized that Mr. Dunachie's prayer had been fully answered.

Later, I unpacked my trunk bound for India to air my things. Because they'd been in the basement, my blankets were damp, so I hung them over the clotheslines in the basement where you'd hang your wash in the wet weather, and turned on the electric fire to get rid of the dampness. Just as I was going up the stairs, somebody slammed the door, blowing the blanket over onto the electric fire, where it began to burn! I ran back and quickly doused it.

Referring to the Church of Scotland's emblem, the burning bush of the Moses story, Blair said, "You don't need to take it *literally*, and burn everything before you go! The quicker you get to India, the better for us all!"

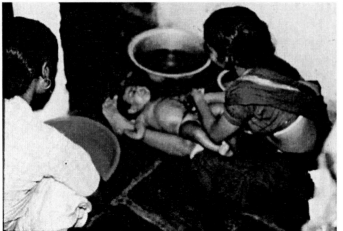

Mother bathing her baby at the Health Center.

Bob (in shorts) preaching in a village

A typical scene in Shantinagar

Chapter 9: Good Brakes and a Very Good Horn

Word came over the loudspeaker. At 10 p.m., the ship would begin sailing through the Suez Canal. "There will be a full moon tonight, Nancy," said Dr. MacPhail. "You *must* stay up to go through the canal at midnight because there is a saying: 'If you sail through the Suez under a full moon, you will always feel the pull of the East.'"

My cabin mates were all too tired, but Dr. MacPhail joined me up on deck. I will never forget the eerie beauty of the desert in the moonlight. The moon was brilliant, the sands gleaming white. We slowly glided through the canal on our huge ship, with only inches to spare on each side. It was chilly, but we few hardy passengers sat in deck chairs with blankets, too thrilled by this fantastic landscape to give it up for sleep.

The beginning of the trip had been not nearly so glamorous. January 21, 1949, was a dull, cloudy day. I had arrived at the Southampton docks by train, identified my luggage, met with immigration, and received my compulsory physical exam. My tickets and passport were checked and double-checked before I was allowed to walk up the gangplank. I stowed my suitcase under my cabin bunk and went up on deck, where I could look down on the busy docks of Southampton.

Leaning on the deck rail, I thought back to all that had happened since my graduation from St. Colm's. Joan Hume and I had spent two months on the Island of Iona as youth leaders to teenage campers. In September, under protest, Nancy Patterson, Joan, and I had gone to London to study phonetics under Miss Lambert. In November, I had suffered an attack of appendicitis, then had my appendix removed at Edinburgh Royal. Happily, this had put me at home with brother Blair and his family for Christmas, where I had nursed Mr. Dunachie until he died in early January. Muriel and Blair's two children, Dorothy, seven, and Nigel, two, my only niece and nephew, were especially dear to me, and it had been lovely to share that time with them.

Though I had been expecting it, it was still somehow a surprise to get word, "You leave next week on the *Maloja*." Joan and Nancy Patterson had left just after Christmas. When they got word, they had called to say, "See, if you'd stayed in London, you could have come with us," but I saw God's hand in the delay because I was able to be in Scotland to care for Mr. Dunachie.

Now, all the farewell parties were over. I smiled as I remembered Dorothy's request, "Aunt Nancy, don't get married in India! Promise me that you won't!"

"That's an easy promise!" I laughed. "I won't get married in India, but why do you want me to make *that* promise?"

"Because I want to be your bridesmaid!" So there were tears and laughter in my departure. It would be hard to be away for so long, especially from the children.

The blast of the ship's horn startled me from my daydreams. Shifting from the past to the present, I began to take in the fact that I was on my way to India, on a ship full of strangers sailing to a land full of strangers. But with this thought, the peace of God came into my heart with his words, "I am with you."

As the ship pulled away from the dock, I walked along the deck and whom should I meet but Dr. Ronald MacPhail. He was a Scottish missionary doctor, world famous for his new methods of removing cataracts. He had performed hundreds of surgeries in north India. We greeted each other like long-lost friends. Dr. MacPhail had spoken to us at St. Colm's, and then I had met him again on Iona. He was in his late 50s; a quiet, soft-spoken man with a quick sense of humour, but the humour belied a sad story.

Years before, in India, his wife had suffered a mental breakdown. This trip to Scotland had been to bring her, at last, to live in a mental institution. Mrs. MacPhail no longer recognized her husband, and the psychiatrists said, "You're just as well to go back to the work you love because it breaks your heart every time you see her. She'll never know you." So both of us were sailing away from family and our native land.

Our ship the *Maloja* was a P & O liner. It was a big liner and I, of course, was in cabin class, which is the lowest. We left Southampton in winter, but as we turned the corner into the Mediterranean Sea, suddenly everyone was sweltering. There were six sharing my little cabin, and space was at a premium, so we stored everything below in the hold except for our suitcases.

Two of my cabin mates were exceptionally memorable. One was the frightfully polite, frightfully British Diana. She was married to a plantation owner and had lived outside Calcutta in the good old British style. She was returning to post-World War II India, and she often worried aloud about "how things will be so terribly changed" now that the British had left India, and she would just have to see whether or not she could survive it.

I no longer remember her name, but the other memorable woman in our cabin was from Assam in northeast India. She had married a British Tommy soldier during the war, and had come back with him to Scotland. Her husband had little education and couldn't find work, so they lived in the slums, a real comedown from India, where she and her parents had owned their own small wooden house. The couple had a son named Patrick, and although she was very much Assamese, both she and Patrick spoke English with a broad Glasgow accent.

Patrick shared the top bunk with his mother. When all of us were trying to get dressed at the same time, she'd lift him back up to the top bunk out of the way, where he could look out the porthole. I often worried he would fall out.

"Aach," she said, "he'll be all right."

The ship's protocol decreed that children were to be fed at one sitting, and then their parents would go back for their own meal. The British adults didn't want messy children in attendance at their own meals. So Patrick's mother left him with us while she went to eat at the first adult sitting, then we would eat at the second adult sitting, and that went on three times a day. Little Patrick wasn't a bad boy, but he had the most horrible, swearing vocabulary. Whenever his mother went off to eat, she'd say to him, "You've got to behave yourself, you know. I'm going to ma breakfast and if you do anathing wrong, I'll gae you such a scalpin' when I come back. In fact, I'll gae you a scalp now," and then she'd whap him one on the head!

No matter how many times we asked her not to do that, she'd give him a whack that left him howling, and we would have to calm him down. This was the daily routine.

As the voyage went on, we learned her story. Once home in Scotland, her husband was ashamed of the Assamese woman he had married. He became involved with another woman, but still would beat his wife if she even tried to leave the apartment. Her in-laws would have nothing to do with her. After the baby was born, she could occasionally slip out to the corner store. A kind Scotswoman at the store was very sympathetic to her, and would often give her extra of whatever she was able to buy—"A wee bit for you, and a wee bit for the bairn"—because the woman was terribly thin.

Then one night her husband beat her up very badly, and threw little Patrick to the floor. When her son was endangered, she could no longer tolerate the abuse, so she ran to the corner store and asked for help, and the kind Scotswoman took her into her own home. There, she and her husband slept on the floor, and gave their bed to this Assamese woman and her baby. While the couple hid her there, the woman from the corner store went to her Church of Scotland minister, who instigated an investigation that confirmed the terrible way the mother and son were being abused. Sadly, there was a lot of this sort of thing after the war. So the church people took her into one of their homes for women, then gave her money for the passage home to her family in India, and that's how she came to be on the ship.

In the cabin next to ours was an Indian family from Poona, the Dikshits, a husband and wife with their two little girls. He had just completed his master's degree in chemical engineering in Glasgow. Between the years of study and the travel restrictions during the war, the family had been in Scotland for a number of years. Both girls had been born and learned to speak there. It was so incongruous to hear these Indian children with such broad Glasgow accents.

One day in the passageway, I heard Prithi, one of their little girls, screaming, so I asked what was wrong. They explained that she had a very sore, infected finger and was supposed to receive daily penicillin injections from the ship's nurse, but she had refused to cooperate. Now the infection was so serious that red lines of infection streaked up her arm.

"Do you think she would let me give her the injections?" I asked. Prithi and I had talked and played dolls up on deck on a previous day. With everyone's permission, I put a bandage on the doll, and said, "The doll has a sore arm and she isn't getting better, so we need to give her an injection." The girl had a plastic hypodermic syringe, so I gave her doll an injection. Then I asked Prithi, "You let me give an injection to your doll. Would you let me give *you* an injection?" Yes, she would.

I explained to the staff in the ship's hospital that I was trained at Edinburgh Royal, and they were happy to let me take over. Every day they handed me the syringe with the antibiotic already in it, and I gave the little girl her injection. In this way, the Dikshits and I became friends.

There were other Indians on the ship and because I was friendly with the Dikshits, they all adopted me. Mr. Dikshit was the only engineer; the other six were all doctors, and they had all pursued different specialties in Edinburgh. I introduced Dr. MacPhail to the group, and we all walked the deck together and played games or cards in the evenings. Three of the doctors spoke Marathi. I was still very nervous about language, but these doctors and Mr. and Mrs. Dikshit, Nanda and Pushpabai, were simultaneously teaching Marathi to me and the little girls, who needed to know it to speak to their grandparents at home in India. Every time my Indian friends greeted me, they would say, "Casa kai?" *"How are you?"* When I replied, "Barra hai," they would congratulate me on my Marathi. "Wonderful, wonderful!" and they gave me courage.

As we relaxed on the deck in our deck chairs, our volunteer Marathi tutors would tell us the words for this and that. They were so encouraging to me, a far different experience than with Miss Lambert! I look back on that journey with gratitude and believe that God was gently preparing me for India.

Our first stop was Port Said, and we passengers had the day to explore this Egyptian port city at the northern entrance to the Suez Canal. There were no travellers' tours then, so Dr. MacPhail and I joined some fellow passengers on a bus into town. We wandered into bazaars, where we were fascinated by the exotic foods and crafts, and enjoyed coffee served the Egyptian way. When we hurried back to the ship, we found there were small boats surrounding our ship, and merchants were sending their goods up by rope basket for consideration by potential buyers. The leather goods, the carvings, and the jewellery were exquisite and so amazingly cheap that we were quick to send our money down to the boats by return basket.

The bargaining was interrupted by the announcement that we would sail at 10 p.m. through the Suez Canal! Dr. MacPhail's saying proved true; I believe I did lose my heart to the East that night. The beauty of the sand in moonlight was indescribable, and I felt God's presence, very close, reassuring me, and I thought, "This is the desert through which God led his people so long ago. He will surely lead me."

Our Indian friends and my cabin mates all came to know one another. The Indians were very accepting of little Patrick with his terrible language, but Diana was determined to make a gentleman of him. "Because when he gets back to India, he is going to shock, not the Britishers, but the Indian people!" So Diana decided that for his sake and the sake of his mother, she was going to teach him proper manners and to pronounce things "pro-pa-ly."

Diana frequently borrowed books from Dr. MacPhail, and one day she couldn't find those she intended to return. We hunted all over and couldn't find them anywhere. The next morning, when I woke up, Patrick had already had his head bashed, and he was howling. "Oh, Patrick, just be quiet!" I said, and all of a sudden he was. Suspicious, I stood up to see what he was doing, and he was throwing a book out the porthole! We had repeatedly warned his mother about that porthole. Now here he was throwing Dr. MacPhail's books out into the sea! That marked the *end* of Diana's efforts to turn him into a gentleman.

Once through the canal, our next port of call was Aden in what is now Yemen. Aden was a major British port, and we had missionaries near there in Sheikh Othman. Our arrival was delayed by the ship ahead of us, which had gotten stuck in the canal, so we arrived two days late at Aden, and well into the evening. The missionaries had invited Dr. MacPhail, something of a missionary hero, to visit their hospital, but with the considerable delay, he didn't expect to see them. I had stayed up to see Aden and was having tea with my friend when over the loudspeaker we heard, "Dr. MacPhail, you have visitors."

"That must be the missionaries," he said to me. "Come and meet them." We had not yet made it to the main dock, but there they were in a little launch, waving at us. We climbed down the rope ladder to their launch, which sped us to their awaiting Jeep. From there we drove for miles down a long desert road. Far from the lights, the sky was dark blue velvet, with tiny stars, the sand reflecting the descending moon. Finally, we arrived at the little Arabian village where they had a mission hospital run by a Scottish doctor, a Scots-educated Arabian doctor, and two Danish nurses.

We toured the hospital, which looked very different from home, with Arabs passing in their long robes, and patients lying on the floor because all the beds were full. From the hospital, we went to the home of one of the doctors, where we were surprised to find all six missionaries waiting for us with a spread of sandwiches, cakes, and tea. It was well after midnight, but they all wanted to meet "folks from home!"

One of the doctors' wives told me how one had to battle against the sand. "It is everywhere—in your drinking water, in the sandwiches, in your bed, and in babies' nappies. You can never get away from it, even in the operating room."

Having had my face sandblasted for miles during the Jeep ride, I was sympathetic and asked, "How do you stand it?"

"Oh, you get used to it," she said philosophically. "After all, the Arabs have to live with it, so we learn to accept it!" They were quite isolated at Sheikh Othman, but they all seemed happy to make their home where God had put them. The night was quickly gone. The doctors drove us back to Aden about 4 a.m., and an hour later, the ship sailed for India. It had been hot and muggy in Aden, there being no such thing as air conditioning, but cool breezes met us as the ship sailed into the Arabian Sea.

Our next port of call was Karachi in what had just become Pakistan when the 1947 partition separated it from India. We all stayed on board there, impatient to get on to Bombay.

When at last we sailed into Bombay, Dr. MacPhail, Diana, the Dikshits, the lady from Assam, and I stood at the rail, looking for those who were to meet us. As we waited for a pilot ship to take us to the dock, I looked around and thought, "I've come here, and I'm going to be living with two older ladies who are both due to retire. They say that one is an angel, and one has a terrible temper." There was also a Dr. Bailey, who was said to be young and very aggressive. The only familiar face would be Dr. Nancy Brash, a quiet woman I knew from St. Colm's.

"I'm not like any of those people," I said to Dr. MacPhail. "I'm going to live and work with four missionaries, three of whom I don't know at all. What if they don't like me? What if I'm no good at my job? What will I do?"

Dr. MacPhail laughed, took another puff on his pipe, and said, "You'll do fine. They'll like you, and you'll like them. It will all work out." Nice to hear, but he was leaving on a train to go across India to Calcutta. Dr.

MacPhail had been such a fatherly figure to me on the journey, and such a wonderful mentor, that I began to feel scared to land in India alone.

We stood clustered at the rail, waiting for permission to dock. A passenger on board our ship had a rash, and had to be examined by a doctor before we were allowed to dock in the city of Bombay. At last we were approved, and as I worked my way through customs, I saw Nancy Patterson, who had arrived only the month before. "Welcome, welcome! The whole mission was here to greet you, but the ship was late docking, and all the other missionaries had to go back to Wilson College for the graduation services. But I'm here and here's the car!"

In a daze, I got into the car with Nancy P., and we drove to Wilson College, a C. of S. mission, to join the graduation ceremonies. Nancy quickly locked my luggage in a room, and we headed for the chapel. Just as I was beginning to feel overwhelmed by this exotic country and all the strangers, Nancy pointed out what was written above the chapel archway: "Lo, I am with you always, even to the end of the world!"

I was *not* alone; I had arrived in the land where God wanted me to be. My fears and nervousness left me, and I felt a surge of excitement. Just as these young students were going out into a new life, so was I! And I was not alone.

We stayed in Bombay for two days to attend the missionaries' annual meeting, where I met the staff of Wilson College as well as about 30 missionaries from all over the region. One was Dr. Ara Rankine, the medical superintendent of St. Margaret's, the mission hospital to which I was appointed. I also met Miss Gertrude Sloan, the person I was replacing, and Dr. Bailey. They and Dr. Brash were all there to greet me. I'd been writing to them, and Miss Sloan had written such nice letters. The one influential person I had yet to meet was Watsella, the woman in charge of midwifery. I was apprehensive about meeting her because she had been there for a good number of years, she knew the language, and she taught in the nurses' training school. I worried, "She'll think, 'Who is this young punk that is coming out and going to be put in charge? Is it just because she's a white person, or just because she's British?'"

We left Bombay by train, and we got into Poona about eight o'clock in the evening. We got off the train, and I was counting the luggage. One of the coolies said I only had three pieces, but I broke in in Marathi, and said, "Nine pieces!"

Miss Sloan turned to me and said, "Oh, that's wonderful, bless your heart!" And I had only said one sentence!

The hospital car was there, and we were taken to the St. Margaret's Hospital compound, right in the centre of Poona. St. Margaret's was a 150-bed women's and children's hospital and training school for nurses and midwives. We drove through an archway, around the garden, and pulled to a stop. There stood an honour guard of nurses greeting me with garlands of flowers! I was overwhelmed to see them. Then an older woman came up, put a garland around my neck, kissed me on both cheeks, and said, "I am Watsella. I am so happy you have come. God answered my prayer. I was so afraid I would have to be matron if Miss Sloan died."

And I thought, "God knew what he was doing after all; I am supposed to be here."

The nurses enthusiastically welcomed me, and the first thing they taught me was how to properly put on a sari. They're very fussy about how many inches it hangs from the floor, and about how the folds go. Before I knew it, I was quickly folded into the established hospital routine. We staff members each had a bedroom above the hospital, but when the weather turned hot, we slept on the roof. We had a common sitting room and a dining room.

There were servants including Ramchundra, the butler, who made my eyes pop out because he wore a stately turban and a long white coat, and was very much like any English butler. At first, I would say "Good morning" to Ramchundra, but he never replied because we weren't supposed to talk with servants. I learned that there was a system, and you followed the system. The butler dusted the sitting room and the dining room, looked after the china, and saw that there was always sufficient water and coal on hand. The cook went to the marketplace and prepared the meals. We also had a water boy who brought up water.

Not long after I arrived in Poona, Nancy Brash and I went to visit the Methodist missionaries, and while we were there, we received an urgent phone call. We knew that Dr. Bailey, Winifred, was ill, and suspected malaria, but the phone call was a summons to come back at once because

Winifred felt she had poliomyelitis. She had recently been in Bombay to shop and to visit a Congregational missionary whom we all knew, Miriam Rogers. Now Mim had been diagnosed with poliomyelitis. When we got back, Dr. Bailey was hysterical. She was the surgeon, and she couldn't move her hands! Another doctor soon confirmed the terrifying diagnosis.

Miss Sloan was Dr. Bailey's aunt, and she said, "I can't put Winifred here in the ward, because she's such a demanding patient." The Indian nurses were all frightened of Winifred, so Miss Sloan asked me if I would look after her. True, Winifred was difficult, but she had a sense of humour and that got us through the whole affair. We became, and remained, close friends.

I'd been nursing Winifred for about 10 days when I developed a very high fever, a terrible headache, and pain that shot down the length of my arm. My arms were also very weak, a frightening symptom I felt pointed to paralysis. Everyone was very worried, and there was a great deal of prayer on my behalf. When, in time, I recovered, Dr. Rankine decided that I had had a very common, and less severe, form of poliomyelitis.

When Winifred was sufficiently recovered, she was sent home by boat to Scotland. Amazingly, after several years of treatment, she was able to return to India, where she served under the Church of Scotland until her retirement. Her legs were paralysed, so she walked encased in metal braces, but her hands were fully functional. Years later, we visited her while on furlough, and the once terrifying surgeon was the most gracious, loving person you could imagine, very like a grandmother to my children.

***

During the war years in Britain, there had been no cars for private use, so when I arrived in India at age 27, I had never driven a car. Our hospital had one car to be used by five missionaries, and it was primarily used to take the doctors on house calls. The car was an Ambassador, British-made in India, and a very solid and sedate sedan. We always had a driver, who not only drove, but also maintained the car. However, one day the driver took ill, and in short order I was sent to take driving lessons!

Learning to drive in the city of Poona was a thrilling experience. Lesson #1 was on the racetrack. Subsequent lessons were on the roads outside the city. My principal instructions consisted of the two laws of driving in India. First was "Always use your horn!"

When I queried, "When is 'always'?" I was told, "Whenever you pass another car, or bicycle, or cart, you must blow your horn. How else will they know you are passing?"

The second law was "Pedestrians and animals have the right of way. You must stop for them."

Now in Poona, a good-sized city by any measure, pedestrians and animals freely wandered the streets. There were donkeys, cows, goats, horses, an occasional elephant, cycles, horse-drawn carts, carts drawn by men, and pedi-cycles, plus pedestrians rushing in amongst them all! "If I have to stop for animals and pedestrians," I asked, "when can I go?"

With an exasperated sigh, I was told, "That's why you need a horn! You blow the horn once; they don't pay attention. Then you blow it two times, and people jump aside. So do animals! There are two things your car must have—good brakes and a very good horn!"

In addition to these two principles, there were also the usual traffic laws like we had in the West, so I had those to learn as well. When I went for my practical driver's test, before the inspector took me out on the road, he tested the brakes and the horn. Then, for my test, I had to drive a figure eight between flowerpots, then out onto the road, right into the heart of a crowded bazaar! The roads were clogged with animals, people, stalls, trucks, motorcycles, and me, trying to steer our Ambassador through it all! I made full use of the brakes and horn. I had been warned that the Indian inspectors rarely passed women drivers on their first try, especially Britishers, so I was quite surprised when I passed on my first attempt. Now I was licensed to drive the hospital car for official business. Still, for our personal travel, we went everywhere on bicycles—complete with a loud bell, and good brakes!

I had only been in Poona for a few weeks when I was sent to Mahableshwar for three months of intensive language school. Soon after I arrived, Elsie Nelson, an American missionary, was in a serious bicycle accident. The other Americans brought her straight to our bungalow because among the Church of Scotland missionaries were two doctors, and a nurse—me. During the course of treating the badly injured Elsie, I met another missionary from the American bungalow, an engineer named Robert Ramer.

With Elsie carefully cleaned and bandaged, we invited the Americans to stay for dinner, and in that more relaxed time, Bob mentioned that he hailed from Colorado. Knowing that famous song, I asked him, "Are you 'The Big, Bad Man from Colorado?'" He had never heard of the song, and denied being big and bad, blushing furiously. Nevertheless, after that gaffe, we began to spend our rare free time together.

At that time, I had no interest in dating and no desire to get married. I was a nursing superintendent in a hospital that was training nurses for India. Well-known and highly regarded, our hospital was situated in a city alive with movies and shops, not to mention other women missionaries. Although we had fun together, Bob was headed for a rural area, and I was committed to my work in Poona. As we spent more time together, I didn't want to mislead this nice man about my intentions, so I wrote a letter to tell him that I thought we were getting too friendly.

"I'm getting kind of fond of you, and I have just started on my missionary career. This is not the time to get friendly, we're not even allowed to date," etc. At the language school I was sharing a room with three other gals, and they all insisted on reading it. They had all become very friendly with American missionaries themselves, and said, "Oh, don't give him the letter; he's so nice; don't give him the letter."

Nevertheless, the next time we were out together on our bicycles, I had the letter in my pocket. We were standing, gazing down at the lake, when he put his hand on mine and I thought, "This is the time."

"Bob, I have a letter that I've written to you."

"Oh, just tell me, whatever it is. Why did you write a letter?"

"Well, because I'm getting rather fond of you …," I said.

And before I could get another word out, he said, "That's wonderful! I've been praying for that! That's wonderful! I know God wants me to marry you!" I was so utterly taken aback with him saying that we should get married that I forgot all about the letter, and I just absolutely gave in!

I told him, however, that I had made a commitment to the Church of Scotland, so we would have to wait two years, and we did. The time at St.

Colm's had prepared me well for just this eventuality. So, with only a few weeks in at St. Margaret's, I wrote to give notice that I would be leaving after my two-year appointment to marry and move to the town of Sangli.

Upon my return to St. Margaret's after language school, I fell into an agreeable routine. Because Miss Sloan, my predecessor, was still there, I was something of an extra hand. I rose at 6:30 to begin my day. The ayah (a maid who in other circumstances might also mind children) would bring me a cup of tea, a banana, and a slice of bread with marmalade for my chota hazri (or small meal), as they called it. At seven o'clock I went on duty, making quick rounds of the ward, reporting on patients and seeing that the nurses were all where they were supposed to be. Then from 7:30 to 9:30 the language school pundit, or expert teacher, came, and I studied language, grammar, pronunciation, vocabulary, and so on, with him. The pundit Mr. Desai had studied with Miss Lambert, too, but he was very jolly, and language study with him bore no resemblance to the Miss Lambert ordeal.

Then it was back on duty from 9:30 to 10:30, during which I would see that the operating room was set up for the surgeries to be done that day. Meanwhile, the rest of the staff had been doing clinics. At 10:30 we had our breakfast in the dining room. Operations began at 11:30 and continued often until about 4, if you had no emergencies. Then we would adjourn upstairs for a cuppa tea. At five o'clock Dr. Rankin started her evening clinics, when private patients came to see her or one of the other doctors. Those private patients provided income that helped to support the hospital.

I was usually free from five o'clock until seven to prepare my language study for the next day. But if Dr. Rankine had more than the usual number of private patients, or if she needed to go to a patient's house, she would call on me, and I'd have to leave my studies to go with her. Occasionally, the private patients were missionaries from other missions, the Australians or the Free Methodists, most of whom were in Poona to do language study. There were also upper-class Indian women, ranis (princesses) of small states, who wouldn't come to the hospital, so I would accompany Dr. Rankine to see them. We ate our evening meal about 7:30 or 8:00, when it was cooler. After dinner, about nine o'clock, if there were no emergencies, we were free to do as we pleased.

As I assumed supervision of the nurses, I noticed they were very careless in some aspects of care. When I said, "That's not the proper way to do it," they would counter, "That's the way Miss Sloan taught us."

Even before I had arrived in Poona, I'd been warned that Miss Sloan had a terrible temper. "I'd better not say too much," I thought, not wanting to offend my predecessor.

Then one day Miss Sloan came up to me and said, "I know I'm old-fashioned, but do they really teach you that you don't need to wash the arm with spirit (alcohol) before the injection?"

"They certainly do not!" I said.

"I thought so. Those nurses tell me Sister Orr says that's the way to do it now." Thus, we caught on to what they were doing, playing us against each other to make their lives easier. Thereafter, I never knew Miss Sloan to lose her temper without good reason. In fact, Miss Sloan was very loving and understanding when I told her I was engaged to Bob, and very grateful that I would stay for the two years. But Ara, Dr. Rankine, was furious! She was so enraged that, for the longest time, she refused to speak to me. That's what she did any time she was angry. She would just walk away, refusing to talk to anyone, and that's very hard to live with.

With such a busy life, it was a challenge to stay in touch with Bob. He started writing to me every day. Then, of course, I had to write every day, as well, but that had to be done about ten o'clock at night after all the other work was finished.

At St. Margaret's we had one day off a week, and we took turns. I asked and was given permission to save my days off, so that I could visit Bob in Sangli once a month, and he arranged things so he could visit me once a month. He'd arrive in Poona on a Friday night and stay with other Scottish missionaries because Dr. Rankine had said that it would be a bad example to allow a *man* to stay at the hospital. On Saturdays, I was on duty in the mornings, but we didn't usually have clinics in the afternoon, so I was free to go out with him then. On Sunday, I taught Sunday School in the hospital compound, and then we would go to church together with the nurses. So even when he was there, our time together was limited.

***

At the hospital we had a lift (elevator) to take patients up and down between floors, and it operated on a pulley system. One day Miss Sloan turned to me and said, "I want you to look at the lift; I don't think it's working right."

"I don't know anything about it," I begged off. "I've never seen one of these contraptions before."

"Well, your Bob's an engineer; he'd better come and see about it." So Miss Sloan went to Dr. Rankin and told her, "I've got an engineer to come see about the lift on Saturday morning."

"Oh, all right," said Dr. Rankin. "How much will he charge?"

"I don't know, but it's for use with the patients, and we can't take any risks with them. But the engineer's coming, and he really knows what he's doing."

So Miss Sloan sent a driver to the railway station to meet Bob when he came in, and to tell him that he was to come to the hospital because an engineer was needed. Miss Sloan met Bob at the door, and solemnly took him to the lift. Well, Bob had never seen such a lift in his life, but he knew the principle of the wheel, so he said, "I think you're using too heavy an oil."

Miss Sloan turned to Samuel, our driver and maintenance man, and said, "Do you hear that, Samuel? The engineer says we need a lighter oil." Then she added, "Go tell Ramchundra there'll be one more person for breakfast—I've invited the engineer."

So Miss Sloan brought Bob to breakfast and introduced him to Dr. Rankin, and they began to chat. I stood at my chair at the table, not quite knowing what to do, while Miss Sloan continued the introductions. "And this is Nancy Brash. Oh, you met her at language school. And this is Dr. Bailey. Oh, yes, you met her, too. You know Nancy? Well, you just sit over there."

Dr. Rankine began eating, then suddenly catching on, she looked up and said, "Are you Nancy's fiancé?"

After Bob said, "Yes," Dr. Rankin wouldn't speak another word.

It was awkward, but Miss Sloan just said, "Oh, I've known Ara for years, that's just her." Dr. Rankin never again mentioned Bob's name. You wouldn't expect this kind of behaviour from a gang of missionaries, would you?

Despite the rarity of visits with Bob, I was too busy for time to drag. I had constant language study for the whole two years, but the next spring, I went up to Mahableshwar for only one month, instead of three, because I was now just a temporary employee. It was my month's "holiday," when I went, but I still had language study for eight hours a day. At least Bob was there, too.

By this time, the staffing situation at St. Margaret's had become quite desperate. Miss Sloan had retired, and Dr. Bailey left when she contracted polio. Nancy Brash transferred to Ludhiana, because she couldn't get on with Ara. Nancy was very quiet, and never lost her temper. If something hurt her feelings, she never made a fuss about it, so when Dr. Rankin would go into a huff, it just drove Nancy crackers. She couldn't let it go. When Dr. Rankin would give her the silent treatment, she'd come to my room to talk it over, and I'd say, "Just forget it."

"I never know what I did wrong. I can't stand this strain," so she wrote to Scotland, and they transferred her to Ludhiana to the medical college where she remained as a professor until her retirement.

This left us with only Dr. Rankin, so we eventually got two wonderful new doctors, Dr. Samuel and Dr. Pinto-Phillips. Dr. Samuel was married and lived in a house just by the gate of the compound. Dr. Pinto-Phillips, Yvonne, was a Goanese woman. She had already done her post-graduate work, but because she wanted more experience, she agreed to come to help Dr. Rankin. So, once again, we had three doctors. Yvonne and I had similar personalities, and we became the closest of friends. She'd come up to my room and say, "Ara's off again. What do you suppose it is this time?" and we would go over the day. "Well, maybe the butler did her wrong this morning…"

Then Dr. Rankin developed pneumonia and was very ill. We tried our best to nurse her, but despite the fact that she was over 70 years old and had pneumonia, she still insisted on running everything. She would ring the bell, and then direct the nurses to do this or go there or find out what Dr. Pinto was doing.

Dr. Rankin's best friend was Mother Doreen, the mother superior at an Anglican convent in Poona. Ara often spent her day off at the convent and had a fine time there. When the nuns were ill, we nursed them, and we became great friends. Wonderful people, the nuns. An outside doctor, a professor, came to see Dr. Rankin, and said later, "You know, that woman never relaxes and gives herself time to heal."

So I talked to Mother Doreen, who was a lovely person, and told her, "Ara doesn't need nursing now, she needs time to convalesce, and she won't do that at the hospital because she keeps going down the stairs and getting involved in things. Could you take her at the convent?"

"Yes, bring her over." So she took Dr. Rankine to the convent where she finally recovered. Meanwhile, we were once again short staffed. Then Dr. Samuel, who was pregnant, delivered her baby early, so for a while, Yvonne and I were in charge of the entire hospital. For weeks, there was never so much as a half-day off. Fortunately, Yvonne's parents lived in Poona and used to bring us cakes and treats to cheer us up. Late one Saturday night we were stretched out on the veranda when monotony overpowered exhaustion, and I said to Yvonne, "Let's do something different."

"What can we do?" she said. "We can't leave the hospital."

"Well, I would like to wear a sari and pretend I'm a lady tonight."

"Come on, you can wear one of my saris," she said, jumping up.

"OK," I said, "and you can wear my clothes." So Yvonne slipped into a western dress of mine and topped it off with an unlikely hat, complemented by white makeup and lipstick. Then she dressed me in a lovely sari and painted my face in Indian makeup. We were laughing in front of the mirror as only the exhausted can, when a sudden emergency careened to the hospital gate.

Running, we met a woman being brought in on an oxcart. She was trying to deliver her baby, but instead the entire uterus had come out. She was in a terrible state, and we rushed to save her. The poor woman wove in and out of consciousness, moaning in pain, but it wasn't until we both leaned over her that she became hysterical. Eyes wide at what must have looked otherworldly, she screamed in Marathi, "Oh, now I know I'm going to die!

I'm seeing a black woman wearing white clothes, and a white woman wearing Indian clothes. Oh, everything's mixed up!"

Unfortunately, it was too late for the baby, but our oxcart ambulance patient survived, thanks to a hysterectomy and some units of blood, and despite the shock of seeing an Indian woman dressed "white," and a white woman dressed as an Indian.

∗∗∗

Now and then, Yvonne would comment to me, "Nancy, I'd love to have a baby, but I don't want to be bothered with a man."

"You'll have to adopt one."

"As soon as I finish my course, I'll adopt a baby. I just don't want to be bothered with a man."

When Yvonne left St. Margaret's, she went to Delhi where she became a professor of obstetrics and gynaecology. Some time later, I received a letter from her father, who had five daughters.

"I just wanted you to know, I have obeyed Yvonne's directions; I have not arranged a marriage. She has arranged her own." She was 34 or so at the time of her marriage, and her Goanese husband was the dentist to, among others, Jawaharlal Nehru, the first prime minister of independent India.

Chapter 10: Bob's Backstory

The woman we always called Gramma Ramer was a stern, opinionated German from the old country. Against her express dictate that her son marry the good German girl *she* had chosen, Manuel married "that foreigner" Helen, a native-born girl, and Helen paid the price—stone cold silence. For months, her mother-in-law refused to speak to her, but remarkably, all was forgiven on February 27, 1921.

That day in Denver, Colorado, Helen gave birth to Robert Peter Ramer, a grandson to carry on the Ramer name. Gramma Ramer spoke only German, but Helen didn't have to *Deutsch sprechen* to understand that she was now being accepted into the family. Mannie wanted to name the baby for his twin brother, Peter, and Helen wanted to name him for her favourite brother, Robert, so Robert Peter he became.

About a year and a half later, little Bobby was presented with a baby brother named after his father, Emmanuel Edward (Mannie), and two years after that came a beautiful baby girl, Elizabeth Ruth. When Bobby was six, a final brother was born, Philip Arthur.

Life seemed to be going well. Helen and Manuel had their own home and four healthy children. Manuel and his twin Peter were business partners in a combined grocery store-butcher shop, where Manuel was the butcher, and Peter the grocer. Then came the stock market crash of 1929. Suddenly, many were jobless and couldn't pay their bills. Manuel and Peter gave their customers food on credit to the point where they couldn't pay their own bills. Peter tried to persuade Manuel to leave for California where conditions were said to be better, but Manuel had a wife and children and couldn't easily pull up stakes and move. Then one morning when Manuel went to their shop, he found that Peter had left for California.

With little money coming in, Manuel and Helen lost their house, but luckily, he had bought a plot of land near Sloan's Lake. Like Helen and Manuel, Manuel's older brother Walt had lost his house because he couldn't meet the payments, so the two brothers built a basement house on Manuel's plot of land. Walt and his family of four moved into one end of the basement, and Helen and Manuel moved their four children into the other end. So, while Helen and Manuel had lost their house and their business, they did have a good, warm basement home, and were sharing with others. Manuel, later known as Pappy, got work as a meat cutter with a large grocery store, the Piggly Wiggly, and slowly, he was able to pay off his debts.

As Bob remembered it, the families never went to bed hungry. There was an orchard in back of their house, and on Saturday nights Manuel brought home what was left over at the grocer's. The children rather enjoyed the basement house where cousins were always available to play. As time went on, Walt got work, and he and his family moved to a rented house. Manuel then began to build the rest of the house on the foundations of the basement.

But it wasn't exactly smooth sailing from then on. Manuel developed rheumatoid arthritis, and his doctor predicted that he would require a wheelchair for the rest of his life. So crippled by the arthritis that he could only get around on his hands and knees, Manuel lost his job. Despondent, he figured that Helen and the children would be better off with his life insurance money than with him. One day he went into the bathroom and shook out a handful of pills, an overdose that would surely put him out of his misery. But before he could get them to his mouth, he heard a voice, "Fool, are you going to spend eternity in Hell?" Startled into awareness, Manuel promised God that if he were healed, he would spend his life telling others about Christ, and in a matter of months, Manuel was back at work, completely well.

Several years later, when Bobby was about 10, the family was on the road in their truck, with Bobby and Mannie.Jr. in the back, enjoying the breeze. Suddenly, a car ran a red light and hit them, and father and son were thrown from the truck as it overturned. Mannie's head was caught under the truck, and he suffered severe head injuries. The spare tire smacked Bobby squarely between the shoulders. It was extremely painful, and he cried from pain and shock. However, he was able to walk and didn't complain much, so attention quickly focused on extricating his brother. As a souvenir of that accident, Bobby carried a lump near the top of his spine. The family ignored it, as did the Navy recruitment doctors years later. Almost four decades passed before Jim Donaldson, orthopaedic surgeon at Miraj Mission Hospital, said to Bob, "I'm curious about that lump on your spine. Let me X-ray it."

"OK," agreed Bob, "but I've never had any pain there since a few days after the accident."

The X-ray showed that Bob's spinal column had been fractured, but that it had healed itself by calcifying over the break. Jim was amazed. "You should have been paralysed, but somehow your spinal column was protected." There are so many miracles in our lives, but we often don't even recognize them at the time.

Mannie's injuries kept him in the hospital for a long time, and under treatment for years. Long after Bobby was grown, the family was still paying medical bills related to that accident.

Helen was a Methodist, and Manuel a German Lutheran, so they compromised on the Presbyterian Church, not far from their home on Yates Street. Highland Park Presbyterian Church became the centre of the family's social life—until the occasion of a vociferous argument about the Sunday School curriculum. Angry, Manuel walked out of the church vowing never to return. But at Helen's behest, he continued to take Bobby to Sunday School. He himself would sit in the car, smoking a cigar and reading the Sunday paper. One day Bobby questioned why *he* had to attend Sunday School, but Manuel no longer did. Manuel replied that it was good to know what the Bible teaches: "It helps you live right."

Bobby countered, "Do you know the whole Bible, Dad, and do you live by it?" Even a stubborn German had to reconsider under those circumstances, and the next Sunday Manuel was at Sunday School, and the whole family in church. Manuel became the teacher for the adult Bible class, and taught it for some 40 years.

Bobby's church activities revolved around the Friday night youth group. The kids attended youth camp as a group, and also went out together to dance, watch movies, and picnic. In that group Bob formed what would become a lifelong friendship with a boy named Walt Bohnet.

After school, Bobby worked as a delivery boy, first for newspapers, then groceries. One Saturday he overslept, and when he showed up late to work, he was unceremoniously fired. Deeply dismayed, Bobby trudged the downtown streets looking for a new delivery job, and was pleased to see "Delivery Help Wanted" in the window of the camera store. Eagerly, he applied. His interview centred on the question, "Do you have a bicycle?" He was hired on the spot, and worked at that camera store throughout high school, leaving only to join the Navy. Bobby soon rose from delivery boy to developer and photographer, even taking the photos for his high school yearbook. It was the beginning of a lifelong hobby.

After high school Bobby, now Bob, was accepted to the prestigious Colorado School of Mines. It was impossible for his parents to pay college tuition for Bob, but Manuel said, "I'll give you free room and board, but you must find a way to pay all your other expenses." By working at the camera shop, picking strawberries and tomatoes, taking photos at weddings, and commuting from Denver to Golden with other CSM students, Bob managed to pay for that first year.

The second year of school was even more expensive, so Bob took a year off to earn some money working in a foundry assaying metals. One of the unanticipated benefits of working there was meeting the first love of his life, Carol, the boss's daughter. By working weekends at the foundry, Bob managed the second year at CSM, with enough extra to take Carol out on a modest date now and then. After his second year of college, Bob needed to work and save for another year. By then he and Carol were going steady and had eyes only for each other.

Meantime, the United States declared war on Japan and Germany. Walt went off to the Navy to be a medical corpsman, and Bob made his contribution to the war effort by working in the foundry. One night there was a concert for which Bob had gotten tickets for a special date with Carol, but at the last minute he was called to the foundry to do an urgent job.

He begged to be let off for the concert, and although the boss was Carol's father, he was immovable, saying only, "This is wartime." It happened that Walt Bohnet was home on leave, so Bob asked Walt to take Carol to the concert. The result of this arrangement was that Walt and Carol fell in love. Although Bob felt there would never be another love like Carol, he and the happy couple remained friends.

At the end of Bob's third year at the Colorado School of Mines, he was offered a full scholarship for his fourth year. At last he graduated with a major in metallurgy and a minor in civil engineering. Upon his graduation, the college invited Bob to teach a summer class on surveying at a field site in Wyoming. Bob's students were mostly rough and ready men who had only a nodding acquaintance with religion, and Bob began to feel the call to be a pastor, perhaps a chaplain in an engineering college.

Just as his summer job finished, Bob was called to the principal's office at CSM. The Army desperately needed metallurgists for a top-secret job at Oak Ridge, Tennessee, and the college had recommended Bob, who had specialized in the study of uranium. The pay and the perquisites were fabulous; the downside was that he could have no contact with the outside world until this particular project was completed. Bob had 24 hours to think it over. He was savvy enough to realize that the project probably involved bombs or other means of destruction. While he was a loyal American, and felt the war was justified, he refused to kill, so it didn't take long for him to make up his mind.

Then, without even going home first, he signed up with the Navy, volunteering as a medical corpsman. He was soon called up and sent to boot camp. His first assignment was a classic military snafu. Bob, a *metallurgist,* was assigned to study the weather, about which he knew nothing. *Metallurgist* and *meteorologist* were all the same to *someone* in the Navy. So Bob served his Navy years stationed in Hawaii where they spent their days studying the clouds over the Pacific. During his term as a weatherman, Bob applied for training as a Navy chaplain.

With the end of the Second World War, Bob's ship went to port in Seattle, where the sailors worked on the ship and waited for demobilization orders. Finally, Bob's orders arrived—two official notices from the Navy, on the same day.

One notice informed Bob that he was released from the Navy and was entitled to the GI Bill of Rights, a suit of civilian clothes, and a ticket home. The other notice congratulated him on being selected for training as a Navy chaplain! After much prayer and thoughtful consideration, Bob decided to refuse the appointment to Navy chaplaincy and try to go to seminary on his own.

When Bob returned to Denver, his days were filled with reunions and welcome home parties. When some semblance of normal life resumed, Bob went to Highland Park Presbyterian for a long talk with his minister, who was startled that the church's chief prankster, and an engineer to boot, felt called to the ministry. There were references made to God's sense of humour.

Then it was time to discuss his plans with his father. It was late on a Saturday night and Manuel had just returned from working at the store, when Bob told his father that he felt called to the ministry. Manuel was shocked. He had lived through the Depression and struggled for years to raise a family while paying off creditors and medical bills. He could be forgiven for being incredulous at hearing that his son, an engineer with a good Navy record and prospects for a well-paying, secure job was thinking of throwing it over for the ministry.

Manuel cautiously questioned Bob, reminding him that he could offer him no financial assistance. The GI Bill would pay tuition, but not living expenses, and it would be three more years until he earned a regular salary. Even then he would never earn what he could command as an engineer. Did he plan to marry and support a family?

Bob assured him that he had considered all that, but felt he must go to seminary and prepare himself for whatever God had in mind. So Manuel and Helen supported him in all the ways they could.

After much consideration, Bob applied to San Francisco Theological Seminary in San Anselmo, hoping to start in September 1947, more than a year later. In response, he received a letter saying he was accepted and should report to classes *this* September, 1946! When Bob explained that he would need to get a job, the seminary recommended him for a position as housefather at a nearby orphanage. Soon Bob was driving off to San Anselmo in an old Chevrolet Suburban, which had already endured many trips through the Rocky Mountains.

After years of studying math, chemistry, and other science, it wasn't easy to learn history, Greek, and Hebrew. However, Bob made an acceptable academic showing and by the end of the year, he had also made many friends. Without singing a note, he had become a valued member of the seminary choir, using the big Suburban to transport instruments, robes, and other necessities as the choir toured to various churches. Besides, Bob could fix anything that broke down, and did so good-naturedly.

During the summer of 1947, the Presbytery appointed Bob to be student assistant to Rev. Ed Bollinger, the minister for Leadville and Red Cliff Presbyterian Churches. It was the perfect appointment—right in the centre of the Rockies, assisting a wise and congenial pastor. The majority of the congregants worked in the mines, so they were delighted to have "a miner" as a student pastor. In those days, these mining towns were rough places, not at all the elite tourist destinations they are now. No fancy, ivory tower seminarian, Bob went down the mines with the men and visited them in their homes. The good old Chevy Suburban came in handy for the youth camps, for hauling kids and camping equipment up and down the mountains.

At one of the youth camps, Bob met the Alters, missionaries on furlough from India. When the Alters heard that Bob was an engineer, they tried to persuade him to become a missionary to India because the church had technical schools there. Bob laughed and said, "I would have a hard time learning the language, so I wouldn't be much use. No, I think I have found my place. I would like to serve the churches where there are miners."

Bob's second year at seminary was a happy one. He still struggled with Hebrew and Greek, but the study became more interesting as Bob prepared and preached sermons to his classmates and professors. At the seminary a group of students had formed an early morning prayer group, and six of them—Larry Driscoll, Al Solomon, Bob Hampel, Harold Lang, Malcolm Carrick, and Bob—continued as prayer partners for many, many years. They were all older than the average student, had experienced war, and were convinced that peace would come only through influencing others to follow Christ's teachings. Three of these six became missionaries—Larry and Malcolm to Japan, and Bob to India. The other three ministered at home. All were extraordinary in their service to God and their communities, and over the years they circled the globe with encouraging letters, sustaining each other in their work.

In 1948, the summer after his second year of seminary, Bob was happy to be appointed once again to Leadville and Red Cliff, and headed back to Colorado with a sense of rightness in his life. Back in Leadville, Bob was assisting Rev. Bollinger again, and camping in the Rockies with the youth of his two churches. For the second year in a row, one of the speakers at camp was a Presbyterian missionary from India. This man, too, said to Bob, "You ought to be a missionary in India. We need engineers, and you could teach in one of our industrial schools." Bob laughed and told him, "I'd never get the language! I've just struggled through Greek and Hebrew!"

"Oh, you don't need Greek or Hebrew," he said, "and you'll find the spoken language is easy." After many discussions, the missionary said, "Just sign this application, and the Board will send you material about

India. You still have another year to think about it." So Bob signed the application and sent it off and thought no more about it.

Back in Leadville, Bob met three young students from Bob Jones College (now University). They were very aggressive evangelists and had come to Leadville to hold a youth rally. Bob attended their meetings at night to hear what was going on. During the day, these three young men went from house to house evangelising. Bob and the three had long talks over coffee. Though their theology was vastly different from his, Bob was impressed with their zeal and energy. After they left, Bob remembered their commitment, and he prayed, "I don't agree with them, but I am impressed with their love for Jesus. Lord, grant me the vision to give up all and trust you."

Summer ended, and Bob headed back to San Anselmo, happy to see his friends and begin his final year of study. About the second week of the term, he received a long telegram from the American Presbyterian Board of Foreign Missions: *The need for you in India is urgent and immediate. Please contact us at once.*

When Bob phoned, he was told that the Sangli Industrial School was in desperate straits. The principal was seriously ill, and if another engineer could not be quickly found, the school would close. The Board asked Bob to leave seminary and come to New York, then go on to India. It was the shock of Bob's life. He had been given a scholarship and was looking forward to his last year at seminary. If he left now, he would lose his GI Bill benefits, which would make finishing after India much more difficult.

After much prayer, Bob took the telegram to the principal of the seminary, Dr. Baird, a wise and considerate man. He discussed the issue with Bob at length, and concluded, "I think God is calling you, but you have to make up your mind as to when and how you will answer the call."

"I want to be ordained," Bob protested, as much to himself as to Baird. "Wouldn't it be wiser to finish seminary? You know what a struggle I have had with my studies, and now I am getting the hang of it. How will it be to come back after five years?"

Dr. Baird reassured him on that count and added, "Your experience in the mission field will always be an asset." Bob left the office still in turmoil and went to see his Greek professor. He showed him the telegram, and said,

"Tell me the truth. You know how difficult it is for me to learn languages. Do you think I could ever learn and work in a foreign language?"

His professor laughed. "Hebrew and Greek are dead languages. In India you would have people speaking all around you. Go to it, and come back to us in five years!" Five years seemed forever, and just when he felt he would soon be ordained. On he trudged to his missions professor, Dr. Jones. Showing him the telegram, Bob asked, "Do you think I would be a good missionary? How can the Board people know if I'm the right person?"

Dr. Jones clapped Bob on the back and said, "Of course, you will be a good missionary; you fit in with all types of people. What a privilege to be called to go to India! What an opportunity! Go, and the Lord go with you. We'll all welcome you back when the time comes." So, Bob soon found himself on the road to Colorado in his old Chevy Suburban.

At home in Denver, there were letters awaiting him with background on the Sangli Industrial School and details of what he needed to bring to India. He was to report immediately to New York to attend "the outgoing conference," a sort of orientation and celebration for new missionaries. There was no time to waste; Bob immediately set to packing up the old Chevy. His brother Phil, sister Betty, and Betty's husband Dan all decided to drive with Bob to New York, then bring the van back to Denver. Having celebrated his return from the Navy only too recently, with little warning Helen was seeing her son off for five more years, to a land on the other side of the world.

Except for the usual minor mechanical emergencies, the drive was uneventful, and the quartet made many happy memories on that trip. Reaching New York, Bob was advised that he would sail for India on a freighter leaving in a week. Phil, Betty, and Dan soon turned their thoughts and wheels to home, and Bob devoted his attention to the conference. There, for a week, he lived with a group of extraordinary young people, all well qualified, all about to set sail for countries most had never seen. On the last night there, a farewell banquet was held, and missionary children, young people who had grown up in the mission field, were in attendance. Bob made a point of talking to them, asking them what it was like to be separated from their parents and sent off to boarding school. "I was so impressed by these young people," Bob was later to comment. "I thought if my children would turn out like that, how thrilled I would be."

Soon came the day of the ship's departure. Bob was given responsibility for far more than his own suitcases—he was also to shepherd along a shipment including a refrigerator and other much-needed equipment for the missions. Although there were a number of missionaries on board, Bob was the only one from the Presbyterian Church.

After three long weeks at sea, the ship docked in Bombay, where Bob was met by the Presbyterian mission treasurer, who helped him through customs. The next day, Bob caught the morning train to Kolhapur with the huge mountain of baggage. About nine o'clock at night the train rolled into Kolhapur, where Bob was overwhelmed by the tide of people who surged toward him with a hearty "Welcome to western India!" and garlands of flowers! Already convened for the annual American Presbyterian (A.P.) meeting, 40-some missionaries and their spouses gathered at the station to welcome Bob. Even coming home from the Navy, he had never experienced a welcome like this.

The first order of business was to begin learning the language, Marathi, so Bob remained in Kolhapur, where he stayed with Gordon and Peggy Ruff and their children, Barbara and Arthur. However, he couldn't wait to see Sangli, where he would be stationed, so on his first weekend he headed to Sangli, 30 miles away. The memory of that first visit never faded; Bob saw so many things he could do.

In 1949 transportation between Kolhapur and Sangli was either by a highly irregular bus or by train, which took three hours. After several frustrating weeks, Bob found he could bike to Sangli in less time, so he took to leaving early Saturday morning, arriving in Sangli 90 minutes later, then pedalling back in time to be ready for class on Monday morning.

The language study program was intensive. Students were required to spend eight hours a day studying their language. The language pundit spent one hour teaching a class, then two hours with each student, with Saturdays and Sundays off. With his difficulty in learning languages, Bob expected this to be torturous, but to his surprise, he found it quite exciting. It helped that Marathi has its own script that makes it easy to pronounce a word, even if you have no idea what it means.

This system of study was soon replaced when in February the Marathi Language School opened in Mahableshwar. Mahableshwar was a beautiful hill station with a lake, built as a cooperative project by missions of several denominations. The school employed Indian college graduates, mostly Brahman, who spoke clear, "high-class" Marathi and had been educated in the teaching of Marathi as a second language. The school itself consisted of corrugated iron shacks built on the hill by the church. There classes were held from 8 a.m. until noon. In the afternoon the pundits went from house to house, giving each student an hour of individual instruction.

At Mahableshwar Bob lived with the other A.P. missionaries, Marvin and Elsie Nelson with their baby daughter Kathie, and Gordon and Peggy Ruff with Barbie and Arthur. Mount Douglas, the A.P. mission bungalow, had a marvellous view, but no running water, and only boxes for toilets. But the waterman brought up water, and the sweeper took away the boxes, emptied them, and cleaned the bathrooms, so no one much minded the limited amenities. The families brought their cooks and ayahs. Like their officially appointed husbands, the wives had to spend eight hours a day in language study. The women rotated responsibility for housekeeping, supervision of the cook, and maintenance of the accounts.

It was in February 1949, on their initial trip to Mahableshwar, that Bob first demonstrated his ingenuity to his new colleagues as he drove an old van up the hill with Marvin, Elsie, and baby Kathie Nelson as his passengers. The climb up to Mahableshwar was steep and unpaved, making for a hot, dusty drive. When they stopped at Wai, someone pointed them to a shortcut up the back pass. It may have been shorter, but it was rugged. They chugged slowly over stony paths until with a thump and a sputter, the van broke down.

Long the master of old, used vehicles, it didn't take long for Bob to diagnose a leaky water pump. He rigged up a bandage and got water from a stream, and on they went, but every few miles the radiator leaked dry. Everyone was tired and dirty, but baby Kathie was utterly miserable, so in a desperate attempt at a longer lasting "fix," Bob said, "Let's try chewing gum," and they all set to chewing big wads of it. The solution was imperfect, but an improvement, and finally, very late at night, they lurched into the Mount Douglas compound where they were welcomed by a flock of worried Presbyterians. By this time, Bob was convinced of the desirability of facing life's adventures with a partner, and decided it was

time to look for a nice girl who might become his wife, and in a toast to
the plan, he soon invested in a double bed.

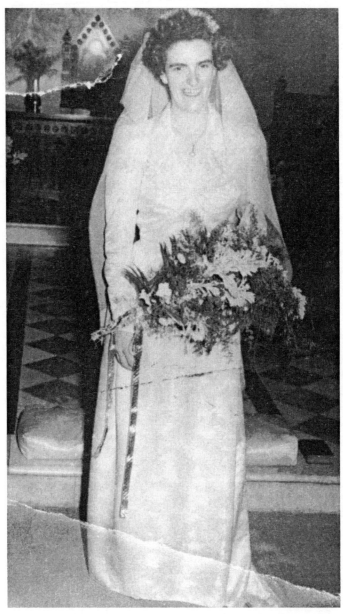

Nancy on her wedding day

Chapter 11: Jasmine and Jacaranda

On June 1, 1951, I awoke to beautiful sunshine, shaded a little by the drape of my mosquito net. Instead of the usual jumping up at the last minute to dress and begin my rounds, I lay quiet, listening to the noises of a busy hospital. Today, surrounded by friends, Bob and I would be married.

On my last night as missionary staff at St. Margaret's Hospital, I had slept on the roof garden where it was cooler. Unlike many brides today, for whom the day is frantic, I felt no need to hurry. My wedding was to be at noon, and I lay there, going over the arrangements in my mind. I had worked at the hospital until 5 p.m. the previous night, handing over to the new nurse superintendent the nurses' files, workers' records, and most importantly "The Book," in which I had written all the details that a new nursing superintendent needed to know. My replacement, Janet Callun, had come from the Mukti Mission to take over my job for a year until a new nursing superintendent would arrive from Scotland. Janet had been my supervisor at Yorkhill, so I could leave in clear conscience, knowing she was amply qualified.

The previous night, my stand-in father Bill Todd, a Scottish doctor about my own age, had arrived with his wife Muriel and baby Heather. Bill was a clever surgeon, a short man with a broad Glasgow accent, and we had become acquainted at language school. Bill's presence in the women's and children's hospital was quite newsworthy. Our medical superintendent had *never* allowed men to come up to the "women's apartments," so Bill and his family had only grudgingly been offered the guest room for the night.

I was looking forward to wearing my beautiful wedding dress, which had a story of its own. It was made of ivory Chinese silk, embroidered with a willow pattern. The silk came from a Chinese merchant who had escaped when the Communists took over. Somehow he had successfully smuggled out several bales of extraordinarily lovely cloth. Two years ago the merchant had come to the bungalow in Mahableshwar, where we were staying for language study. As he rolled out the precious cottons and silks, this beautiful willowed ivory immediately caught my eye. "Oh, I want that for my wedding dress!" I had joked. Bob and I had just become engaged. The merchant tried to persuade me to buy the silk, but there was no question of buying it; I just didn't have the money. "Come back in two years!" I countered.

"It will be sold by then, and I cannot get any more like this from China!" Resigned, I had to let go the idea.

A year later, the same merchant came to St. Margaret's, saying, "I have only seven yards of the willow pattern silk. You take it, pay me later!" By then I was able to scrape together enough to buy it from the persistent merchant, who agreed to accept payment in two instalments. Some time later, I took it to our wee tailor Nikam on Main Street, Cantonment, Poona. Cantonment was the military part of Poona, where the British had lived, and tailors there were experienced in making European clothing. I had seen the dress I wanted in a magazine, and showed it to Nikam, whose work, it was known, was sometimes excellent, sometimes horrid. I wondered if I could trust him with the irreplaceable fabric.

When Nikam saw the silk, his eyes lit up. "Good, good cloth. I do frock well!" And he did. The gown had a fitted top, and a skirt with a flowing princess line and a short train. There was a sweetheart neckline with a back collar edged in tiny loops. A panel of small pleats formed the bodice, and long sleeves tapered to a point over my hands. Nikam had created a gown for a princess. At my final fitting, he handed me a remnant of the silk, saying, "This is enough to make sandals to match. Go to Chinese shoemaker, he do it!" I followed his advice, so I had lovely sandals to match.

Now, everything was ready, though the flowers had been touch and go. Under British rule, the flower shops of Poona had been famous for their flowers, but that was no longer the case. Prime Minister Nehru advocated that only Indian products be sold, so there were no imported flowers to be found.

Knowing this, I had begun talking with the local nursery in January, and was assured that they were planting the flowers I wanted for June. Again in March I checked, and was assured that everything was under control. But when the time came for delivery, they had only two small white, lily-like flowers. Two white flowers after promises of roses and gladioli!

Fortunately, our watchman said, "I get flowers—I know many malis (gardeners)!" He did know many malis, and he brought great bunches of beautiful blooms to the church. I had not yet seen them, but Kathryn Ramsey, another Scottish missionary, had phoned to say, "Don't worry, we have lots of gorgeous flowers!" I pictured my Scottish colleagues decorating the church with flowers from the many lovely private gardens.

As it was, many friends had contributed generously to make it a beautiful and memorable day. First, the Chinese merchant had allowed me to buy the silk for my dress in instalments. Then there was the matter of the veil. I still had my mother's wedding veils, but no headpiece to affix them to. I happened to mention to Multibai, principal of the Scottish Girls' School, that I was looking for a headpiece and she said, "Nancy, I've got a headpiece for you."

"You do?"

"I have a spray of white orchids just coming out in bud, and I've put a net over them so the birds can't get at them. I'm watching them every day, and I think they'll be just right for your headpiece. I'll bring them to you on the morning of your wedding!"

Pleased at how things had turned out, I got up to enjoy my quiet time. I was just finishing my prayers when Ayah brought in tea, toast, marmalade, and a banana. "Would you like egg?" she asked. "Long time till lunch, have an egg!" but I was too excited to eat much.

At nine o'clock my two bridesmaids arrived. Yvonne Pinto-Phillips, our resident surgeon and my close friend, was going to wear her grandmother's dusky pink sari. The matron of honour, Nancy Patterson, principal of the Church of Scotland Teacher Training College, was a dear friend from my St. Colm's days in Edinburgh. The two swept in saying, "We are here to give you a bubble bath!"

"I can jolly well bathe myself," I protested. "Besides, Yvonne, you have dozens of patients from the prison clinic waiting. So off you go—I'll bathe myself!" The prison clinic usually meant 30 to 50 women who needed penicillin shots for venereal disease.

But Yvonne was already giving orders to bring up the hot water. Nancy P. explained, "The prison matron brought a busload of patients early, and Dr. Samuel and two nurses were all in the clinic by 6:30 a.m. giving injections and medicine. She lined up the women and told them, 'It's Sister's wedding today—quick, quick, quick! No fussing today!' Everyone worked so fast, and the women were so cooperative, that they were finished by 9 a.m. Yvonne has even done her rounds of the ward!"

Back from requesting the water, Yvonne said, "This is the Indian custom. We bathe you and do your nails and hair. Then we cover you with sweet oil, and leave you to lie down and relax. After an hour, we return and put your dress on!" My friends laughed and teased as they submerged me in the bubble bath, and we laughed even more as they both massaged me with jasmine oil. Finally, a cool dark cloth was laid over my eyes, and they covered me with a sheet and departed.

I did rest, and then took a quick shower so the *strong* jasmine smell would be a bit less overwhelming. A couple of my nursing staff popped in with sweet wishes. At 11 a.m., Yvonne in her sari, and Nancy in a beautiful blue formal gown, came over to do my hair and help me into my wedding dress.

They had just finished when Dr. Rankine came in. Ara had been so angry at my leaving to get married that she had made everything difficult. Diplomatically, I thought, I had first asked Ara to give me away, but still surly, she'd answered, "I will not!" Furthermore, she had been insistent that only off-duty staff could go to the wedding, leaving sadly disappointed the nurses and ayahs who were scheduled to work that day. That's where Dr. Coaji came to the rescue. Dr. Coaji was the medical superintendent at the nearby government hospital. She had served her residency under Dr. Rankine, and took our emergency calls when Dr. Rankine was at St. Mary's convent, recuperating from pneumonia.

About a month before my wedding, Dr. Coaji came to assist Dr. Rankine on an emergency case. As we worked in the operating room, Dr. Coaji asked, "Sister Orr, have you arranged for all the nurses to go to the wedding?"

I looked at Ara. Sniffing, she replied, "Only those who are off duty can go! I'm not going either. Somebody has to think of the patients!"

"Surely you can go for a short time, Dr. Rankine!" said Dr. Coaji. "I know! I'll come and stay at St. Margaret's for two hours. I'll bring two buses with nurses from my hospital—ayahs, too! Then the buses can take *your* nurses and all your workers to the wedding! Then after the wedding and reception are over, a couple of hours at most, the buses will bring your nurses back here, and then take all my staff back to the municipal hospital!"

"Not at all," said Dr. Rankine. "How could we possibly pay for all that? It is not necessary!"

But Dr. Coaji was not to be thwarted. Smiling, she said, "This is my wedding present to Sister Orr, and Ara, it *is* necessary for you to go. Sister Orr ran the hospital when you were so ill, and personally nursed you, too! So it is all arranged!"

At 11:30 a.m., just before I was to leave for the church, I was giving myself a last look over when Ara walked into my room. She came over to me and laid a beautiful gold necklace with an aquamarine pendant around my neck. She hugged me, and with tears in her eyes said, "Forgive me for being so difficult. I just couldn't abide seeing you go!"

I was so touched. "You look lovely, Ara. I still wish you would give me away."

"No, don't ask me to do that, but I do give you my blessing. The entire staff, all of us, will be at the wedding. Dr. Coaji brought her staff over in buses just a bit ago." Ara again kissed me, and then went off with Muriel Todd and the two bridesmaids.

Bill Todd, acting father, came to my room to take me downstairs. He whistled and said, "Nancy, you do Scotland proud! You beat all those American lassies!" I felt such peace and great confidence that God was leading me into a whole new life. We were taking the hospital car to the church, and to my surprise, the staff had decorated it beautifully. In the car, as we approached the church, Bill leaned over, patted my knee, and said in his broad Scots accent, "Now, Nancy, if Bob Ramer is nae good to you, if he is cruel to you, and you are nae happy, you just come to Muriel and me. We'll see you straight! Just dunnae forget, I'm not your faither just to walk down the aisle, but a faither who will see that his daughter is treated well!"

I was deeply moved and squeezing Bill's arm, I assured him, "I'm sure Bob will be kind, but I will always remember that you are in the background!"

St. Andrew's Church, the Scots' kirk, is a beautiful wee church, built to serve the colonial Presbyterians. We drove through the gates, and as Bill helped me out of the car and walked me into the nave, we could hear Robert Miller, a professor at Wilson College, pumping the organ with great vigour. I gasped when I saw the sanctuary. Every window ledge was full of flowers; the sanctuary was aglow with blooms. Before I could really take it in, my bridal bouquet was handed to me, and Robert began the bridal march.

The Church of Scotland missionaries were all there. From Mahableshwar came the Fletchers and the Vaughns. Harry Brown, the senior missionary in Sangli, came down. Ian and Isabel Patterson were there, too. Ian was a minister with the Church of Scotland, and a professor at Union Seminary in Poona.

As Bill led me down the aisle, I could see that the church was packed. Nearing the altar, I looked up and saw Bob standing there in an India-made, somewhat ill-fitting light grey suit, with an awestruck look on his face. I smiled, and Bob broke into a wide grin, as he stepped forward to meet me. At Bob's side was his close friend Rev. Marvin Nelson, an American Presbyterian missionary, and Nanda Dikshit, the Hindu Brahman whose family had been on the ship with me when I left Scotland. Nanda's mother lived in Poona and had adopted me. It was unfortunate that Marvin's wife Elsie was in Kodai and couldn't be there. It was because of her bike accident that Bob and I met, and the Nelsons were always good friends. The officiating minister was Dr. James Kellock, principal of Wilson College, Scottish missionary, and, at that time, moderator of the United Church of North India.

Dr. Kellock's homily had great dignity and warmth. "Nancy and Bob," he said, "God has called you into this marriage. You will make your home an outpost of heaven. Share this great love for each other with all who enter your home. May they feel Christ's presence in your lives as you welcome all nationalities, all people of different faiths, young and old, the sick and needy, because Christ is the head of your household." Excited as I was, I heard every word, and we often spoke of his loving charge to us. Such a few words, but so perfect that I remember them now, more than 50 years later.

We left briefly to register the marriage in the church Session room, then Dr. Kellock led us back into the sanctuary for the benediction, after which Bob and I walked down the aisle, joined for life. I was so proud to be "Mrs. Robert Ramer." Robert Miller pounded that organ with joyful abandon. His face was tomato red from the exertion, and I heard later that he broke the pump!

At the door of the church was the most beautiful sight. Sixteen nurses in their white saris had formed a guard of honour. Holding branches of gulmohr and purple jacaranda, they made a lush and fragrant arch for us to walk through, a beautiful portal to our new life. Dr. Kellock, in his white robes and red stole, preceded us through the bower, announcing, "I introduce to you Mr. and Mrs. Robert Ramer." Then to us, "Go in love and peace."

The opening hymn at our wedding service was "Praise to the Lord, the Almighty," the same hymn that had sent me to my room in tears at St. Colm's when I learned I would have to go to India instead of China. "Hast Thou not seen how thy desires e'er have been granted in what He ordaineth?" I surely saw now my heart's desire granted in what he ordained!

After pictures were taken, we went over to the Church of Scotland girls' hostel, where Multibai had prepared a reception of cold lemonade with cookies and bridal cake. Isabel Patterson had baked the cake and decorated it by painting Mahableshwar scenes on top. Two of the servants from Bob's Sangli household had come to help serve.

The servants had all said, "Oh, you should have a big dinner," for that was a firmly established Indian custom, but we couldn't afford it. At the time I was earning 200 rupees a month, and Bob was earning 400 rupees, and we had to pay for our keep out of that. In a good month, when food was cheap, one person's food bill might be only 150 rupees, but often it was more, so our salaries barely covered our expenses. In Sangli, the mission provided Bob's unfurnished house, but we had no furniture, and no money to purchase what we needed to set up housekeeping. So we had been extremely careful about our wedding expenses, and determined not to spend a lot of money.

Despite our economic limitations, it was a wonderful celebration. Bill Todd made a great speech, as did Marvin Nelson and Dr. Rankine. After the reception, the bridal party went to our hospital quarters for lunch. I only wished we could have provided lunch for everyone; so many had travelled so far.

We left the reception in time to catch the three o'clock train to Bombay to begin our honeymoon. People followed us in their cars to the railway station and saw us onto the Deccan Express. I had changed clothes back at the hospital, and was wearing an aqua green dress with a lace top and a silk skirt—very smart—so my necklace from Ara still complemented it. Everyone at the station threw the flower heads of marigolds that they use for garlands as we were getting on the train, and off we went to Bombay.

At that time the Presbyterian Church had beautiful guest rooms on Marine Drive, looking right out on the Indian Ocean, and that's where we spent our first night. Our friends the Prentices, who were staying there, had said, "As a wedding gift, we're going to go away for the weekend to give you the whole flat. It will cost you nothing. We've given a menu to the cook and ordered all your meals for you. The servants will disappear, and you will have the apartment to yourselves."

So we went there and had a wonderful, wonderful first night. Bob and I had never had sexual intercourse. We both felt very strongly that there shouldn't be sex before marriage. It had been difficult, very difficult at times, but we managed to stick to it, so that first night we were very excited, so excited that we were overtired and unable to consummate the marriage. But the next morning we woke up fairly early and by gum, we had a wonderful consummation! Afterwards, we lay in each other's arms and began a beloved ritual of our marriage, a tradition of praying and thanking God for the wonderful gift of marital happiness, and for the gift of sex. It was so wonderful to lie together in one another's arms and praise God, and that's one of the things I miss very much now.

On that Saturday we went shopping in Bombay because we'd been given monetary wedding gifts, and thought we might buy some much-needed lamps for the big rooms in our home in Sangli. On Sunday we went to the Anglican Church. It was nearly empty because the British were gone, and they hadn't yet built up their Indian congregation. There were only about 15 of us. To my dismay, most of the congregation mumbled the Lord's Prayer at a rapid pace, so I deliberately spoke it loudly and slowly, and the congregation slowed down and followed me. As we went out the door, the minister was standing there, and I thought, "Oh, dear, I ought to apologize."

Instead he graciously thanked me for helping them to remember how important it was to say it properly. "Because we forget, and we rattle it off. Thank you for reminding us."

On Monday we made the administrative rounds, getting my name changed and registering at the American consulate, then at the British consulate. The passport we left for later because on Wednesday we were off to exotic Kashmir.

Kashmir had been in play between India and Pakistan since the partition into those two countries. According to the constitution, each state was to choose which they wanted to join—Pakistan or India. Members of the Kashmiri ruling class were Hindus, as was the raja, but the majority of the people living in Kashmir were Muslims. The decision was made, not by everyone's vote, but by the ruling class, and the raja, and their congress voted that Kashmir should belong to India. This greatly pleased Prime Minister Nehru, who was a Kashmiri.

Originally, we had planned to honeymoon in Kodaikanal because it had to be somewhere cheap, but our commissioner, Dr. Strickland, wrote early on, "You should go to Kashmir for your honeymoon." We knew Kashmir would be wonderful, but you had to have very special permission to go there because the military was occupying Kashmir just then. Pakistan was trying to take Kashmir back from India, and there was a great deal of unrest. But Dr. Strickland convinced us that visiting Kashmir was the experience of a lifetime and not to be missed. His wife, Martha Strickland, made all the arrangements. We were able to obtain special permits because the district superintendent of police was Scottish.

The vale, or valley, of Kashmir is just a beautiful place with saffron fields and flowering meadows, lakes and rivers, surrounded by the snow-capped peaks of the Himalayas. There are orchards of walnuts, almonds, apples, apricots, peaches, and pears. We were headed to the lake city of Shrinagar.

The first leg of our journey was the train trip to Pathankhot, which took two days and was anything but luxurious. There were four people to a compartment and it was brutally hot in June. There was no air conditioning, so the windows remained open all the time. It didn't help that Bob and I were rather overloaded for easy travelling. We had a huge bedding roll, two suitcases, a duffle bag, and all of Bob's camera equipment. I was also carrying a thermos and all our food for the journey. Fortunately, we had coolies to help us get to a taxi that took us from the railway station to the bus station. It was about 110 degrees in that crowded bus station where we waited for the bus to rattle in.

It quickly became apparent that despite Mrs. Strickland's careful plans, things weren't going to happen as scheduled. Our train got in about eleven, but the bus didn't leave until about four o'clock, and we were *supposed* to arrive in the lowland part of the state of Kashmir by six o'clock that night. The reality was that we got to Jammu at midnight, and the bus took us to the hotel where we were all to go. But when we got to the hotel, there was no room for any of us from the bus! So they told us to sleep in a recess in the corridor. There were six men already sleeping there, and Bob tried very hard to get a room for me, but I said I'd rather stay with him than with a whole lot of strange women. So we claimed a corner, and Bob and I slept in that big hallway. Of course, there was no place to dress, and the bathroom was just a little lavatory, but Bob curtained off a corner to allow me to put on some clean clothes.

In the morning we set off on the bus, which kept breaking down, getting flat tires, and running out of water. Although we should have arrived in Kashmir the next evening, we were a whole day on the road, and ended up at a little hotel because it was dark, and the driver said he couldn't drive over the Banihal Pass. As this was a very high and dangerous pass, we didn't argue with him. The hotel was a classic Indian hotel up above a coffee room. There was no bathroom—you had to go to the bushes—but at least we had a tiny little cupboard of a room where Bob and I could sleep on the floor. We had to leave all of our luggage on the bus and trust that no one would steal it. It was hot and miserable, but we were happy with each other, and decided to look on the experience as an adventure.

The next morning, off we went in the bus again, to go up the mountainside. It was after midnight when we finally arrived at our destination. Because it was so late, we were troubled by how we would get to the houseboat where we planned to stay. But as we climbed out of the bus, we heard, "Ramer, Ramer!" It was the butler from the houseboat. He had waited for hours to pick us up. Soon he had loaded us, and all our belongings, into a canoe-like boat that floated threateningly low in the water.

When we arrived at the houseboat, all the other guests were asleep. As we stepped onto the boat and inside, we were amazed to find ourselves in a beautiful sitting room. We went on to a lovely bedroom with a double bed. The whole houseboat was furnished with the beautifully carved furniture for which Kashmir is famous. A British woman living in Delhi had bought and furnished the houseboat, and when it became apparent that the British would be leaving, she gave the whole enterprise to the three men who had worked there for her. Thus, three families were supported by the business of running this lovely houseboat inn. Bob and I enjoyed two wonderful weeks there in Shangri-La.

Our wedding, June 1, 1951. Left to right: Isabel Patterson, Muriel Todd, Heather Todd, Dr. Bill Todd, Rev. Ian Patterson, Rev. Marvin Nelson, Bob, me, Dr. Rankin, Nancy Patterson, Dr. James Kellock, Dr. Yvonne Pinto-Philips, Nanda Dikeshit

Chapter 12: Mangl Sutra

After the honeymoon, we returned to Sangli and were warmly welcomed. Bob, of course, had already been working there, but I was a new addition. Everyone was very friendly, and the missionaries gave us a lovely dinner, but the most memorable welcome came from the children at the Marathi elementary school Bob managed in addition to supervising the Sangli Industrial School.

It was one of our first appearances as Mr. and Mrs. Ramer. In one classroom the teacher explained to the children that Mr. Ramer had gone to Poona, which was well known for its beautiful flowers, and he had picked one of the most beautiful flowers to bring back to Sangli, and that was her way of introducing *me*. The children sat on the floor looking at us with big brown eyes as their teacher explained, "They got married in Poona, but we weren't there, so we didn't see it, but many other people did. Because they're not Indian, Mrs. Ramer doesn't have a mangl sutra on, so today we are going to give Mrs. Ramer the mangl sutra."

The mangl sutra is the wedding necklace worn by all the Indian wives. Just as in many western cultures the bridegroom gives a ring to the bride, in India he gives her a mangl sutra, which means "auspicious thread." The mangl sutra was composed of two rows of tiny black beads and, at the very front, two small, shiny disks of hollow gold. As it was explained to us, the tradition of this auspicious thread was that one disk signified the husband's promise to provide his wife with shelter and care, and the other, that he would provide food and water. As time went on, if he could afford it, the husband would buy his wife additional disks for very special occasions, particularly for the birth of a child.

The teacher motioned a little boy to come forward to give Bob the mangl sutra. When Bob placed it around my neck, the children sang the hymn that goes with it, about God putting the wedding band around one's neck.

***

When I arrived in Sangli, I learned that for two years the missionaries there had been writing to America, begging for a public health nurse, only to be told that public health nurses were few and far between, and that there was little chance of getting one to come to Sangli. One of the missionaries, Mrs. Brown, told me that when Bob first went up to language school and wrote back to say that he was engaged to a Scottish woman who was a *trained public health nurse*, "I got down on my knees and thanked God!" I was pleased to know that I would be able and welcome to put my experience to good use.

I soon learned some of the background of the Sangli mission. The missionaries there prior to my arrival had done a very wonderful thing. In Sangli there was a slum called Shantinagar, where people lived in squalid huts and had little access to education or clean water. The residents were mostly outcastes, or those who had been put out of their own villages for misbehaviour. The mothers in Shantinagar were desperate to improve the lives of their children, and the missionaries wanted to help. The nearest school was a mile and a half away. Because it was too far for little children to walk, they just didn't go to school. So the missionaries bought a nearby piece of land and built a one-room schoolhouse, but they soon realized that the people needed far more than a school.

There was a town water tap several blocks away from Shantinagar, but people from the slums were only allowed access to the tap between 2 and 3 a.m., and 2 and 3 p.m. Most families needed more water than they could haul home in the afternoon hour, so someone had to get up in the middle of the night to get water at 2 a.m., and this was a nightly occurrence.

With 200 people in this shantytown, there were long lines of people with water jugs whenever they were allowed access to the tap. If someone was taking too long—sometimes people would take their clothes there to wash—tempers would flare, and there would be fights and shouting, especially in the hot season. So some of the senior missionaries, led by Mrs. Lyon and Mrs. Brown, had bought land in the slum area and dug a well there, and for the first time the people had easy access to water and some hope for sanitation.

One thing led to another. The parents needed hot water for bathing in order for their children to be clean to go to school. So the well led to the Health Centre. It was sadly apparent that the little ones weren't getting enough to eat, so it was arranged to obtain and distribute dried milk powder through the centre. It was evident that much could be done to improve the health of the people in Shantinagar if they only had a public health nurse to work out of the centre.

Here was the opportunity I had dreamed of all of my life.

In those days, a wife was not appointed as a missionary. As the wife of an American Presbyterian missionary, you were commissioned as a "missionary wife" and expected to do whatever particular job (unpaid, of course) the mission executive had for you to do. My responsibilities were twofold. First, I was to work at the Sangli Health Centre every morning from 8 until 10 or 10:30. Then I would come home to hold a clinic for any who might be sick among the 100 Industrial School boys and the 200 people working on the school compound.

Cleanliness may or may not be next to Godliness, but it's an important first step toward good health. At the Health Centre we provided hot water and soap for the mothers to bathe their babies. At home they lacked not only running water, but also any way to *heat* the water they carried home from the tap. So the mothers would come to the centre, where we had towels and soap for them, and they'd bathe their babies there.

Before the mothers arrived, we would pump water from our well, fill the big copper boiler and light a fire under it. By the time the mothers arrived, we could give them half-buckets of hot water to which they would add enough cold to make it comfortable. We didn't need bathtubs. One corner of the centre sat a little lower than the rest and had an L-shaped ledge like a kerbstone. Mothers would sit on that ledge with their legs outstretched, clench their big toes together, and put their babies in the cradle formed by their legs. Then they'd take a cup of the warm water and pour it over the babies, soap them all over, and pour water over to rinse them. Then they'd turn the baby over like a pancake and wash the other side.

But the mothers did one thing that made me crazy every time. They put kohl, a dark cosmetic eyeliner, on their babies' eyes. There was nothing wrong with that; it was done for beauty, and it also kept the flies away. But when they bathed the baby, they would wash the kohl off with soapy hands. The soap invariably got into the babies' eyes, and they screamed!

Many times I urged the mothers, "Don't do it with the soap, just take your cloth and wipe it," but I was never able to convince them to keep the soap from their babies' eyes; this is just the way they did it. Then they would take the towel and dry the baby. We took children up to age five, and the older children could just stand up while their mothers poured water over them and washed their hair.

In addition to bathing facilities, the mothers were provided with milk for their little ones. From UNICEF, and later Church World Service, we received great bags of milk powder. We made up the milk at our house in large milk cans, then sent it down to the centre with somebody on a bike. I'd follow them on my bike to ensure that the milk wasn't stolen along the way. We also had Pablum, a very nutritious baby cereal, one of the first prepared foods you could give a baby. American churches would raise money specifically to buy Pablum and send it to us.

At 11, after my shift at the Health Centre, there was a teacher who taught first and second graders because the children were all outcaste kids from the slums and weren't allowed in any regular Indian school. After second grade they were old enough to walk about two miles up to the mission compound, where we had a school that went through the fifth grade. Then their parents could pay about $1 a month for them to go to the mission boarding school for Indian children in Kodoli, about 75 miles away. After eighth grade, they could go to the boys' or the girls' three-year high school in Kolhapur. If they were capable, they could then go on to college—quite a contrast in opportunity from being allowed in no regular Indian school at all.

The money for these programs came from the Presbyterian Church in the U.S.A. to the treasurer of the executive committee, who then paid the salaries of the missionaries and the Indian employees. The executive committee met once a year, and if you, as a missionary, wanted money to do something, you had to bring it before the executive committee. When I began, we ran the Health Centre on about $1000 a year, money sent by the Presbyterian Women's groups in the U.S.A.

***

The needs addressed were so profound because the mission worked with the 40% of the population considered "outcastes." Outcastes were landless labourers, most of whom had no regular jobs, but were paid by the day whenever they could get work. They did all the nastiest jobs, the ones considered "unclean." They worked with skins as cobblers or tanners, and were the scavengers who cleaned the streets. It was the outcastes who cleaned latrines and removed dead bodies to the funeral pyres.

In the Hindu cremation ceremony, just before the body was placed on the fire, they cracked the skull so that as the body burned, the spirit escaped.

Then within 40 days you were reborn into a situation reflecting what you deserved, according to what kind of life you had lived.

Outcastes were not cremated at death because the cremation process involved freeing the spirit, and outcastes were considered to be spiritless. They were buried in the ground like animals because there was to be no rebirth for them; that was the end. So among the outcastes, there was a terrific hopelessness. They were relegated to the outskirts of the town, and were forbidden to walk through the main street of the village unless they were cleaning it. They were forbidden to enter any temples, and could enter upper-caste houses only to clean them. The outcastes were called the uspursha, or untouchables.

This was all a function of the Hindu caste system, which was carried on by the British government during the colonial period with the attitude of "just let them do their own system." Children were born into the caste of their parents and remained part of that caste throughout their lives. Outcaste children were not educated. They were told that they were outcastes because in a previous life they had been bad and, consequently, the gods had ordained that they would be born as outcastes, the equivalent of animals.

One of our Indian bishops, Ramchandra Bhandare, grew up as uspursha. One day, while returning from looking after the goats in the fields, this little boy ran around a corner and, by accident, bumped into a Brahman woman. She was so angry with him that she removed her chappal, or sandal, and beat him with it, which was a very grave insult. He had made her clothes ritually unclean, or untouchable, and she was on the way to the temple. There wasn't so much as a speck of mud on her sari, but because of the encounter she had to go back home, bathe, and put on another sari before going to the temple.

A week or so later, Ramchandra happened to see the same lady on her way to temple when she accidentally stepped in water buffalo excrement, which is smelly and soft. The filth was stuck to her chappal and the edge of her sari. The woman asked someone for some water, which she took and poured over her chappal and sari before heading on her way. In a defining moment, he realized that in her mind he was lower than the excrement of a water buffalo because she hadn't considered *that* defiling, but his unintentional touch *was* unclean. That was the attitude when we went to India.

Now Gandhi and the Congress Party were very much against that. They made it constitutional law that there were to be no outcastes. Gandhi changed their name from untouchables to "Harijans," or "children of God." So the former outcastes were no longer to be called uspursha, a word we missionaries never used. This was one of the reasons that Gandhi was shot; the Brahmans objected to the former untouchables being called children of God.

***

It makes me angry to hear people speak so critically about the old missionaries, because they lived in different times, and they were a part of their times. It was the 1800s in our area of India when the early Christian missionaries began to try to improve the lives of the people known as outcastes. In the early mission records, one can read of the controversy among the missionaries in western India due to the Presbyterians' three-pronged approach, which included education, medical care, and evangelism. They are often assumed to have been single-minded, but the truth is that the missionaries were not just focused on making people Christian, and building up a Christian community.

One of the old pastors, Tatoba Phandare, told me this story, and it illustrates the history of the mission. Tatoba was born an outcaste. When he was a boy, there was an epidemic of the plague, followed by an epidemic of cholera, which killed both of his parents. He was taken in by missionaries, enrolled in their little 20-boy school, and fed and looked after. Over time Tatoba became a Christian. The outcastes had only first names, no surnames, but when they became Christians, they adopted a surname of their own choosing. Tatoba chose Phandare, which means "white." He finished eighth grade, which was as far as they could go in Sangli at that time. He was tall for an Indian, about six feet, strong and healthy, and he became very involved in wrestling, one of the many games and sports the missionaries taught the children.

At that time Sangli was a kingdom, ruled by a raja. Even under the British, the Indians were able to keep their small kingdoms as long as they paid taxes to the British. This raja heard of Tatoba and took him into the palace to be trained as a professional wrestler. The raja had a team of wrestlers that competed against wrestlers from other small kingdoms, and Tatoba became very famous. From time to time, he left the palace to see an uncle in the village, or to visit the mission school and his teachers, including housemother and evangelist Miss Enright.

Miss Enright was a very proper lady, and quite strict. She used to go out in a one-horse carriage to preach in the outcaste area of the village. In part because the outcastes were forbidden to enter the temples, there were idols along the side of the road where they could give offerings as they passed by. Sometimes a bus would stop along its route so that passengers could break a coconut in front of the idols. Miss Enright wanted to be a witness for her faith, as she understood it, so she would get out of the carriage, and with her umbrella, she'd smash the gods to bits! She was able to get away with this because she was white, and the rajas knew that it was in their best interests to protect the white missionaries. The rajas didn't *help* the missionaries, but they protected them.

One day Tatoba had gone to visit his uncle when Miss Enright began preaching in the village. A crowd had gathered and was shouting at her for having broken the roadside statues. Then somebody picked up a stone and threw it at Miss Enright, hitting her in the head. She fell unconscious and was bleeding profusely. The reluctant Tatoba did nothing, simply watched her carriage driver pick her up and take her home.

Tatoba suffered a very guilty conscience after that, and later went to the compound to apologize, but she refused to see him. Some time later, he was again visiting his uncle in the village when Miss Enright showed up to preach. This time he walked up to her and said, "Don't be afraid, I'm here to protect you." Miss Enright was a tiny woman, barely five feet tall, and Tatoba, at six feet tall and a professional wrestler, offered considerable protection.

Decades later he could clearly recall, "She just looked up at me and said, 'I don't need you. I have Christ. You go.'" Feeling like a worm, he went home and wept. He'd gone all through boarding school and was nominally a Christian, but had not really committed himself to his faith. But now he felt called, and for weeks he struggled with the idea that it should be *him* preaching in the village, not Miss Enright. Finally, he gave up his easy life as a wrestler, and went back to Miss Enright, who saw that he was sincere and said, "You're not educated enough; you've got to go back to school."

So this strong, six-foot wrestler went back to school with kids much younger, then on to Poona, 150 miles away, to a Bible college run by the

Church of Scotland and the Presbyterians. When he finished, he returned to Sangli, and proudly announced that he had been ordained as a missionary by the *Presbytery of New York*, which must have sounded very official and prestigious.

Tatoba and several other men took tent meetings from village to village, creating a mass movement of people becoming Christians. He was 100 years old in 1985 when I spoke with him, so this must have happened in the early 1900s. The previous year, 1984, had been the 100th anniversary of the arrival of the first missionaries to Sangli.

Perhaps surprisingly, this swell of Indian Christians brought controversy among the missionaries. There were not enough churches for the new converts to go to, and there was much discussion about whether and when they should be baptized. There were hundreds of illiterate people, unable to learn more about the tenets of the faith by reading. Was it right to baptize them before they had really learned enough about what they were getting into?

Some said, "Yes, baptize them immediately! Phillip just jumped out of the carriage and baptized the Ethiopian in that Bible story." Others were reluctant because the people wouldn't be able to read the Bible until they'd had years of education.

Another group had a different, pragmatic outlook. "If we take them in right away, then it will become a church of the untouchables, and we want to reach the high castes, too, so that *they* will be the ones to preach the gospel." The whole idea was to have the nationals, the Indians, take over, so they needed to get the upper, educated classes into the church.

But the Indian pastors said, "This is spiritual, they've now got the faith, so start teaching *after* you've made them Christians. Don't let them fall by the wayside." So that's what they did, building schools and compounds for the former untouchables, the newly Christian Indians who were scorned by their non-Christian families and villages—untouchables rejected even by other untouchables.

Indian girls who wanted to preach were educated to become "Bible women," and they, too, worked in the villages, often marrying a pastor, or living with their own families in the village. Thus, the village churches became the strength of the church in India. In the Sangli district there were over 50 churches, and we had 40 people working in the villages, including pastors, Bible women, and teacher evangelists, all working under a district superintendent who was a missionary.

Tatoba also told me of one of our previous missionaries, Rev. Bryan, who had been a wrestler at Princeton University. When Rev. Bryan became the district superintendent, Tatoba was out in the villages working under him. When Bryan found out that Tatoba was a wrestler, they started wrestling for fun when Tatoba came into Sangli for his pay. One day both were out in the village of Nandri, when someone recognized Tatoba as a former wrestler and accused him of becoming a pastor because he could no longer make it as a wrestler.

Tatoba denied it and offered to wrestle anyone in the crowd. When no one accepted, he said, "Sahib [Rev. Bryan] is a wrestler, too. Does anyone want to wrestle him?" Again nobody came forward, so Tatoba said, "I challenge *him* to wrestle."

Suddenly, everyone was interested. "A sahib wrestling an Indian!" From then on, wrestling was part of their performance and ministry. The two didn't want to create trouble in the village, so somehow Tatoba, the Indian, always won in the end. After the match, the two wrestlers would put an arm around each other and declare, "We are one in Christ!" In the experience of these villagers, the Indian and the white man had never been "one" in any sense, so that solidarity and inclusiveness made a powerful impression.

This sense of brotherhood wasn't just for show. At the mission tent meetings, in an unheard-of mingling, the missionaries, white and Indian, and all the Indian workers, regardless of caste, ate together and slept in the same tents. Tatoba explained that this was a tremendous witness, and more and more people came to Christianity.

***

Soon after our honeymoon, I became pregnant. When I was about two months along, we were invited to the home of Dr. Gorde, a very gracious and influential Christian doctor, who lived some 15 miles away. So we took the jeep, the only vehicle at our disposal, and headed out, having heard that the road was a good one. But what is "good road" to people on bicycles is not the same as "good road" to people riding in jeeps. It was terribly bumpy, but Bob drove very slowly and carefully, trying to avoid all the bumps.

It was a nice dinner, but we arrived home exhausted from the drive, and I had just lain down when a note was delivered. A nurse who had worked with me at St. Margaret's was in the hospital with TB, feeling desperately discouraged. "Please come see me *today* because I want to kill myself, but I know I shouldn't do it, so please come right away."

I couldn't ignore the plea of one of my former nurses, but I couldn't face the jeep again either, so Bob and I biked the 2½ miles to the Wanlesswadi TB sanatorium to visit and pray with her. Meanwhile, her family had come to visit, and she was cheered up, so later that evening we biked home. Exhausted, I lay down on the bed and instantly fell asleep.

The next morning I felt OK, so I went to the Health Centre and was just doing some laundry when I began to have some bleeding. We sent for Dr. Evans, who prescribed bed rest for at least two weeks. He also gave me an injection of morphine. At the time neither of us knew that I react badly to morphine. As the drug took hold, I began to hallucinate! My pulse raced, and I thought the walls were caving in on me. It was terrifying! Bob sat up most of the night with me, and the bleeding increased. The next day was August 15, India's Independence Day, and a Dr. Cecil was coming from Miraj to raise the flag at school for the celebration. After the flag raising, Bob got Dr. Cecil to drive me very carefully in his lovely car to the Miraj hospital.

At the hospital they took one look at me and rushed me to the operating room. Dr. Evans told me, "Nancy, you've bled so much that your blood pressure is dangerously low, and we can't give you an anaesthetic, but we're going to have to remove what's left of this baby by dilation and curettage." So he did the necessary D & C, which was very painful.

When it was all over, they put me into one of the cottages to recover, but I became violently sick and then fainted away. It turned out that I had a blood clot in my lung, a very serious condition. The whole hospital was called out for prayer. I had to have a blood transfusion, but there was no such thing as a blood bank there. A Dr. Caruthers, a professor of medicine, volunteered, "My blood matches hers, O group," so they gave me a pint of his blood.

It helped, but more was needed. A desperate call for blood donation went out to the missionaries, but none had compatible blood. Then Dr. Caruthers's Indian intern said, "I don't know what my blood is, but try it and see." It matched! So he gave me his blood. Constant prayer continued in the chapel. From every department of the hospital a person would come to pray for a few minutes, then go back to work to be replaced by another, as was the custom in Miraj hospital. I learned later that everyone talked about how terribly sad it was that Bob and I were just married and now I was about to die.

In addition to bleeding, I was constantly throwing up, which made it all the worse. Dr. Evans remembered an old physician telling him to give iodine drops orally to calm the nausea. The drops of liquid felt good in my throat. The nausea stopped, and I could feel the pain receding. A nurse held my hand, and I told her, "I'm better, I'm better! After that second pint of blood, I just felt God's hand was laid on me, and I'm going to be better." The blood clot had dissolved.

It took time, but I recovered and was soon back to running around normally. When I went back to Dr. Evans in September, he said, "Now, everything is normal. Go ahead and try to have another baby because you mustn't get into the habit of having miscarriages." Habit?

***

I continued to wear the mangl sutra every day. As with wedding rings in the West, Indian women always wore their mangl sutras. I took mine off to bathe, then put it back on, but sometimes in the morning I was in a rush. It was a bit difficult to attach the mangl sutra—one end screwed into the other—and sometimes I just forgot amid getting breakfast, having family devotions, and giving the day's menu to the cook.

As I pedalled my bike to the Health Centre in Shantinagar, I always met the third and fourth graders walking up to our school, and they would greet me with "Salaam, Madam Sahib! Salaam, Madam Sahib!" But if I'd forgotten my mangl sutra that morning, there would be one kid who would say, "Oh, she doesn't have her mangl sutra on! *You* don't have your mangl sutra on!" and I would feel so bad.

One particular morning I was rushing out the gate when I remembered that I didn't have my mangl sutra, so I left my bike at the gate and ran back home to put it on. Pleased with myself for remembering, I got on my bike and headed out. That morning all the kids met me with "Salaam, Madam Sahib! Salaam, Madam Sahib!" and gave me especially big grins, so I gave them back a big smile. I arrived at the centre and was busy getting things started, giving out medicine, and so on, when I began to notice two staff members looking at me and snickering. Typically Indian, they put the end of their saris over their faces when they giggled. Then they whispered something to another woman who drew her sari across her face and giggled. I looked at my two helpers, Mrs. Sheik and Mrs. Gorde, who smiled, but said nothing.

Finally I went to Mrs. Sheik and said to her in Marathi, "What is wrong? Everybody is giggling."

"You have your mangl sutra on backwards."

I was wearing it with the little disks down at the front, but the hollow black sides of the disks were facing out, so I said, "OK," and changed it. This brought another round of giggles, so I asked Mrs. Sheik again, "What is all this about?"

She started laughing and said, "In our tradition, we cannot argue with our husbands; we're living with his family. So if we're mad at our husband, we take our mangl sutra and turn it so that the black side shows out, and then everybody knows we've quarrelled, and they'll all ask our husband, 'What did you quarrel with your wife about?' And his mother will get after him, and say, 'Why did you quarrel with your wife?'

"He'll say, 'Oh, it was nothing,' but people will torment him. Tradition is that you don't change it back until he has apologized and given you a new sari. Then you change it back and wear your new sari, and everybody rejoices that the quarrel is over!"

That evening at home I told Bob about the significance of the reversed mangl sutra, and that story became a staple of our speaking engagements whenever we went home on furlough and were "at deputation," speaking to groups about the work in India.

Several years later, we were home on furlough, driving through New York City, headed for Philadelphia, when Bob spotted a photography shop he knew from a catalogue, but had never visited. He pulled over to the curb, and jumped out of the car, saying, "I'll just be a moment; I want to ask something," leaving me in the car with a two-year-old and a baby on the busy streets of New York. The children and I sat and sat there. He was away for almost an hour while I entertained fidgety, unhappy children. Of course, I was mad when he came out. He took one look, saw that my mangl sutra was on backwards, and knew, without my saying a word, that I was angry.

As he later told congregations we visited, "The mangl sutra saves you saying a lot of things you might be sorry for later."

Our house in Sangli

Shantinagar Health Center, giving out medicine while the Bible woman tells a story

Chapter 13: Buffalo Milk and High-Class Marathi

When I was a little girl, it was not uncommon to hear a parent on the street say, "Now you behave yourself, or the black man will get you." Nevertheless, as I biked along the streets of Shantinagar, I was amazed to hear women standing at their doors saying, "Here comes a white woman. If you don't behave yourself, we'll give you to the white woman, and she'll beat you!"

This made me so angry that I'd go over and say in their own language, "I never beat *anyone*. If you want to come to our centre, you'll *see* that you get milk and cunji (cereal), and nobody *ever* gets beaten."

Though it angered me, it turned out to be a great thing because a lot of the women then said, "Oh, you speak Marathi?"

"Yes."

"Do you really give free milk? And cereal, really?"

Shantinagar means "Village of Peace," but it was just the opposite. A slum on the very edge of Sangli, it was home to the outcastes who came to work in Sangli City. The children on the streets were always very welcoming and friendly to us, but the adults often regarded us with suspicion.

There were encouraging times and times of despair. Many days I'd come home from the Health Centre, or from someone's home, in tears, thinking, "Why do I have so much, and these people so little? How would I survive if I were them?" There were always people at our door asking for help, so many that we couldn't help them all. I tried not to lose patience at the constant requests, thinking, "If my child were starving, where would I go? There are no social services, no welfare, no food clinics—where would I go if my kid were starving?" And I knew I'd go to a missionary who gave food to kids.

The Shantinagar people were squatters who built their shacks from whatever could be found, improving them when they could. Commonly, they collected sugarcane stalks and bound them together with mud and clay to make walls. Roof tiles were formed from river clay and baked. The tiles were small and light, but they would keep out the rain for two rainy seasons before they needed to be replaced. A door might be made of old metal cans, flattened.

As they could, the people replaced the cane walls with materials they scavenged, sometimes bricks or stone from older buildings that were being torn down. There were no latrines; children were taught to go outside and squat in the gutter. The poorly designed gutters frequently became blocked, and sewage overflowed into the streets and homes. The floor of the house was made of a mixture of dung and water that, when dry, made a sweepable, clean floor.

Our church in Sangli had that same kind of dung and water floor. I often saw children coming into the church without any pants and urinating on the floor, and others did more than that. The mothers would get a leaf to pick up the bowel motions., but they would just forget about the urine, so there was a constant smell in the church.

I decided to try to raise funds for a rough tile floor in the church. The common such material was the slate-like shahabad stone. Friends at home, members of supportive churches in the U.S.A., were good enough to help us raise money for the church floor. My next project was to put a stone floor in the Health Centre. We had lots of kids having accidents there, and accidents don't clean up easily from a dung floor. Eventually we were able to do that, too.

***

My empathy for the needy children around me only grew when I became pregnant with Robbie. In this cherished second pregnancy I often suffered with morning sickness, but I was able to keep going down to the centre and doing my bit, as the doctor said everything looked fine.

Then one morning I got up and looked in the mirror, and saw that the whites of my eyes were yellow. "Bob, I have jaundice." I was afraid it was a jaundiced pregnancy, but it wasn't. It was infectious hepatitis, possibly from that second pint of blood I received during my miscarriage. Thanks to that pint, I was alive, even if I did have jaundice.

For some time I'd been praying God, "I want a nurse to carry on the work" at the centre. We had two employees, Mrs. Sheik and Mrs (Hirabai) Gorde, who both had experience as ayahs and bountiful good sense, but I was the only nurse. Then one day I learned that there was a new mechanical drawing master at the industrial school whose wife was a trained nurse working in the Miraj hospital, five miles away. In those days, that five miles took an hour by bus because of the bad road, so she stayed with relatives in Miraj.

Hearing that, I asked Mr. Gorde(who was not related t Hirabai Gorde), "Would your wife consider coming to work at the Health Centre?" Sulochana Gorde was a midwife with valuable experience, having been a nurse in the army during the war, and the matron of a small hospital. If she would come to the centre, the mission would provide a cottage for their family. I said, "I can't pay her what she gets in the hospital, but would you ask her if she would come?"

Come she did, and she took over easily because she was a native of the state of Maharashtra and well qualified as a midwife and to run the clinic. I had no money to pay Sulochana, but I wanted her to start right away, so Bob and I figured out a way we could pay her out of our own pocket, which wasn't easy because we didn't have much money. As missionaries, we didn't have to pay rent, but we were required to have servants and to pay them from our salary. Meanwhile, we wrote to one of our supporting churches, the one in Indianapolis, I think, and after two months that church's women's group took on paying her salary, which was wonderful.

Once Sulochana was hired, she and I divided up the city, and every week we visited a different area. One day I said to her, "Right next to this poor area is the middle-class area, and any infection from the poor area is going to spread there because there isn't any sanitation." Even middle-class homes didn't have latrines; they squatted outside, too. So we decided to talk to them about taking simple sanitation precautions. When you don't have a lot of water, and you don't have a strong government, sanitation suffers the most.

But Sulochana said to me, "I can't go there." When I asked why, she said, "Those are upper caste living there. They won't listen to me, but they will listen to you."

"Why would they listen to me? I'm a foreigner."

"You speak better Marathi."

"How do I speak better Marathi?"

"That's what you've been taught." Until then, I hadn't really realized that we had been taught very *proper* Brahman Marathi. It's like it was in Britain. If you had a good Oxford accent or a good Edinburgh accent, then you were considered to be better educated than other people. Sulochana said, "I'll go with you, but you do the talking."

I was a bit leery about this, but together we went to these middle-class homes, and I saw the truth of what she said. When I spoke Marathi, I didn't know all the vocabulary, but that was forgiven because I talked in the right *class* of Marathi.

Now, despite the agony of language study, I was very grateful for language school in India and for those awful months with Miss Lambert. Though I couldn't wait to get away from her at the time, I saw how wonderfully God had prepared me for this job that I was doing—all the years in nursing, and the years in language class that gave me the right accent to talk with all kinds of people.

I had been so determined to go to China; then that door was shut. But I did go through the door that opened and came to India. I had thought I would be stuck doing administrative work in a hospital all my life, but God opened a more wonderful door—I met and married Bob Ramer, and I was able to use all my training and background and "right-accented" Marathi in the work amongst the poor in Sangli City.

Incidentally, if I had gone to China, it would have been a disaster. The language is tonal, so the same word spoken with different tones has different meanings, and I'm almost tone-deaf! I never would have been able to master the Chinese language. But Marathi has broad vowels and rolling *r*'s, and, of course, that is the Scots' way—broad vowels and rolling *r*'s. Many times I was complimented on my Marathi, and I always thought of the many who had helped me, including the Indian men on the ship who had taken away my fear of speaking Marathi.

***

Because of my earlier miscarriage, I was advised to stay in bed for nearly three months with my second pregnancy, but the work in the Health Centre continued. Sulochana and Hirabai came twice a week to report on how things were going, and others took on making up the milk for them, which I used to do, so the work carried on.

As I lay in bed, I did all the accounts for the Health Centre and all the reports that had to be done. Still people were saying, "Poor Ramer, his wife is so delicate, she has to be in bed a lot," but I think I made up for that once Robbie was born. I was still in my bed over Christmas, then in February they said I should get away. We were advised to go way up in north India, 1500 miles away, to the location of Woodstock School, one of our schools for missionary children. There was another mission school in the south, about 750 miles away, but I was advised to go up north where the weather was cooler.

In those days the train from Poona did not stop at Sangli, so we had to take the jeep to madhadnagar to catch the train. Six months pregnant, I had packed a large, clumsy canvas holdall with a mattress, our blankets, and all the things we had to take up north. There was no platform where we boarded, so the train was high off the ground. I had boarded the train, and Bob was pushing our stuff in the door when the mattress got stuck, and the train began to pull away!

"Don't hit him!" I yelled, pulling on the emergency chain with all my strength. The train screeched to a stop, and the guard came down and apologized. He hadn't seen Bob still struggling with our things. With the help of a couple additional men, the canvas holdall was pushed and kicked through the door, and Bob climbed over it and got in, too. By this time, I was in tears wondering how I would ever have found Bob and handled all this stuff if we had gotten separated, pregnant as I was.

After overnight stops in Bombay and Delhi, we made it to Woodstock. Landour, where the mission bungalows are, is very high up on the mountain. Others climbed that stretch, but they said I couldn't climb in my condition, that I had to ride in this awkward chair. Like a stretcher for sitting up, the chair sat on two poles, each of which was supported by two men. It was terrifying going up those narrow paths with the chair swaying back and forth with every step. When we finally got to the top I told Bob, "I am *not* going in one of those chairs again. I will walk down, or slide down, but I'm not going in one of those chairs!"

All went well in the cooler north, and in May we were able to return to Sangli, where I went to the Health Centre about twice a week to keep tabs on things. There was a lot to keep tabs on. I had gotten one of the doctors to come from Miraj every week to offer a prenatal clinic for all the poor women in Shantinagar who never went to a doctor, who could never *afford* to.

There was a government hospital in Sangli, but for the first 10 years we were there, it was one of the most miserable places you ever saw, and very poorly staffed. So the women refused to go there, instead asking, "Would you come and be with me when the baby is here?" So I ended up doing quite a number of deliveries.

When the Lyons family went on furlough, their cook came to work for us, and just before I was to deliver Robbie, the cook's wife called for me to come do *her* delivery! It was very hard because I was nine months pregnant myself, and she was on the floor, so I had to get down on my knees for the birth. But we did it and the baby, Timothy Kolhapurkar, came through all right.

∗∗∗

When I was working at St. Margaret's in Poona, I had become very close to the staff nurses, called "sisters." Sister Lena worked in the operating room at St. Margaret's, and Sister Margaret had worked with me in training young midwives. Lena and Margaret were trained to be women's and children's nurses, and could not be required to do male nursing, but times were changing, and now nurses were required to know male nursing to be on the registry of nurses in India. Because ours was a women's and children's hospital, I had made arrangements for nurses who wanted to go to the municipal hospital for their male nursing training. I would teach the accompanying classes, and they could then sit the exam.

When I wrote from Sangli and said that I was pregnant with Robbie, Lena and Margaret wrote, "We'll come to Miraj (the American hospital) and learn male nursing, but before we do that, we'll be your nurses when you have the baby!" In those days, the rule at Miraj was that you provided your own nurses, so this worked out very nicely. Nevertheless, Dr. Rankine at St. Margaret's was very annoyed with me because I wouldn't come back to Poona, 150 miles away, to have my baby!

∗∗∗

The first contractions came at 5.00 on a Sunday night when we were at church in Sangli. After dinner, Bob and I went to Miraj where we sat and talked to the Fletchers, my doctor and his wife. When night came, Dr. Fletcher put us in a hospital cottage for the night, and we slept. Two ward boys with a stretcher were stationed outside on the veranda, ready to carry me to the labour room. But when the time came, it came quickly, so we commandeered the car of someone visiting a neighbouring cottage, and off we went to the labour room. Dr. Fletcher was in emergency surgery at that point, so Dr. Servid and Sister Margaret were there with me.

Robbie finally arrived at 7.30 on Monday night, June 23, 1952, nearly 27 hours after labour began. We were *thrilled* to see him. On our return to the cottage for recovery, the ward boys wanted their due, so they carried me on the stretcher, while Bob and Robbie rode in the car.

"Robbie baba," as the Indian folks called him, weighed in at nine pounds. Bob sent off telegrams to our family in the U.S.A. and the U.K. My brother, Blair, read out the telegram to his family: "Unto us a son—Robert Blair—9 pounds. Mother and baby well. Praise the Lord!" Hearing this grand announcement, my six-year-old English nephew was puzzled. "Only 9 pounds (£) for a boy? I thought they would have to pay more than that for a boy!"

So when we returned to Sangli, it was with a baby boy—and nappies (diapers) and bottles. Although I breastfed him, in those days the thing to do was to give babies a little glucose in water in between feedings. Because of the nature of the water, the bottles and the nappies always had to be boiled. We would wash the nappies, boil them, rinse them, and then hang them out in the sun to dry. When the weather was humid, it took forever for those nappies to dry.

After a while, we began to notice that there were always one or two fewer nappies than we had hung on the line. At first we just puzzled over it, but then we started to count them, and we found that they were regularly disappearing. Then I began to notice the babies of the staff who lived on campus—the staff of the industrial school, the elementary school, and the agricultural centre. For the first time, their babies were wearing nappies! We used big 36-inch-square towelling nappies folded into a triangle. Here the staff was taking them and cutting them in half and making two smaller nappies, perfectly adequate for their smaller babies.

Bob said to me, "Well, there you are. You see, you're teaching them not just to squat any old place but to cover up and protect themselves from infection."

"This," I thought, "is an aspect of public health they never taught us about in school!"

On October 5, 1952, in the evening, Robbie was baptised by Rev. Haribhau Rukedekar and our Sangli pastor, Rev. Bedekar. The church was full, and after the service our missionaries from Miraj, Wanlesswadi, and Sangli, as well as our Indian colleagues, all came for a tea at our house. The Indian Christian tradition was to have a large dinner party to which *all* the church members would be invited, but we could not afford that, so we served tea and simple Indian sweets. Our more modest reception did nothing to reduce the joy of welcoming Robbie into the church family.

From the time he was about three months old, little Timothy Kolhapurkar shared Robbie's playpen and sandbox. In fact, all the Indian kids came onto the veranda to play with Robbie's toys. Ayah would chase the older kids away, but Robbie loved company. Soon Robbie was crawling all over the house, pulling all the books off the shelves, satisfied that he had done a good job of emptying the bookcase.

We were busy, but soon became busier when the Lyons family went home on furlough. Mr. Lyons was the churches' district superintendent, so Bob had to take over when he left. There were 52 villages to be covered, and about 20 "established churches," which meant they had more than 50 people but didn't have their own pastor. There were smaller churches with perhaps 20 in the congregation, maybe two or three Christian families, but they all had to be attended to, and provided with communion at least four times a year. So Bob was not just teaching in the industrial school and managing the elementary school, he was also in charge of the district.

Both of us were busy in the extreme. Often Bob came home very tired about six in the evening, and he'd say, "Let me have Robbie." He and Robbie would sit in the rocker on the big veranda. Of course, Robbie loved it, too. He'd chortle away and talk to his daddy, and his daddy would talk away to him. Bob said it was the greatest comfort to be able to have that time with Robbie.

In many ways, it was a wonderful life. I'd come back from working at the Health Centre about 10.30, and feed my baby. Then I held the clinic for the compound schoolboys and staff. Fortunately, the clinic was in a back room of our house. It was really part of our guest room, but we shut it off a bit, and stocked a big cupboard with the medicines. There was a bathroom, so I could wash my hands. We had a big cedar chest that we padded and covered so patients could lie down to be examined or to have their dressings changed.

The boys came to the back door where they waited on the veranda for their turns. I gave them medicine, treated or bandaged them, or just gave them a bit of motherly comfort. There were always at least a dozen boys waiting because they wanted to get off school. I soon changed the beginning time from 11 to 11:30 because they had their lunch hour from 12 to 1:30, and most of them just wanted to get out of class.

I loved the work at the Health Centre and the clinic, but it meant that I had to have an ayah, or babysitter, for when I was away. We also had to have a cook because fresh food had to be bought daily at the bazaar. When the Lyons family went on furlough, they lent us their refrigerator. This meant we could boil up the buffalo milk and put it in the fridge. By morning it had a thick cream on top. We skimmed the cream off and beat it, making the most delicious whipped cream to go with our cereal. The whipped cream was delicious, but the milk had a strong taste, and in all the years we were in India, we never succeeded in getting our children to drink buffalo milk. There was dried milk, but we never gave that to our own children because that milk was for the children at the Health Centre.

Because of my training in public health, I got the idea to visit people's homes in the evenings. By evening, the water had been brought in, and the children were home from school, so families could often be found sitting in the doorways of their shacks, chatting with one another. In their homes I saw flies crawling on uncovered food and kids squatting just outside the house and passing urine within the house. Slowly, I tried to teach them about sanitation, that it could help prevent disease if they at least squatted in the ditch instead of in the house. That still wasn't great, but we got after the municipality, and about once a week, they would come and clean the ditch, so that all helped. Sometimes I was able to convince people to dig a hole in the fields behind their houses, and then cover it up. Over time many began to do that.

I also made a major effort encouraging immunizations because typhoid fever and cholera were very prevalent. When I visited homes and talked about immunizations, they often said to me, "Why would we do that? You take a typhoid injection, and you're sick the next day. Who wants to be sick just because we took a typhoid shot?"

"It will save you from getting the worse disease," I'd say.

"Oh, we won't ever get the worse disease."

"It's all around you; you see people with typhoid or cholera every season."

"Karma," they said. "If it is the will of God, what can we do about it?"

Then I discovered that the person I had to convince was *the mother-in-law*. You hear about women being under the feet of the men in India, and to a great extent that was true. But inside the house, the mother-in-law is the authority until her husband dies, and she is the one who decides everything: how money will be spent, if the children may go to school, issues of cleanliness in the house, and many other details you might not think about. Having realized that, I set about making friends with the mothers-in-law.

One evening about eight o'clock I got an urgent call to come to Hirabai's house. Her young son, about eight years old, had had a very high fever for three days. They'd gone to the doctor, who had done nothing, but I immediately recognized typhoid fever. Bob and I put him in our jeep and rushed him to Miraj, where he was admitted and officially diagnosed with typhoid.

The doctor confirmed that we should begin inoculations in the city. I persuaded one of the doctors to come along with me to tell people about the inoculations. I'd been promoting them, but having a doctor say so, too, would be more persuasive. It was Dr. Anand Gaikwad who agreed to come. He was a young man then, but went on to become a famous urologist. Dr. Gaikwad came by bus to Shantinagar, and we asked people to come to the centre for a class, but that didn't really work. Then we found if you went to someone's house, the neighbours would come by to see what was going on. So we would go to a person's house and start talking about inoculations, and soon a big crowd would fill the road outside, curious to see what a doctor and a foreign nurse were doing at their friend's house.

Some agreed to have the typhoid shot, so we would give it to them along with some aspirin for the one-day fever that would follow, and there were very few adverse effects. It gradually became routine that just before every rainy season I would go 'round to the homes with inoculations. There was always one child that ran away, and I'd have to chase after them, catch them, and give them the injection.

We were able to get the immunization drugs from the Hafkin Institute in Bombay at a greatly discounted price. We had spirits to disinfect the arm, and a little portable stove that we used to sterilize the needles. We immunized hundreds of people. The needles became dull with use, but it was expensive to replace them. Fortunately, one day Bob was reading a medical magazine and found out how to sharpen the needles. So when I came home from one of these immunization outings, he would sharpen all my needles, and we would boil them all up again. It was a somewhat primitive system, but I only remember one infected arm in all the years that I did immunizations, and we did 400 to 500 inoculations of *each* disease in season. You had to do two injections for typhoid, a week apart, and a month later we would do injections for cholera.

Sometimes at a house, we would run into a mother-in-law who said, "You're not touching my children. We're Hindu, and we don't believe in these Christian things." But over time those mothers-in-law began to see that those who took the injections didn't get typhoid. Gradually, people began to seek out the immunizations, coming to our little one-room clinic and bringing their children. It takes years to build that kind of relationship in an area. It was maybe two years until I really began to feel that I was earning the trust of the people. Slowly, I got to know the people in Shantinagar, and they accepted me into their lives.

At Indira Gandhi's reception in Sangli. Gandhi is center front in the colored sari. The second person to the right of her is Shalini. In the middle row, Laxmi is third from the right and I am eighth from the right.

Chapter 14: Long Nose, Short Hair

One of the signs that I was becoming accepted in Sangli was being included in local events, such as the visit to Sangli by Indira Gandhi. At this time, Indira was the Secretary of the Congress Party, the first *woman* Secretary. Important in her own right, even then, she was also the daughter of Prime Minister Jawaharlal Nehru.

When it was announced, months ahead of time, that Indira Gandhi would be visiting Sangli, the Congress Party decided that local women should hold the reception. This was a great event, and all communities were to be represented. When our Christian community was asked to nominate somebody, they all wanted me, but I said, "No, I'm not an Indian; you have to do it."

"Oh," they said, "They'll just make fun of us."

"Why would they make fun of you?"

"Because of our accent everybody knows we are outcastes, and they wouldn't like it. This is a *Brahman* town." That was the first time I realized how deeply ingrained caste was, because within the Congress Party there was to *be* no caste differentiation. Eventually, three of us, the principal of the school, Sulochana Gorde, and I agreed to be representatives. There ended up being about 45 people on the committee, and we met weekly for months. Of course, the chairwoman was a Brahman, and all the officers were Brahmans, but the other castes were represented.

The monumental question was where to receive Indira. She was coming in the middle of the day, so it was decided to receive her in Ambrai Park, a big park that had been given to the city by the raja. Then there was the discussion of what to wear, and it was determined that we would all wear white, as advocated by Mohandas Gandhi, Indira, and the Congress Party. (Indira was not related to Mohandas Gandhi; Gandhi was her married name.) The idea was that instead of fancy silk and embroidered saris, women should wear white cotton saris, which made everyone equal. The men wore white shirts, khaki pants, and little hats. This style of dress identified members of the Congress Party.

The state of Maharashtra was strongly pro-Congress Party. Many of the Congress Party women had been freedom fighters, supporting the men who sabotaged railroads and committed other acts to try to force out the

British. The Brahmans had given a great deal of money to the cause of Indian independence, and they were strongly nationalistic.

So, although the three of us registered as the Christian representatives and attended the committee meetings, it soon became apparent that no matter what we said, it was ignored. If we made the slightest suggestion, the next comment would be on an entirely different subject. When we broke for tea, we three would go to speak with some of the other women, but others wouldn't speak to us, so after about three meetings, we decided that we were wasting our time, and might just as well not be there. But I'm a stubborn Scot, so I went back to the meetings, sat at the back, and just kept making small suggestions into the void.

Often I found myself seated next to a large woman named Laxmi. She was Brahman, but she wasn't wealthy. Her husband owned a little shop in the town. On the other side sat the Gujarati women. They didn't speak very good Marathi because their tongue was Gujarati. No one would speak Hindi, the national language of India, because at the time it was considered disloyal to our state.

A great deal of discussion was devoted to exactly how Indira was to be received when she arrived at the park gates, who was to escort her into the park, and all that fuss. We were all to be directed by a very efficient lady, Shalini Yadov, the Secretary of the Sangli Congress Party. A week before Indira was to come, we had a rehearsal during which Shalini directed everybody, "You stand here, now you stand here ..."

After the weeks of meetings, at last the day of Indira's visit arrived. My job was to stay in a little cut-off bit of the park surrounded by a hedge, where all of the women of the committee were to meet to have their picture taken with Indira. I was to control access to the area, so that nobody but the committee people entered. Indira was to arrive at 11:30 a.m., so we were all to be in place by 9. This was midsummer and, though there were trees, it was still quite hot to spend hours standing in the park. Fortunately, we were all dressed in white, as we were told Indira would be dressed.

There had been a good bit of rivalry over who would receive Indira, and it was decided that she would be greeted by two women. The police would keep people back while the greeters walked Indira to the area where the photo was to be taken, the bit of park I was to control.

We had all arrived at nine o'clock as instructed, and waited as noon came, then one o'clock, then two. We'd brought our water and our lunches, but after five hours, those were long gone. Many of the village women had massed in a big area in the park, near the stage where Indira was to speak. I'd been standing with the photographer for hours, guarding my bit of park. People would want to come in and sit for a while, but I had to say, "No, you're not allowed to come in."

With little warning, the motorcade pulled up, and the two women marched forward with their garlands. But after running late all day from reception to reception, Indira was very impatient. She waved off the greeters and strode off by herself, with the crowd quickly filling in behind her, leaving her greeters well behind. Stationed at the other end of the driveway, I hadn't seen any of this, so I had no idea Indira had arrived.

Suddenly, this woman in a dark sari with something over her head came walking in, and I said, "Oh, I'm sorry, you can't come in here."

"I beg your pardon," she said stonily.

Recognizing her then, I stammered, "Oh, come in!" But none of the committeewomen were there! "Just a minute," I said, "You've come without your reception!"

"I know I'm to stand here and have a photograph taken!"

By then someone had alerted the women, and they came flooding in. I couldn't have stopped anyone. "Come on, photographer, take the picture, take the picture," Indira insisted, but the photographer knew the plan and waited for the women to assemble before snapping the photo.

Unfortunately, Shalini, who was responsible for directing the visit, didn't make it for the photo. She was up at the stage where she was to introduce Indira. All the local Congress Party leaders were sitting on stage waiting when someone brought a lost baby to the podium. So Shalini stepped up to the microphone to say, "Here's a lovely baby. Whose baby is this? Whose baby is this? Come and get your baby!"

Meantime, Indira had fled the moment the photo was taken, and was coming up on stage. As she approached, Shalini said with relief, "Oh, the baby's mother has come!" Meanwhile, the men of the party were all dumbfounded at this baby business, but recognizing Indira, they stood up, and Shalini realized the terrible mistake she had made.

After all our organizing and rehearsal, nothing went according to plan. I ended up standing next to Shalini as Indira addressed the crowd. Because Indira spoke in Hindi, I didn't understand a word, and neither did most of the women who had waited so long to hear her. Nevertheless, when the people on stage clapped, I clapped, too. Shalini stood still and quiet, which I attributed to shock.

Finally, Indira sat down, and we all clapped heartily and shouted, "Indira Zindibad!" "*Long live Indira!*"

Shalini turned to me and said, "Do you know what she said?"

"I haven't a clue what she said."

"She said, 'The women of Maharashtra are uneducated, and they do not know how to arrange things properly,' but she's the one that's made a mess of everything. She said, 'It's time that the women of India come forward and learn to organize properly, that they learn to move efficiently.' She gave us such a lecture—I'm glad I'm not up there!" The Congress Party men and Shalini spoke Hindi and knew what she'd said, but none of the masses had understood.

Then Indira left the stage and swept down the driveway, once again outrunning the women with the garlands. Just as she got to the car, one of the women caught up with her and reached into the car to hand her a gift, saying, "This is from Sangli!" Then the car sped off.

By then it was half-past four, and we were dead beat. I had cleaned up my little corner where the photo had been taken, and we were all about to go home when I heard one of the two official greeters say, "It wasn't worth all that trouble!"

The other greeter turned to her and said, "Who does Indira Gandhi think she is? She's just like our Ramerbai—long nose and short hair. She's just the same, but Ramerbai speaks *Marathi*, and Indira can't even speak Marathi!"

"Well, long nose and short hair," I thought, "That's me." That was the first time I was mistaken for Indira. But over the years, on occasion I would be in a shop or on the street, and people would gather around, thinking I was Indira. I finally figured out that all I needed to do to convince them otherwise was to speak to them in Marathi.

As for Indira's visit, I understood that she'd been to all these other little towns, and everywhere she went people gave great, long speeches. She had arrived 2½ hours late in Sangli, having refused to stop for a meal because she didn't want to make it any later. So she didn't want any folderol. She knew what she was supposed to do, and she did it.

It may seem that all those committee meetings were a waste of time, but that's not the case because I formed good friendships with all those Gujarati women, and with Laxmibai, the Brahman woman who sat next to me and was such fun. She was a very religious Hindu woman and had no respect for the caste system. From her and the Gujarati women I learned so much about the lives of other Indian women, so different from the lives of our Christian women. After those meetings, I sat on a number of committees, such as the flower committee, the city garden committee, and the first aid committee. When these friends had their special festivals, they invited me to come.

One of my new friends was Mrs. Deshmukh, the wife of the Sangli health officer. Dr. Deshmukh was a Brahman, and he had no use for missionaries or any other kind of foreigner. He was unfailingly straight-faced and abrupt.

I had encountered Dr. Deshmukh early in our years at Sangli when Bob was in the hospital for hernia surgery. Robbie had just been born, and I'd left him home with Ayah and hurried to catch the bus to Miraj. I waited and waited, but no bus came. Finally one came, but it was so crowded that they wouldn't let anyone else on.

Three overcrowded buses went by, and I was desperate to get to Miraj. Then a car came along, so I stopped it and asked, "Would you be kind enough to take me to Miraj?" It's a straight, five-mile road, so anybody coming along was bound to be going to Miraj. "Can you please take me to Miraj Hospital because I can't get on the bus, and my husband's operation is going to be in half an hour, and I want to be there."

"Why should I take you?" asked the man, Dr. Deshmukh as I later learned.

I just looked at him and said, "I just thought Indian people were so hospitable. I would pick up somebody and take them, so I thought you wouldn't mind."

"Get in front with the driver," he said, so I did, though to be directed to sit with the driver was a very intentional insult.

When we drew close to the hospital, the driver said, "Madam."

"I know," I said, "I get off here."

So I got out and thanked the man, who said only, "Drive on." Fortunately, thereafter, when I needed something from him as the health officer, I would go to his office, and his secretary would help me, so I never had to address him. However, his wife was on the Indira committee, and we became very friendly.

***

About every five years missionaries were sent home on furlough, both to tell people at home about the work being done and to help us missionaries stay in touch with our own families and countries. Our first furlough seemed to come along very quickly in 1953. Bob had been there five and a half years, and I had done four and a half years, so it was time to go to America and Scotland. Bob was going to complete seminary and be ordained, so that when we returned, he could head the industrial school *and* be district superintendent of the churches. It made him more versatile. So I was turning more things over to Sulochana, and getting ready to go on furlough.

When I visited houses, women would often ask me about my marriage. It always puzzled them that Bob and I had what they called a "loove" marriage because in India marriages were always arranged, and here we were in India with Bob's family in America and my family in Scotland.

I'd say, "Yes, it is a loove marriage, we love one another," but to them a loove marriage was when somebody "had to" get married. Because we had been engaged for two years before marrying, that obviously wasn't the case, so this was all very puzzling.

Even the young people would say, "My parents know me better than I know myself, so they will choose somebody for me they know I'll get on with. We'll fall in love with them after we get married. I don't understand how you can really know a person just by 'going out' with them."

One woman said to me, "You're going home, and you're going to stay with your mother-in-law?"

"Yes, for a while we're going to stay there."

"Aren't you afraid of what she's going to say to you? You married her son without her permission."

Then another woman popped up and said, "Oh, that'll be all right. She's got a son now, so grandma will be happy, and she won't have any trouble."

When we got to Denver, I told Bob's parents about how the women were so worried about how my mother-in-law would mistreat me, and this was a great joke with them all. Helen Ramer was one of the kindest, gentlest people you could ever meet, and the idea of being frightened of her was a remarkable thing.

When Robbie was 13 months old, we prepared to leave Sangli on one year's furlough. Our belongings had to be packed up because others would occupy the house. I sorted and packed our things according to a complicated system. One barrel was to go by ship direct to the U.S.A., another trunk was to travel with us by ship, then across the country to Denver. In other barrels we packed things to be left for our return to India. There were still other trunks for things to be sent to the U.S. in the event that we didn't return.

It was a nearly impossible task complicated by having a toddler. We couldn't lock the three doors into that room, so while Ayah and I were busy at one end, Robbie would toddle in, pick up things from one trunk, and put them in another! I nearly went crazy until I employed Sugandh, a teenage carpentry student with a broken arm, to take Robbie out and keep him occupied. He was excellent at thinking up things for Robbie to do or to watch. Sugandh became Robbie's big brother—indeed big brother to all our kids—for he was in our employ for 27 years.

We sailed off on furlough in July 1953, arriving in New York for our debriefing with the Mission Board. From New York we drove to Lincoln, Pennsylvania, with baby Robbie howling all the way. The transition from India to the U.S. was not as easy as one might think. Robbie's greatest trauma was his first American haircut. In India the barber came to the house, and cut Robbie's hair with scissors, while friends and neighbours sat by his chair, chatting and playing. So it was a pleasant social occasion, climaxed by cookies and lemonade all round!

Not so in America. On our trip across the U.S. to visit partner churches, we were staying with a minister's family in Ohio when the minister's wife declared that Robbie needed a haircut. I replied that we would take him in the afternoon, as Bob and I were speaking at a special lunch meeting that day.

When we got back, we learned that *she* had taken Robbie to the barbershop. Bob and I rushed over to find Robbie in the barber chair, two people holding him down while the barber shaved his head with electric clippers! We both rushed to stop it. Poor Robbie was hysterical—all these strangers and that terrible buzzing noise. His hair was half crew cut, half long! It had to be finished. We finally got the crew cut done, but the haircut trauma lasted for years, long after we returned to India!

We made our way across the country to Denver, where we stayed with Grandma and Pappy Ramer until August, when we headed for San Anselmo. There Bob completed his last year of seminary, graduating in June 1954, just in time for us to be in Denver for the birth of Robbie's new sibling!

It was the 4th of July, my due date, when I felt the first contractions. Robbie had a high fever that day, and there was an epidemic of polio in Denver at the time, so I postponed going to the hospital to see about him. My sister-in-law recommended her paediatrician, and when I got Dr. Russell on the phone, he asked right away, "Where are you from?" It turned out that, like me, he had studied at Yorkhill Hospital in Scotland. I took Robbie in and was considerably relieved when Dr. Russell diagnosed tonsillitis and fixed Robbie up with some penicillin. After all that, my labour stopped, and I ended up being induced on July 10, 1954, and giving birth to little Nancy Helen, called Lyn.

After Bob, along with his brother Phil, was ordained, it was time to return to New York, where we set sail for the U.K. on the *Queen Mary*. It was wonderful to see my brother Blair and his family, and our Scottish friends, but we weren't so welcome everywhere. Signs informed us that some people didn't care to rent to "No dirty missionaries."

After three months in Edinburgh living with a toddler and a newborn in a cold-water flat, we were ready when the time came to sail again for India. In December 1954 we arrived back in Sangli to a warm welcome.

Chapter 15: Repaid a Hundredfold

After our warm welcome back to Sangli, life slipped into a routine—of sorts.

One morning, when Lyn was about 18 months old and Robbie about three and a half, I heard Lyn screaming and Robbie yelling, "Mom, come quick!" I raced into the bedroom to see Robbie hanging onto Lyn's dress and trying to pull her away from the door. Lyn was reaching her hands out, trying to pick up something. I grabbed Lyn and saw what *she* was trying to grab—a scorpion!

The Sangli house we lived in during all our married years had been built in 1905 as a famine relief project, to employ people and provide some income to them. It was built of very large, square blocks of stone joined together with mud mortar and red clay. There were three connected bedrooms, then a dining room and sitting room that made a "T" to the bedrooms. The kitchen was built outside the house, so that the cooking wouldn't heat up the rest of the living quarters. The floor was made of the local tile. The house had been built with three verandas or porches, which made the house much cooler. They were about three feet wide and were covered by a sloping roof supported by columns.

Cooling was a primary consideration in construction. The ceilings of the bedrooms, sitting room, and dining room were 20 feet high, and the walls were two feet thick. Because of the verandas, the bright sunshine never came into the house. Near the high ceiling where the hot air rose, there were windows with mosquito netting that opened and closed with pulley ropes. At night we opened those windows and all the doors, and we kept the house open until about 9 a.m., when we would close everything to keep out the day's heat.

Bob and I slept on the screened-in veranda at the far end of the third bedroom because we'd made the third bedroom into an office for him. There was just room enough for our bed, a cupboard, and a chest of drawers.

During the very hot weather, before we went to bed at night, we would throw a bucket of water against the screens and the whitewashed walls. As the water dried, it cooled the air. We often sprinkled our sheets and pillowcases and left them open so they became cool, too. It was one of the tricks of living in a hot climate.

Over the years we wrote many circulars, letters telling friends and family who supported our mission work what we were up to. In a 1958 circular letter, Bob wrote, "The hot weather has been kind this year. We have had few days over 100 degrees and with the help of fans (gift from Casper church people and Auke-Bay Alaska churches) at home and in the office I have hardly noticed the heat. We had never had a fan before and were amazed at the difference it makes."

When we returned from our furlough, we still had Sulochana Gorde with us, which allowed us to expand our health services. Once a week, Dr. Anand Gaikwad came by bus from Miraj for the antenatal clinics. On another day, Dr. Ranabhise came to treat the chronic medical cases, such as patients with heart problems who couldn't travel to Miraj. Being more senior, Dr. Ranabhise could usually commandeer the hospital car for his trips to Sangli.

When a new chief district health officer came to Maharashtra, he was excited to meet others who shared a vision of expanding public health. We developed cards that told the story of each prevalent disease and how to avoid it. This included dysentery, malaria, smallpox, scabies, and malnutrition, all things that parents at home could do much to prevent. The health officer suggested that our nurse go into the schools to talk about disease prevention, and this was exactly what we wanted to do.

In one particularly bad cholera year, we worked together to immunize as many people as possible. The municipality provided a jeep with a loudspeaker to announce our intentions, and a man to keep records of immunizations. We went into schools and immunized the children. We told them the shot would feel like an ant bite, and very few cried, except for the little ones. They cried mostly because the older kids had frightened them with "You don't know what is going to happen to you when you get in there! There's a white witch in there!"

Not knowing I spoke Marathi, the kids were shocked when I'd turn around to them and say, "I'm white, but I'm not a witch. And I'm doing this to keep you healthy!"

We also had a tuberculosis prevention program. The mission TB sanatorium was 2½ miles away and was directed by Dr. Takaro, a very talented specialist. TB patients could be admitted for two months at government expense, so for two months, and only two months, they would get good food and their injections. Dr. Takaro started a fund for continuing the shots after people were discharged. He sent the streptomycin to me, and I would go to the patients and give them their shots. Some of the patients lived just across the river, so Bob would take me there on the Lambretta scooter.

One day the younger brother of a former sanatorium patient came to our door with tears in his eyes. His brother, Mr. Kade, had been treated in the sanatorium and been discharged, but his health had broken down again. His brother had walked five miles to our house to ask for help.

"My brother is again very ill with tuberculosis. Our two older brothers have died of it. Our father had a good farm that he sold to pay for treatment for his sons, but now he's used all his money, and we live in a shack in Sangliwada. There are only four of us left, my mother and father and this brother and me. Will you please help us save him?"

Bob took me on the scooter to see Mr. Kade, and he was obviously very ill. I got in touch with Dr. Takaro, and he agreed to readmit him to the san because his first round of treatment had been prior to Dr. Takaro's arrival in India. When Dr. Takaro examined him he said, "We have to operate on him to remove part of the lung. He must have this operation, and I'd really like to do it free, but the minimum cost to us is a few hundred dollars."

Thanks to the many friends at home who knew the reality of life in India, we had a small special fund account with discretionary funds, so we told Dr. Takaro to go ahead and operate.

Before he contracted TB, Mr. Kade had been a photographer, and he asked Bob to buy his camera so he could help pay for his operation. But Bob said, "I'm not going to buy your camera. This is your way of earning a living, and you're going to earn a living again. When you get better, I will help you buy developer and supplies so you can revive your business. But right now, you have to get better, and we will see to the expense."

Much improved after the surgery and some months in the san, Mr. Kade was discharged, and a treatment of bi-weekly inoculations was prescribed. Mr. Kade was of a higher caste, the warrior class, which is just under

Brahman. Sangli was a strong Brahman city, but Sangliwada was mostly warrior class, high caste, but often poor. Whenever we visited people, we asked them if we could pray for them, and if they would like to read something about Jesus. Mr. Kade said yes, so we gave him a New Testament and prayed with him.

One day we were on the scooter on our way to see Mr. Kade when a kid began throwing stones at us. We skirted around him, thinking, "Oh, it's just a kid." The next time we came, at the street corner near the Kades' house, there was a group of boys who threw a shower of stones. Bob stopped the scooter and attempted to talk with them, but they ran away.

On a third trip, there was an even larger group of boys. Before they started throwing, Bob stopped the scooter to talk, and they denied any intention of throwing stones. "We just wanted to see you white people and your scooter. We've never seen a scooter before."

When we started off again on the scooter, we were hit by a shower of stones and mudballs, and my back was splattered. When we arrived covered with mud, the Kades were very upset and said, "We will see that this doesn't happen again."

When we next saw the younger brother, he told us, "My father went to the patil (Hindu chief) of the village and told him you were coming to save my brother, and the patil said he felt very bad about what had happened." It seems that the Hindu kids had been encouraged by some of their parents to throw stones to keep us out of their community.

The next time we went to treat Mr. Kade, the patil was standing on the corner. We expected to be told not to come again, but instead he said, "I am so sorry this has happened. It won't happen again." From then on, whenever we came to the Kades' corner, there was always a Sangliwada elder standing there to ensure that there was no stone throwing.

Happily, Mr. Kade recovered. The two Mrs. Gordes, Sulochana the nurse, and her assistant Hirabai Gorde, began taking the bus over the bridge to follow up on Mr. Kade's care. They were able to walk freely into the wada, but not only that. They were invited to speak in the schools about health issues, and to distribute the disease prevention cards. This was possible because we had attended Mr. Kade.

Although he always remained thin, Mr. Kade, with the help of some supplies from Bob, was able to start up his photography business again in a little shed by the river. He was a very independent man, gracious and grateful. One day three years later, he came to Bob and said, "Christ made me better, and Christ brought you people into my life. I want to be baptised and become a Christian."

So Bob said, "That's fine," and referred him to our Sangli church.

We were later horrified to hear that the Sangli church had refused to baptise him and have him as a member. When Bob questioned the minister, he was told, "My congregation [which was Indian] doesn't want him because he's high caste, and if you let the high caste come into the church, pretty soon they'll run the church. They'll look down on us, and won't listen to us, so we don't want any high-caste people." It was as if in the U.S., there were a church of former slaves and a white person wanted to join.

We were shocked at this and tried to cope with it, but the church was self-governed, and we couldn't mandate that they accept Mr. Kade. Undeterred, Mr. Kade went to a village church, but they, too, rejected him. The admission of high-caste people was a long-lasting and troublesome issue within the church.

We tried to be understanding, knowing this came out of what the outcastes themselves had suffered. Our whole mission effort worked at removing the entire idea of caste, and we would think we were making progress until a high-caste person tried to join the church. Then we would realize how intractable the caste system was.

The situation was a heartache to us, but Mr. Kade said, "It doesn't matter. I can worship Jesus anyway," and he and his family continued to read the Bible and pray.

Mr. Kade married a very loving woman, and they had a son they brought to our house, asking Bob to bless him. Later a daughter, also, was born. Although old Mr. Kade is gone, the family came to have a prosperous business with three photographic studios.

One of Bob's endless responsibilities was the supervision of 10 village schools. When he visited, the schoolmasters told him, "There are so many needing medicine, and they can't get to the doctor. Can you do something?" In response, Bob began to take Sulochana Gorde or me with him, and we'd take a bag of cough medicine, ear drops, eye drops, antibiotics, and other medicines. But the villagers needed much more than one day's help.

Then we decided I could teach the schoolmasters to be health aides. Once a month, the schoolmasters came to Sangli for their pay, many travelling long distances. While they were there, we had prayer and worship, then we met for an hour over a cup of tea. I taught them basic health care, and listened to what problems they were encountering, for example, a wave of dysentery. Each man was given a box with bottles of non-prescription medicine, and the instructions and doses for those medicines. They learned how to keep records of medicine received, and when to send for a doctor. With malnutrition a major health problem, we also began to send milk powder and vitamins out to the district.

As Christians, we were technically outcastes, but everywhere we went we were welcomed and accepted. Bob was invited to join both the Lions Club and the Rotarians. There were already six or seven missionaries in the Rotarians, and none in the Lions Club. For that reason, and because his great friend Dr. Ranabhise was a member, Bob joined the Lions Club, and they made him the chaplain.

That wouldn't be so remarkable in the U.S., but in Sangli the majority of the Lions were Hindus, with a number of Muslims and just a few Christians. But they always respected Bob, and when there was a funeral they would invite him to come and say a prayer. It was a wonderfully inclusive way. The Lions met every week and did important work in eye care, arranging for cataract surgery and providing eyeglasses.

The work we did in public health in Sangli continues as a strong part of the Miraj Medical Centre to this day. It has grown far beyond our wildest dreams; God has shown his presence in this.

***

During the very hottest months, March through June, we missionary mothers took our young children and went to Kodaikanal for a respite. Kodaikanal is 7,500 feet above sea level in the mountains of south India, 750 miles from Sangli. It took three days of travel on three trains and a bus to get there. Our three-day route was from Miraj to Bangalore, Bangalore to Trichy (trichinopoly), and Trichy to Kodai Kanal.

While we were in Kodai, the older children who were there in boarding school could come and stay with their mothers and siblings. In May the mission schools for the Indian children were closed. Even the hospital work slowed, for no one went to the hospital in that awful heat unless it was life threatening. It meant that we wives were separated from our husbands, but the men would take off the month of May for *their* annual holiday, and join us at Kodai.

One year, 1958, Bob drove us to the Miraj station in the jeep piled high with the 13 suitcases, food basket, drinking water, thermoses, a small bag for each child with their special toys, and a bag of books so we could read stories on the train. In addition to all that, we had Sugandh and his wife Shalini, Robbie, Lyn, and me squished into the front seat with Bob. I planned to teach Sugandh to cook while we were there, and Shalini would help with the children. Upon arriving at Miraj, coolies poured around us, and the bags disappeared, as we herded our crew in the direction of the train.

It was beastly hot in the middle of March when we headed for Kodai. Robbie was almost six, Lyn almost four, and I was pregnant. The baby was due in May, so would be born in Kodai. This was the first time since we were married that Bob and I would be apart for so long, and I certainly wasn't looking forward to that, but he promised he would arrive a week before the baby was due.

In those days we always travelled first class, but it was anything but luxurious. The second-class coach accommodated 60 on bare, unpadded benches. At every stop people poured into the compartment and more or less sat on top of each other! So with small children, we travelled first class. At that time there was a small car attached to first class for the attendants, so Sugandh and Shalini were put in there. This meant that others would not get into their compartment at the stations.

Since I needed three of the four bunks, there would be only one other person sharing our compartment. We had our own "toilet" in the compartment, but toilet meant a hole in the floor, and the kids were terrified of that, so I carried our own potty. The engines were steam engines, and cinders flew back into the compartment. I always carried eye ointment on the train, for at least one of us was sure to get a cinder in the eye. There were small fans, but it was cooler to have the windows open, and the breeze from them was refreshing.

In those days the train ticket collector wore a white cotton suit and a navy blue hat with a white cover. He carried a whistle and a red and green flag. Robbie was fascinated by the ticket collector, so we had him all dressed up in a white suit with his whistle, his hat, and two flags, and he felt very important.

Suddenly, Lyn and Robbie realized that they had to say good-bye to Daddy, and they began to cry. One did not show affection in public in India because it was quite offensive to some, so Bob and I had said our real good-byes at home. However, I was also able to sneak in a wee, surreptitious kiss while trying to extricate a clinging Lyn from Bob's arms. As the train pulled out, I had candy and a book ready to distract them.

Kodai itself was just a small town with one street of shops known as the bazaar. The Presbyterian Mission owned nine houses on property across the lake from the school. We stayed in a two-bedroom cottage with kitchen, dining room, sitting room, and the basic furniture. Because Kodai is cold, we packed all our blankets as well as pots and pans and all the children's clothes. Of course, I had to bring all the tiny clothes and accoutrements that we would need for the new baby, too.

It was a particular relief that year to arrive at Kodai, settle in, and look forward to the birth of our baby. I had already arranged for Dr. Bailey, with whom I had worked in Poona, to take her holiday with us and deliver the baby in due course. Then I received a long letter from Dr. Bailey, the gist of which was that her mother in Scotland had had a stroke, so she would be going to Scotland, not Kodai. She recommended another Scottish doctor, who would be in Kodai when the baby was due.

Dr. Ellen Larson (not her real name) was to be my doctor. I had been told she had had six years' midwifery experience in Scotland. When Lyn was born in Denver, I had been told that I would have to have a C-section for the next child and should be sure to have a very good obstetric surgeon. At my appointment with Dr. Larson I told her this, to which she replied, "Nonsense, nonsense, you nurses are always nervous."

When she examined me, I could tell right away that she wasn't well experienced. "How long did you serve in Scotland in midwifery?"

"Six months."

"Oh."

Our friends the Eatons were at Kodai, and Mrs. (Dr.) Eaton was an obstetrician. I had really wanted to have her, but they were planning to go to Canada on leave. At the last minute, their leave was cancelled because their replacements didn't come, so she was in Kodai, living in the house next the hospital. Dr. Eaton told me that if I felt I needed her, I should just send Bob next door, and she would come.

When I got up to Kodai, I found that the Mansons, Scottish missionaries, were expecting a baby three weeks before ours. I knew the Mansons, and whenever Noreen and I met at the bazaar, we always checked in with each other.

Bob came up at the beginning of May, travelling the 750 miles on the Lambretta scooter with a top speed of 45 mph! Obligingly, the baby began to come on the due date, May 5, so we went to the hospital. Dr. Larson wanted to give me Pitocin, but I refused unless she gave it by drip. "You nurses are all alike," she complained. "I know what I am doing," and she shot Pitocin into me, which increased the labour pains very quickly. Then, in the middle of the night, Noreen Manson arrived with her husband Roy.

In the morning I was moved into the labour room where Joan Carol Ramer, "Jody," was delivered on May 6, 1958. Bob had been with me all during the delivery, but after Jody was born, he went home to tell the family that we'd had a baby girl, and that everything was OK. I had been taken back to my room to recover, but suddenly I knew I was having internal haemorrhage! I rang the bell for help, and just had time to say, "I KNOW I am having internal haemorrhage! My blood group is group O!" before losing consciousness.

Noreen had just delivered her baby, and Dr. Eaton was waiting for her to pass the placenta. Quickly, Noreen was rushed to her own room, and I was hurried back to the labour room. When Dr. Larson saw the terrible flow of blood, she *fainted*, so the nurse went rushing into Noreen's room and asked Dr. Eaton to come and help.

Dr. Eaton could see that I desperately needed a blood transfusion, but they had neither the blood nor the transfusion kit. Just then her husband, also a doctor, came in to see if she was coming to lunch, so she told him, "I need to get blood!" At this point, Roy Manson volunteered, "I'm group O. I don't know anything else about my blood, but you can take it." So they put Roy on the table and withdrew blood from him, and tried to *inject it* into me because they didn't have a drip apparatus. It wasn't going well, and the situation quickly went from bad to worse.

Just then Bob came back to see me, and was shocked to find I wasn't in my room. "Come and help us!" Dr. Eaton yelled. So Bob held up the bottle for a drip while they took blood out of Roy and gave it to me. For four hours, Dr. Eaton worked to stop the bleeding, and finally she succeeded.

In the middle of all this, a patient came in with a baby that had fallen off a table. She was quickly told there was an emergency, that Mrs. Ramer was desperately ill, and she should take the baby to one of the other doctors in Kodai. When that information got out, Archie Fletcher, my original doctor in Sangli, rushed to the hospital on his scooter, to find the worst was over, and I was regaining consciousness. The nurse was taking my blood pressure and saying, "It's still only 90 over 40, but she's coming around."

"That's normal for me," I said.

She looked at Archie, who concurred. Archie told the doctors to go have their lunch, and he would sit beside me, while the servants saw to the baby. Jody was born on May 6, and May 7 was my 37th birthday, one I almost didn't have. During the emergency, they had held a special prayer meeting. Prayer really does make a tremendous difference, and I am so thankful that I came through that experience.

Dr. Eaton confided to me afterwards, "I never had a patient so close to death and still live. It's a miracle." I later learned that the hospital had put out an alarm for blood donations, and more than 200 people had offered theirs. Appropriately, Marvin Nelson, best man at our wedding, was a compatible donor, and after I got that second pint, I felt much better.

Between the blood lost and the infection that followed, it took me quite a long time to recover. Fortunately, my friend Margaret, one of the nurses who had been with me when Robbie was born, came up to Kodai after

Bob had to leave because I really wasn't able to do much more than feed the baby and look after myself. Margaret took care of Robbie and Lyn and even travelled back to Miraj with us. On top of travelling with two little ones and a new baby, and me still weak from infection, Margaret had an awful attack of asthma on the train on the way home. It was a huge relief to arrive.

***

In 1958, a new missionary family arrived in Sangli. It was our friends from seminary, Jack and Joan Seibert, and their children Mark, Anne, and Karl. Mark was six months younger than Rob; Anne was six months younger than Lyn; and Karl was just about two, and the children became great friends.

We had wonderful memories from our time at San Anselmo with the Seiberts. I had met Joan at a gathering of the wives, hosted by the wife of one of the professors. When I arrived at the "parsonettes luncheon," I discovered that our hostess and I were wearing the same dress. Now in those days, that wasn't a good thing to do, especially for a *student's* wife to have a dress identical to that of a *seminary professor's* wife!

But there was no mistaking it. They were identical red dresses with a little black ornament on the lapel. When I bought that dress, I'd been searching for something very smart to wear for all the speaking engagements we would have while on furlough. I had gone to a store in New York that gave a big discount to missionaries, and a beautiful African-American lady had offered to help me. Having been in India for nearly five years, I told her, "I will have to depend on you. I have no idea of styles, but I'm going to be visiting in churches, and I want to have something smart to wear." It was she who directed me to this particular red dress, and it was just what I wanted. I *love* red. Now here was a professor's wife in the same dress. We laughed, but I could tell she didn't think it too funny, so I was careful never again to wear it where she might be in attendance.

After that embarrassing beginning, I sat down beside this woman, Joan Seibert, and started talking with her. Her husband was also in seminary, and they had a little boy near Robbie's age. We got along well, so soon I asked them to dinner, and we arranged a date.

One day Bob came home and said he had met another student who was also an engineer. He didn't remember his last name, but we decided he should invite this "Jack" and his family to join our little dinner party. So I was expecting Joan and her husband, and Jack and his wife. They each planned to bring their baby, so we cleared out a place for a playpen and set the table for six.

Soon Joan arrived, and as I welcomed her, I turned around to find Bob saying, "Jack, I want you to meet my wife." We all stared at one another. We only had two guests coming, because Jack and Joan were married to each other! We simply hadn't gotten that far in our getting acquainted.

Knowing Jack was an engineer, Bob talked up Sangli to Jack and Joan, and they became interested in the mission field. When Jack graduated, they were assigned to Alaska, but he still yearned to serve overseas.

Meanwhile, we had a request in for another missionary at the Sangli Industrial School (SIS). At this point, a pastor could not get a visa to come in, but an engineer could, and Jack qualified. Jack could take over at SIS, so Bob could continue with the district church work. Joan was a teacher and could take over the elementary school. It took nearly four years for this all to come about, but finally the Seiberts moved in next door to us in Sangli, and we were delighted.

Jesus said, "If you leave father and mother, brothers and sisters for my sake and the gospel's, I will repay a hundredfold," and that is true because he gave us brothers and sisters in the other missionaries, and we all became very close.

***

People sometimes wonder why we sent our children far away to boarding school when the missions worked so hard to build and staff schools nearby for the Indian children. There were several reasons why our children needed to be taught in English from an American curriculum. Although missionaries were sent out for five years at a time, we were foreigners and could be sent home at any time by the Indian government. If that happened, the children would have to fit into the American system. However, our children all learned Marathi as their first language, so they were fluent in speaking, even if they were not being educated in it. In fact, our Indian colleagues often remarked, "Your children speak excellent

Marathi, better than you or Bob." That was rather discouraging for us, who studied the language for many years.

Another reason for the American curriculum was that, after five years in the field, we were sent back to America for "home assignment" for a year, and during that time the children went to American schools. It is hard enough to adjust to life in America after India, but if the children found themselves unable to understand what was said at school, it would be a traumatic experience. So, we did our best to prepare our children for the future.

When Robbie was five, I began to teach him at home from the Calvert curriculum materials, paid for by the Presbyterian Church. After my stint at the Health Centre each morning, he and I hid away in a little schoolroom we had created in back of another mission house. There we had class from 11 to 1 while Lyn, a considerable distraction, stayed with Ayah. At 1 we broke for lunch, then we would do crafts in the afternoon while Lyn napped.

Robbie and I enjoyed our time together a great deal, but it was a very imperfect arrangement. In order to have some uninterrupted time, I instructed the staff not to tell anyone where we were. With a compound full of teenaged boys, someone was always in need of help.

One day when we came back to the house, we found Florence Bond, one of the missionary wives from Miraj, waiting for us. She had come to talk to me about something, and the servants kept saying, "Oh, we don't know where she is, we don't know where she is."

Florence was becoming increasingly frustrated. When she saw me, she rushed over and said, "What are you doing? I've been trying to get hold of you. Where were you?"

"I was teaching Robbie, and I don't want people to interrupt us. I can't get any teaching in if people know where I am."

"Well," she said, "There are always people waiting for you!" And that was true.

The next day Florence returned to say, "I have been thinking. When I come to see any of you other missionary wives, you're busy teaching your child, Huldah is teaching her child, and Ruth is teaching hers. You and Huldah are nurses, and Ruth is an occupational therapist, and you're all *needed.* I am a teacher, but I can't get a teaching position in the Miraj schools because I'm not licensed in India. But I could teach these children the American curriculum. Then you could take them up to Kodai from March through June during the exceedingly hot weather, and they could finish their year at an accredited American school."

Florence was a wonderful teacher, and the prospect was a very attractive one, but Miraj was five miles away. We had a jeep, but it couldn't be devoted to carrying our children back and forth twice a day. Still, we wanted to give it a try. So at first we sent Robbie with a young man who worked in Miraj and had a second seat on his bicycle. When the Seiberts came, there were two boys to transport, and I got a bright idea. We paid Sugandh's father, Kallapa, to take the children to school on the bus, walk them to the compound, take his lunch with them, then bring them home on the bus at 3. In the meantime, he sat in the garden at the Miraj missionary compound and chatted with the others. It worked well, and the arrangement lasted for *years.*

Kallapa had a big white moustache and wore a turban, so he looked like a typical shepherd. He always walked ahead of the children, and every once in a while he'd turn round and say, "Shh-shh," and that meant everybody had to get back into line again. He kept a good eye on the children, four of them by the time Lyn and Anne joined the school-goers. Then the Dilleners came along, and he had some of the Dillener children, too, so there was quite a group to take on the bus. Sometimes the children would pull on the back of his turban, and make it fall off, but he only yelled when he got really angry, and then they'd all fall in line.

I had told Kallapa that if the children fell or got hurt, he was to take them to the hospital. No matter what, he was not to let anybody put dirt on the wound, which was the traditional Indian way to stop bleeding. I was to be very glad that I had taught him that.

In our area, we had quite a lot of tamarind trees, which have big, lemony tasting beans that the children loved to eat. Near the bus stop where the children waited to go to school, there was a large tamarind tree, and the Indian children used to throw stones at it to knock down the juicy beans. The trouble was that the stones would return to earth, and we saw a lot of head wounds from that. So I lectured at home and at school that they must not throw stones.

But one day at the bus stop, some kids were trying to knock down the beans, and one of the stones hit Robbie in the head. As scalp wounds do, his bled profusely, and one of the children ran back to get me. When I arrived, adults were coming with hands full of dirt, wanting to put it on to stop the bleeding, but Kallapa stood firm and said that no one was to touch Robbie. I thanked Kallapa for being so sensible, and took Robbie home to clean him up.

Another time there was a bus accident. Nobody got hurt because the buses didn't go very fast, but all the children had to get off. Kallapa marched them off and stood them all by the side of the road. Many people stopped in their cars and offered to take the children on, but he wouldn't allow it. With all those kids to take care of, Kallapa was a very busy man.

We were very grateful to Florence Bond for teaching the children. There were often about 10 kids, and they would bring their lunches and eat together outside or go over to "Aunt" Huldah's and eat there. Later on, some of the Indian doctors' children attended the school, too. Florence gave the children a solid educational foundation, and we were so grateful that they could have those few years of schooling at home before heading off to boarding school so far away. The children became very close, like cousins. It was important that they felt they were all part of one big family, especially when they headed off to boarding.

When the children were a bit older and went to boarding school in Kodai, it was a 46-hour trip by train. There was quite a ritual to getting the children off to boarding. For one thing, the food sold on the train platforms wasn't safe, so we mothers prepared food for them, at least for the first 24 hours. Then they could buy food at Bangalore. We sent tasty things, cookies and special sweets, but the most important item was comic books.

When the time came to leave, we'd all take them down to the Miraj station to get on the train. The kids would be hugging us, some of them crying. It wasn't easy to say goodbye. After the train pulled out, we mothers would all go back to Huldah Fletcher's or Ruth Donaldson's for a cup of coffee and a bit of a weep. Then we'd start telling stories and laughing until it was time to get back to our work.

At first there were 10 or 11 children going to Kodai, but over time there grew to be 21—quite a shepherding chore. Two adults escorted them, and they had a compartment reserved just for them. Bob oversaw property at Kodai and could check on it while he was there, so he was always one of the escorts. For a while, the mothers took turns being the other escort. Then for quite a number of years when Marvin Nelson was there, it was he and Bob who took the children.

Bob saw to the tickets and the luggage, while Marvin kept an eye on the young travellers. The kids liked to have Uncle Bob and Uncle Marvin look after them because they didn't get in a flap over the kids' behaviour. For example, they let the kids have water balloon fights, which the mothers never allowed. The kids filled balloons with water and threw them at each other. The children loved it, and Bob and Marvin thought it wouldn't do anybody any harm because it was so hot. The kids got soaked, but when it was time to go to bed, the men cleaned up the compartment, and the children changed into dry things to lie on their bunks for the night.

The entourage would leave Miraj about 10 in the morning, travel all day and night, and arrive about 9 a.m. the next day at Bangalore. While one father, with the help of coolies, rounded up the luggage, the other father took the kids to a restaurant for breakfast. Some of the kids took their pets to Kodai with them, sometimes a pet rabbit or a bird, but one of the favourites was the loris, or "pocket monkey." They were tiny little things with the softest paws, just beautiful, and they would sit on your hand. Not all the kids had pets, but some had guitars or sports equipment, so there was plenty to see to.

After breakfast, they would get rickshaws or taxis and take the kids to shop or to see a 1:00 movie. About 3:30, it was time to get the rickshaws back to the station to catch the 5:30 p.m. train to Trichi. They would arrive in Trichi about 6 or 7 a.m., then catch a noon train to Kodai Road. Upon arriving at Kodai Road about 4:00 the next day, all the kids and their stuff had to be loaded onto the bus for a 25-mile ride through mountain jungle. The trip took five hours along the slow winding roads. Because of the elevation, partway up it would be cold enough to dig in their luggage for their jackets. By the time they finally arrived at about 9 p.m., everyone was very weary, but there was still the business of getting them off the bus and into the right hostels. Then Marvin and Bob would go over to the Presbyterian campus, where they would stay for about a week attending to matters of property and gardens.

Though they were busy seeing to the repair and maintenance of the property, every day Bob and Marvin would have lunch with the kids, and see that they were settling in.

One time when I made the Kodai trip, Rob didn't want to go, so he hid in the cupboard. I felt so bad, but I took the crying boy from the cupboard and said, "Robbie, you need to go," and then I started to cry.

Robbie stopped, looked at me, and said, "Mom, don't cry. After two days I'm all right. I only cry for two days." And that didn't make me feel too much better.

***

Back in Sangli, there were getting to be quite a few missionaries. The Seiberts were next door, and at the other end of the campus were Roy and Peg Dillener. At that time, in the 50s, we had Peggy Case for a while, and Betty Hilty, and Kay Schwabe, all living in the big bungalow. All of us missionaries served under the Mission Committee, and they were the ones who told you how long you had to go to language school, what your jobs would be when you came back, and how long you would do that.

After the Seiberts arrived, in no time at all, Rob and Mark Seibert were the best of friends, as were Lyn and Annie. Little Karl tottered after them, and as Jody got bigger, she tottered after Karl. As the kids grew, they didn't want to be separated for meals. Some days they all wanted to eat at our house, and other days they all wanted to eat at Joan's. This got to be a nightmare because you'd prepare food for five in the family, and all of a sudden you would have seven. Or you'd prepare for five and end up with only two.

To solve this problem, Joan and I decreed that if they were going to move, they had to move in equal numbers each direction, and that settled that. Then the other problem was they wanted to sleep overnight. Now we rather encouraged that because we knew that eventually we had to train our children to be away from us in order to go to boarding school.

One night Lyn, who was four or five at the time, was desperate to go and sleep at the Seiberts'. "Are you sure?"

"Oh, yes!" With great hilarity and high expectations, she went over to sleep with Anne.

At about three o'clock in the morning, there was a knock at the door. It was Jack Seibert saying, "Do you folks want to have a little girl? We have a little girl who wants to come and stay with you." That only happened the first time. I can't count the number of times Mark slept over with Robbie, or Annie would be over with Lyn. Our families became very close, and it was a great joy to be able to share our lives with them.

Chapter 16: Diamonds

One day Prasad, the husband of a respected couple (whose names I have changed), came to our house about noon and said, "Mrs. Ramer, you have to come at once! Chota is having one fit after another!" Chota was their 18-month-old boy, the youngest of their three sons.

"We'll have to take him to hospital," I said.

"No, Kamal [his wife] and I both feel that you should come and lay hands on him, and he will be healed." Now Bob was away at meetings, so I said again, "I think maybe we should take him to hospital."

"No," he repeated. "Last night we saw that Chota was much worse. We've been praying, and we feel that God wants you to come and lay hands on Chota."

"I can't refuse to go and pray with them," I thought, so I went.

In all the speaking I have done over the years, I have almost never told this story because it's too easily misunderstood. It's definitely not a story to be told just for entertainment.

At both Ranyard and Iona, we had had classes about praying for healing, but as I walked over there I prayed, "God help me know what to do; I don't *know* what to do." When I arrived at their home, there was Kamal with this dear little boy, and he was having one long continuous epileptic seizure, what we called epilepticus staticus.

Kamal and her husband were both about 35 and very devoted Christians, so we three knelt at the bed, and I found myself saying to them, "If we ask God to heal Chota, all three of us must confess our sins before God and commit ourselves to try not to sin again. Don't ask why. Each one of us has to pray."

At this point I didn't know that early that morning they had called for Dr. Desai, but he hadn't yet come. The Miraj hospital was only five miles away, but it was a 45-minute drive over bad road, so they had come to me.

As we prayed, I laid my hands on Chota, and although I don't remember the exact words, I said something like, "Chota is precious to us, Lord. We have all sinned and offended you, but we want to commit our lives to be new in you, and we want Chota to have a new life in you, too. Will you please heal Chota?"

As each seizure rolled through Chota, he screamed a kind of "Eh, eh, eh, eh, eh," and his whole body shook. Then the seizures would stop for a moment before resuming with "Eh, eh, eh, eh" and the shaking. As we prayed for him, Chota gave a scream, but when we expected the shaking, nothing happened.

He was quiet, and I thought, "Has he died?" I opened my eyes, and he opened his eyes and smiled. His mother looked up and said, "He's not having a fit anymore." The three of us looked at Chota and wondered what was happening.

They say if you have faith the size of a mustard seed, that nothing is impossible, but there had always been doubt in the back of my mind. Still, I knew there was nothing God couldn't do. The doubt was about me.

"Chota," I said, "can you hear us?"

"Yes," he answered in Marathi, adding, "I'm hungry." Immediately, I thought of that little girl Jesus healed. He had then said, "Give her something to eat," so I told Kamal to get some food for Chota. His father was so happy and said, "I just know you've healed him!"

"Well, his fits have stopped, anyway," I said.

Kamal brought hot cereal and fed Chota, and then he took the spoon to feed himself and said, "Why is Madamsahib here?"

"I just came to see you, Chota," I said, "but I'll go now." Unbeknownst to us, as we had knelt praying over Chota in the front room, Dr. Desai had arrived and was standing in the doorway, looking through the screen door. "Oh, Dr. Desai, do you want to come in?"

"What has been going on here?" asked Dr. Desai.

"We'd just been praying for him."

"Well," said Dr. Desai, who was a Hindu, "he may seem better now, but he won't stay better. This is pure emotional euphoria."

"How can a 1½ year-old kid have euphoria?" I thought.

"I saw he had epilepticus staticus, and it's most unusual that he should come out of it," said Dr. Desai, "but this won't be the end of it," and off he went.

Chota recovered very quickly, and was soon laughing and playing with the other kids. When Kamal told the doctors in Miraj what had happened, they weren't sure what to do. They were all Christian doctors, so they decided, "Let's not give him any medicine until we see what happens. If he starts with seizures again, you bring him here."

Chota had been fine for about six months, when, without warning, he had a terrible epileptic seizure. Kamal took him to the hospital where he was once again terribly ill. She called for me to come, so I did, but this time as I stood by his bed, it was entirely different. I prayed, "We love him so much," and prayed for his healing, but I felt there was a wall, that for some reason these prayers weren't getting up. "What's going on?" I thought. "Is it me?"

I went home and talked it over with Bob, but it was just one of those things you can't understand. Both Bob and the church pastor went to the hospital and prayed. I continued praying and we had prayer meetings, but little Chota died.

Because his parents were at the hospital, I was looking after Chota's two brothers at our house when word came by messenger that Chota had died. With the sad news came the request that I tell his two brothers, so I did. One of his brothers said, "Why couldn't you fix him like you did the last time?"

All I could say was, "God has need of Chota, and God has taken him home."

Everyone was very sad, but Kamal came back to work in the clinic, and life went on. One morning about a month later, Kamal came in and said, "Mrs. Ramer, I want to talk with you about something."

"What is it?"

"A woman on this compound says my husband is involved with one of the other wives. Do you know anything about it?"

"I've never heard any such thing," I reassured her. "Some people gossip. I've never seen him with any other woman."

"Well, it must just be gossiping, I guess."

A week later, Kamal came to me in a flood of tears. "I went to work, but I had forgotten some keys, so I went back home, and I found my husband with this other woman!"

Bob called Prasad in, and he couldn't deny it as his wife had found him in bed. Bob talked with him, and at Kamal's insistence, she and I were there, too. It came out that when Kamal had been at the hospital with Chota, before he had been healed, this woman had been making lunch for Prasad and taking it to him at his house. Then somehow they had gotten into a sexual situation.

When Chota got so ill with staticus, his father had a guilty conscience, so he came to me. I had had no idea at the time, but felt led to say that we must ask God to forgive us our sins. We each promised that whatever had been displeasing to the Lord, we would not do again, and we asked for strength not to do it.

About six months after Chota was healed, while Kamal was at work and the two older boys were in school, the liaisons had begun again, and it was at this time that Chota became so ill and died.

It seemed so awful, so horribly unfair, to think that a child would die as punishment to the father. But I remembered the story of King David, who watched Bathsheba bathing when he was on the roof of his castle, brought her up and had sex with her, and arranged for her husband to be killed. When she had a baby, King David did everything he could for the child, but still the child died.

Bob had to ask Prasad to leave, and Kamal felt she had to leave, too, saying, "I cannot go around here and hold my head up. Everybody knew about this but me and this woman's husband." The other woman and her husband had six kids, and Bob thought it was not our business to tell her husband, so we didn't.

***

The Health Centre remained very busy, and I needed to find another nurse. The situation was desperate because another five years had passed, and we were due to go on furlough again.

I prayed so hard for a nurse, and did everything I could to find one, but public health was looked down on in those days, and we couldn't get nurses or even a midwife. I needed a midwife nurse because with Miraj hospital five miles away over rough road we still did many deliveries in the homes. Dr. Evans was very good at doing the antenatal and postnatal clinics, but he was in Miraj, too far away to do the deliveries.

Kamal had already left when one day there was a knock at my door. When I opened it, I saw a small, wiry, grey-haired woman who looked like someone's grandmother. "I'm Hirabai Sawadekar."

"Oh?"

"I heard that you needed a nurse. I've just retired from the J. J. Hospital in Bombay."

"That is one of the biggest hospitals in Bombay! How long were you there?"

"Twenty-five years."

"Where did you train?" She had trained at a mission hospital, St. Luke's in Vengurla, under Sister Margaret Craig, and had all the papers to prove it, but I wondered if such a wisp of a woman was up to the task.

"It's a lot of walking. The position is public health nurse."

"That's what I want to do. I'm tired of Bombay, I have a pension, and I want to do mission."

I was a little unsure because she spoke very colloquial Marathi, but she certainly was a trained nurse, and we desperately needed someone, so I said, "OK, we'll try you." We later learned that she was one of the most beloved nurses in that Bombay hospital.

"Hirabai" means diamond, and she proved to be a diamond in the rough, a gem of a person. Though she had worked in Bombay, she had been born in a village and still had the stamp of a village woman on her, including a tremendous lot of common sense. I took her on, and she lived in a little room in the back of our house and worked at the centre, where the women just loved her. They all called her Adji, which means grandmother, because she treated them like their own grandmothers did. If the women weren't doing what she wanted them to, she'd give them a cuff on the side of the arm—or the head! And they all just took it without complaint. One of the things we were always pushing for was to get the women to keep their houses clean, and the cooking and eating vessels washed. Hirabai would go into their houses and say, "Why aren't you doing this? Why don't you do that?"

Hirabai also knew a lot of village women's cures for problems. For example, when the babies were teething, she told the mothers to soak the leaves of a particular plant in water, dip a cloth in the water, and then let the baby suck the cloth. I was very careful about village remedies, and checked this one with the pharmacist and with the doctor in Miraj, who approved the remedy.

Now there were two Hirabais working at the clinic—Hirabai Gorde, who had been there since before I arrived, and now Hirabai Sawadekar. "Bai" is the honorific added to a woman's name, and "Hira" means "diamond." Hirabai Gorde was fairly tall and heavily built, a quiet, faithful, and honest woman whose husband worked in the court, so she was one diamond. Now with the new Hirabai, I used to say, "I'm so rich now; I have two diamonds."

When the boys came to the clinics, they used to tease Hirabai Sawadekar, but she teased them right back and treated those boys like they were her grandsons. She *did* have a bad habit of spitting. You couldn't help laughing at her because she'd be lecturing about keeping things clean, and in the midst of it she would go spit outside. But she had a heart of gold, she was a good nurse, and so she took over for me when I was going away.

***

Hirabai's arrival solved one big problem that stood between us and our 1960 furlough, but there were many other issues to be resolved before we sailed. Ever since we had come to Sangli, we had had a man named Gundappa helping in the garden. Gundappa was an old man who didn't really know much about gardening, but he watered the plants, washed the floors, and carried in water. At first we had tried to grow vegetables, but we had given up on that because they always disappeared just before they were truly ripe. We were on a compound with school kids passing by all the time, so we just got used to that. Still, what we did have had to be tended to, and Gundappa was very ill.

Once again Hirabai Sawadekar came to the rescue. She brought a young man to us and said, "This is my nephew, and he works in the villages. Will you take him on as your gardener?" She vouched for his honesty, so that was settled.

Furlough always brought a great upheaval, but we found each time that things would eventually fall into place. The Seiberts were taking over the school, and we received the welcome news that Lois and Jerry, a paediatric specialist, and their three children were coming to stay in our house while we were gone. At last, everything was settled in India.

The remaining problem was that we still didn't have a house in America to stay in. The Mission Board didn't handle this; this is something we had to arrange for ourselves. Then we got a letter from Pappy Ramer saying that the church was building a house for the pastor. The basement of the house was finished, so Pappy and Grandma Ramer would live there, and we could live in their home, the house on Yates Street where Bob had grown up.

At last we were ready, and the day came when we boarded an Anchor Line ship and sailed for England. It was such a relief to get on the ship, to have all the packing done, all the staffing attended to, all the injections done, all the kids' clothes for Scotland with us, and all the other clothes and our household goods on their way directly to America.

***

Travelling by ship was thoroughly wonderful. At night we could leave the children in their room because a stewardess would sit in the corridor and call us on the loudspeaker if the children cried or needed attention. This left us free to roam the ship because we were always within reach of "Mrs. Ramer, call back to cabin. Jody is crying." Jody, at that point, spoke only Marathi, which complicated things a bit.

We were met at Liverpool by my brother Blair, his wife Muriel, and their children Dorothy, who was in her teens, and Nigel, who must have been 10 or 11. Muriel was quite a wonderful cook, so meals at their house were quite marvellous. One night, Bob and I offered to make an Indian meal for everyone, including friends our niece and nephew wanted to invite. We dressed the girls in saris and Nigel in a dhoti, the loincloth worn by Hindu men, but he didn't like it, saying it was too much like a nappy. Our guests sat on the floor, and we served them curry and rice on big leaves. Everyone seemed to enjoy it well enough, but Robbie just *loved* it. When he was finished, he greatly embarrassed me by rubbing his tummy and saying, "Now *that's* what I call a *real* dinner!"

From there we went up to Scotland, where we stayed with Mom and Dad Forrest, my adopted parents from my days at St. Colm's. Blair and Muriel came, too, so there we were, back in Scotland with the family. Bob rented a camping vehicle, a van built with bunks and bench seats that folded out. With three children, it worked well except that it was mighty cold in Scotland.

One especially cold, wet night, Mrs. Forrest said, "You know, you can all sleep here in the bedroom. Nancy, you and Bob can be in the big bed, and the three children can be on the floor." But Robbie and Lyn wanted to sleep in the camper, so Bob stayed with them, while Jody and I slept nice and cosy at the Forrests'. You should have heard Bob's description of his night—everyone cold and shivering, awake and needing the bathroom. There was little sleep in the camper that night, and Jody and I had no regrets.

On July 7, 1960, we sailed from Southampton for the U.S., where we travelled across country, visiting churches in towns and cities such as Warren, Indianapolis, Ft. Calhoun, Wray, Ekley, Denver, Leadville, Albuquerque, Casper, and Monterey. Bob, especially, had a demanding schedule, accepting as many opportunities as possible to tell about the work people's mission gifts made possible.

One day, before seatbelts were in common use, Bob, two-year-old Jody, and I were driving through Denver when Jody cried to be up front with me, crawling over the seat and into my lap. I was helping her, so I saw nothing when an inattentive woman in a big Oldsmobile ran a red light. In a split second, I yelled to my husband, "We are hit!" and tightened my arms around Jody as the Olds smashed our little Volkswagen bug between it and a Cadillac. I was thrown from the car, and woke up lying along the road, glass and blood everywhere.

The ambulances came quickly. Jody had also been knocked out when her head smashed into my face but, fortunately, she had no serious injuries. Bob suffered superficial facial cuts and bruises and an injury to his arm, which was twisted in the wreckage. That Volkswagen model year was the first to have a collapsible steering wheel, a fact that probably saved Bob's life. My face was badly bashed up. My nose was broken, my upper jaw was broken in two places, and my left cheekbone had been crushed into tiny pieces. Worst of all, my left eye drooped out of its socket!

I wove in and out of consciousness. Every time I came to, I'd tell everyone around me—good Samaritans, ambulance workers, doctors—"allergic to morphine, two months pregnant, group O blood." When I came to in the hospital, once again I said as loudly as I could manage, "allergic to morphine, two months pregnant, group O blood!"

A policeman leaned over me and said, "We know, you've told us five times already!"

Having gone to a neighbour's after school, Robbie and Lyn were watching TV news when Robbie recognized our car in the story about the accident and went running to the neighbour in the kitchen. Bob's parents arrived as soon as they could, and Bob called Carol Bohnet, our old friend and Bob's former girlfriend, who came and stayed with Jody in the children's ward.

A doctor in emergency removed the radio knob that had become embedded in my leg. The plastic surgeon, Dr. Mammal, spent eight hours putting my face back together. In an amazing connection, he would later come to Miraj as a volunteer surgeon serving people who had leprosy. I was very fortunate. Amazingly, my eyes eventually returned to normal, and I was able to read and drive again.

Thus it was that in 1961, in Denver, Colorado, I became an American citizen, not standing proudly for the ceremony, but sitting in a wheelchair, very grateful to be alive.

I was so thankful that my pregnancy continued without incident, despite the trauma to my body. It would be my last pregnancy. When I had seen Dr. Whitely in October, he had diagnosed some pre-cancerous cells in my uterus and encouraged me to have a hysterectomy. Though Bob was firm that my health was most important, we really wanted a fourth child, so we struck a deal with Dr. Whitely. A pregnancy would inhibit further growth of the cells. Dr. Whitely agreed that a hysterectomy could be delayed if I were pregnant again by January, provided I give him my written promise to have a hysterectomy at the time of that future delivery, and so it was.

With our car demolished, we were even more grateful for the gift of a Chevy truck from the Wyoming Presbytery. With the children, luggage for five, and the mattresses in the back covered by a camper top, we drove from Denver to New York. In New York we boarded the *Queen Elizabeth* to sail to England, and from there it was on to India by ship, for Robbie had to be at Kodai to begin school on June 1.

***

Back in India, we were quickly absorbed in our work. The government was very pleased with our work in public health, and we struck an agreement. We missionaries would establish health centres if the government would take them over in three years. One of the first communities we approached was Kawlapur, where there was a particular need for prenatal and midwifery care. The townspeople were eager to have us and provided free water and a building in the heart of the city. Mrs. Sheik, who had been at the Sangli Health Centre for years, went down by bus every day to provide services.

Mrs. Sheik had come to us from very difficult circumstances. Her parents lived in south India in the early 1900s, and had been Brahmans before becoming Christians. Sadly, her father died, and in those days it was common for the widow and any girl children to be turned out into the streets. Somehow the mother, Mrs. Irrons, was able to take her son, as well as her daughter, when she was forced out. Together they walked hundreds of miles to Poona, where there was a Mukti women's mission that took in widows and orphans and tried to find husbands for the widows.

Mrs. Irrons ended up marrying a carpentry master from Sangli, and the children went on to very productive lives. The boy went to school, then on to college, eventually earning a Ph.D. and becoming principal of Wilson College, one of the most prestigious colleges in all of India. Like her mother, the girl, Salomibai, married a young carpentry master, Mr. Sheik, a teacher at Sangli. Sadly, both of the couple contracted TB. He died and she recovered, but had no way to earn a living. An earlier missionary, Mrs. Brown, had asked me to take her on at the centre, which I did.

In her work at Kawlapur, Mrs. Sheik found that something odd was happening. "There are so many poor women here. I go out to visit their homes, and they're all very friendly, but only a few come to bathe their children at the centre, and I don't know why." Bathing and keeping a clean house are the first principles for avoiding disease, but no one was taking advantage of our free water.

I finally asked one of the neighbourhood women, "Why do you not bring your baby to get bathed? You come in yourself and get medicine, but you won't bathe your baby."

"Well," she said, "we don't want to make them Christians."

"That doesn't make them a Christian," I said.

"Yes, it does. Everybody knows when you pour water over a baby's head, that baby becomes a Christian, and there's nothing you can do about it."

"No, you haven't heard right," I said, and proceeded to explain baptism. "At our centre, you bathe the baby yourself. But to baptise a baby, the baby comes with his father and mother to the church, in front of the members, and the parents say that they want the baby to be baptised. Then the pastor takes the baby and puts water on his head. He doesn't *bathe* the baby." When that message got around the mostly Hindu women, dozens of mothers began bathing their children at the centre.

Soon other villages were clamouring to have centres, but that took money. Then Dr. Ted Stevenson, medical director for all Presbyterian work overseas, came as a short-term volunteer in Miraj to relieve Dr. Fletcher, and to see for himself what was going on in the mission field. He and his wife Bunny came 'round to our Health Centre, visited in the homes with us, and visited the Kawlapur centre.

"This," Dr. Stevenson said, "is the future of medicine—public health. I am going to see that we raise money so that you can get clinics in the villages. *You*," he said to me, "write up a proposal."

So I wrote up a grant request that included regular visits from the doctors at Miraj Hospital. As it was, several of the doctors came when they could, but if no car was available, they might be late. Mothers might wait with children, then have to leave in order to get water for the night, missing their appointments.

Just as I was writing the proposal, Dr. Evans resigned as medical superintendent at Miraj because of eye problems. He was a professor of gynaecology and obstetrics, and had been my doctor in the early days. Because of his diminishing sight, he couldn't see well enough to do surgery, so he was retiring. With hope, I asked this highly esteemed doctor, "Would you come and be our public health doctor?"

His wife was offended. "Don't you realize he was a *professor* of obstetrics? How can you ask him to do public health?"

But Dr. Evans said, "Nancy, years ago, before I ever became a missionary, I was a family practitioner, and I love doing that work. This is what I think God wants me to do." So Dr. Gene Evans was put in charge of the public health program for the whole district, headquartered in Wanless Hospital, often called Miraj Hospital. True to his word, Dr. Stevenson raised money to support the grant, and on his furlough Dr. Evans raised money for our own very fine public health jeep, so he was able to go regularly to clinics.

Dr. Evans became the cornerstone of Village Health Service (VHS), as it was called, and it was wonderful to see the program develop. He went from village to village in his blue and white jeep, driven by Mohan Londe, a motor mechanics graduate of SIS, Sangli Industrial School. Mohan was a great partner. He could drive anywhere, and he maintained and repaired the jeep. Dr. Evans became quite beloved in the villages because he understood the village women and had great love and compassion for them.

Well aware of the contribution that good nutrition makes to health, Dr. Evans was always looking for practical and inexpensive sources of nourishment. The villagers' staple was a healthy flatbread made of milo grain. Peanuts were a popular crop in the area, and Dr. Evans urged villagers to eat peanuts in other forms, such as peanut butter, which was very healthy and could be spread on their bread. So with great affection, they all called him "Dr. Shengani," "*Dr. Peanuts.*"

Dr. Evans built up the Village Health Service, increasing the staff so that there were nurse midwives in all six clinics. Dr. Evans had a public health engineer on his staff because one of our big problems was sanitation. Smoke from the indoor fires was another problem, so we tried to give the villagers smokeless chulas. I served on the VHS committee and continued to manage the Sangli Health Centre, but it was all part of Dr. Evans's work. Eventually, it came time for this wonderful, compassionate man to retire.

When Dr. Evans retired, all the villages had great farewell events. On the day of Sangli's farewell, we had prepared a special program for him in Shantinagar. My friend Margaret Salumke, who was the night nurse in Miraj Hospital, had the day off, so she came to join us for the celebration. The plan was that after the event in Shantinagar, we would come back to my house to change before going to a big farewell tea at the Rotarians, which was to be followed by dinner at our house.

Just as I was getting ready to go, Shalini, the wife of our cook Sugandh, went into labour. I went to her house and sat with her, but her labour wasn't progressing, and I knew I had to go down to the centre because I was in charge of the function. So Margaret, also a midwife, said she would stay with Shalini at Sugandh's house, so that I could go down to the program at Shantinagar.

Just as Dr. Evans was rising to thank everybody, Bob arrived on his scooter and said, "You've got to come quick! Sugandh's been burned!" So I jumped on the back of his scooter, and we dashed home at full speed.

At the house, we had a stove we'd brought from America, and it was connected to a gas tank. Sugandh knew how to use it, but he had been careless. He'd tried to light the oven, but it didn't catch at first. While he took time to find another match, the gas collected in the oven, and when he approached it with the match, the gas had blown up. I went tearing into the house!

Meanwhile, a crowd including Sugandh's parents had collected by my clinic door, and everyone was saying, "Oh, Sugandh's been burned! Sugandh's burned!" Having been taught in Edinburgh about putting mentholated spirits on the scalded parts, I put it all over Sugandh's face, carefully avoiding his eyes. His face, his arms right up to his shoulders, and a little bit of his chest were burned. Fortunately, they were only second-degree burns, so with the mentholated spirits and the worst spots covered with wet cotton wool, Sugandh felt much better. We gave him some tea, and something for the pain, and I kept him lying there quietly because, at that point, there was no way to get him to the hospital. All this time, Margaret had been at Sugandh's house delivering his wife's baby! Suddenly, she burst into the house to announce, "It's a girl!"

"Oh, no, not another girl! This is my bad luck day!" moaned Sugandh. "I get burned, and then I have a *daughter!*"

"Sugandh, don't say that," I said. "She's a lovely little girl, and she was delivered safely."

Then Dr. Evans arrived, took a look at Sugandh, and said, "He doesn't really need to go to hospital. You've done well, just keep him lying there." After checking on Shalini, Dr. Evans was getting into the van when I reminded him he'd planned to change clothes before the Rotary reception. "Oh, yes," he said, "I'd forgotten," but in getting back out of the van he fell and scraped his hands and nose. So it was back to the clinic room to patch him up before sending him on his way.

Then Margaret asked me, "Will you come and see Shalini?"

Thank goodness, by this time Hirabai had arrived and said, "I will clean up the baby and see to the house, Margaret. You go help Madamsahib—she's having 12 people to dinner." So Margaret and I went into the kitchen, leaving Sugandh—the cook for our dinner party—sleeping on the guest room bed. Margaret and I busily prepared for the dinner guests while Ayah bathed Lyn and Jody.

Bob had arrived home and was getting supper ready for the kids when Sugandh walked out and said, "I feel a lot better now. I'm going to help you."

In those days all the missionaries had cooks, and when you went to dinner at another missionary's house, you sent the cook ahead to help the host cook. So one of the cooks from Miraj arrived, and he said, "Mrs. Ramer, I'll take over from here," then to Sugandh, "You just sit down there and tell me what to do."

With sudden realization, I said to Sugandh, "You haven't seen your new daughter yet! Come on, we're going to see your new baby." Despite his initial reaction, he was very touched when he saw his delicate new daughter.

By the time we returned, it began to seem that things might be under control. We all were dressed and had the table set when Dr. and Mrs. Evans and the other missionaries arrived from the tea in Miraj. As we sat down at the table, Dr. Evans looked at me and said, "How many days do you have like this, Nancy? This was fantastic! I shall *never* forget my last day in Sangli!"

We were very glad that the day ended happily. All through this chaos, I had been praying, "Make Sugandh be all right, let the baby be all right. May Dr. Evans not have had a head injury from falling on his nose." Now there was a beautiful new baby, Sugandh would be all right, and thanks to the extra cook, even dinner went smoothly. It all worked out, and we had a wonderful time.

Before Dr. Evans left, he had taken on Dr. M. N. Kamle to replace him in Village Health Services. Dr. Kamle was an older man, a graduate of Miraj who had worked in the village clinics. He was a very quiet and Godly man, and he often took Hirabai Sawadekar with him to talk to the women. Over time, we were able to get nurses and midwives who would stay in the villages.

This was all overseen by the VHS committee, which I was asked to chair. I was the first chair who was not a doctor, and I served for many years. As part of VHS, we had Eric Ram, who was a public health engineer and brought many projects and ideas. After five years, he went on to earn his Ph.D., but he returned to VHS to work for another five years. As people moved on, others rose to take their places, so the work in the villages went on.

Shantinagar had expanded to become a training centre. We were also teaching in the government schools, where our nurse taught simple community health measures to the children. Much of this work was supported by the chapters of Presbyterian Women in the U.S. From all different churches, women were sending money through our board to support this work in the villages. It was a critical time in the health history of Sangli District because we would come in and start clinics, which the government would then take over, allowing us to move further out and start more clinics. We all felt that this was part of our call from God.

As the government took over, their plan was to have a main resource hospital where everything was done. Then 10 miles away would be a health centre, and another five miles away, in four directions, would be sub-centres with nurse midwives. They gradually went on through the whole district with centres and sub-centres, so that Maharashtra has a very good health program.

With the health centres incorporated into Miraj Hospital as part of VHS, I was free of that responsibility. Eric brought in another doctor, Dr. Kalindi Thomas, who took over as the work spread and Dr. Kamle retired.

It was a joy to have Kalindi Thomas with us. Her father had been the first Indian administrator of Miraj Hospital. I'd known Kalindi since she was a baby, and here she was working in the community health system. She went on to Johns Hopkins in Baltimore, Maryland, where she earned her master's in public health, and came back to lead the program, working in Miraj for 23 years.

Dr. Cherian Thomas, Kalindi's husband, was director of Miraj Medical Centre. Eric Ram went on to become International Director of Global Health Programs for the World Vision Partnership, working with the United Nations.

It's exciting to see how God can start with a few missionaries giving out milk to starving children and expand it into a system of health care clinics, and how people who served in our area have gone on to bring better health to people all over the world.

Chapter 17: Lizard in the Curry Pot

Robbie was not quite nine years old on 1 June, his first day of boarding school at Kodai. I cried buckets about sending my little boy away, especially because I was pregnant and couldn't go along to help him settle in. It was all made worse when his birthday parcel arrived too late for his 23 June birthday.

By August, though, things were looking up. When Timothy James was born 25 August 1961, in Sangli, Bob declared it "Christmas in August!" Dr. Fletcher and Dr. Mazarello delivered Tim by Caesarean, and performed the necessary hysterectomy. At the time, Robbie was in the Kodai infirmary with chicken pox, but the nurse later told me that he jumped up and down on his bed when he received the telegram with news of his wee brother. He then proceeded to tell everyone he saw, "I've got a brother!"

Then there was more good news—we would be allowed to import to India the truck, though not the camper top, given us by the Wyoming Presbytery. We never experienced anything like the terrible Denver accident in India, but transportation there was a challenge nonetheless. When I married Bob and moved to Sangli, it was a small rural town of 88,000, and I was surprised to find the roads almost as crowded as in Poona, with perhaps even more cows and water buffalo!

Except for the scooter, the only vehicle we had access to in Sangli was a U.S. military Jeep left over from World War II, and we were one of three families authorized to drive it, and then only for village mission work. It was a sombre brown with a canvas top and plastic doors and windows. Sturdy, but not very comfortable, that four-wheel-drive vehicle would get you through almost anything, but how our bones ached after a day out in the villages! For our local transport, we used bicycles.

We had many adventures in that Jeep. During the rainy season, little rivulets or dry riverbeds, called wadas, would swell into rivers. One day, while driving to a large village, we came to a dip in the road and found that it was now a river 50 meters wide! In ordinary times this was a dry riverbed with paved road running across it, but not now. Knowing there was a paved road under the water, Bob asked some men sitting on the bank, "Has any traffic gone through this wada today?"

All four men looked surprised at the question, and said, "A truck just went through," so we forged ahead, only to get stuck right in the middle. All seven of us climbed out into water up to our thighs, and tried to push it out, but the Jeep was stuck!

Bob called out to the four village men, "Can you get a bullock to pull us out?" After friendly, but lengthy, bartering, the four produced two big buffalos, hitched them to the Jeep, and pulled us out. As Bob paid the farmers, he asked, "How come a truck got through, and we got stuck?"

Smiling, the eldest replied, "Oh, the truck got stuck. We pulled it out, too! This is a good day for us!"

That good old Jeep was with us for 25 years. To celebrate the Jeep's anniversary, our staff painted it silver, a bright, dazzling aluminium silver! You had to wear sunglasses to break the glare. The mechanic students loved to drive her and polish her up. After the arrival of the American Chevrolet truck for use in village work, the beloved silver Jeep was devoted to teaching the Industrial School students how to drive. The canvas top, the doors, and the windows were all worn out, but she still had the most important parts—a good horn and good brakes!

With so many village churches to visit, it took Bob a long time to get around to them all. One Christmas wasn't properly celebrated until February! In a circular in 1963, Bob wrote about that "Christmas" visit to Umalwad:

"As part of Christmas celebration, they had a cycle race and a bullock cart race. The races were to be over a course of five miles, and they thought that it would be a good idea if our truck would pace the bullocks. They assured me it was a good road (good for what, they did not say). At first it was easy, we started off on a smooth road and by going about 20 mph got well ahead of the carts. Then the people in the back [of the truck] wanted to see the carts and told me to slow down, but others, who were afraid the carts would catch up to us, told me to hurry on. So I looked in the rear vision mirrors and kept just ahead.

"Then I saw a big curve ahead and hurried and stopped just beyond the curve so that we could get some pictures. They seemed to slowly approach, and then all of a sudden were almost on us! The people in the back of the truck started to hammer on the body, which was the signal to hurry up, and I did. But then went into a very rough "road," and it was difficult to go even ten miles an hour. The bullocks were catching up! Fortunately, the road got a bit better and so I pulled ahead. But then we came to a very rocky bit, and I had to slow down. The managers of the race began to shout at me, and to bang the car, telling me to hurry up, but all I could do was to go slowly crawling over the rocks. By the time we got to the top, the bulls were almost breathing down our necks. Then at last it was a straight run over the prairie!

"The first cart in the race led the others by a good furlong. Bu there was an exciting race for second place, with the men standing in the carts and whipping the bullocks, and the iron tires striking sparks on the stones and everyone shouting at the top of their voices!"

***

In Sangli City there were only two M.D.'s. One, Dr. R.V. Desai, a Brahman, lived across the street from us. His sister-in-law, Dr. Asharani Desai, a lovely person and also Brahman, was a lady doctor who lived on the other side of town. Both became great friends of ours.

As a young woman, Asharani had shown herself to be very clever. Her mother was a widow, so the rani (wife of the raja) of Sangli took it upon herself to see that Asharani received a good education. There were very few women doctors then, Asharani was the first in all of Sangli District.

Asharani had her lady clinic in the centre of the city in a good area. In the same building were the male clinic offices of Dr. Desai, and the pharmacy of his brother, Mr. R.V. (Raubhau) Desai, who was trained as a chemist. Both of the Desai brothers were R.V. Desai, as was often done in India. Children and wives would have the father's name as their middle name, so they would all have the same middle initial.

Because I was married to Bob, I was Nancy Robert Ramer, and Tim was Timothy Robert Ramer to the Indians. That's why they thought it so strange that I called my first son "Robert," because to them that made him "Robert Robert Ramer." Because of this naming custom, all the kids in an Indian family would have the same middle name, and many parents liked to give their children first names beginning with the same letter. That was a fashion among the Brahmans.

Mr. Desai was the eldest sibling in the family and a highly trained chemist. He was already married to a Brahman woman and had children with her when he and Asharani fell in love. Although Mr. Desai was already married, he and Asharani were able to marry because at that time Hindus could still have two or three wives, though it was frowned upon.

In 1954, it became illegal for Hindus to have more than one wife, but Muslims could have up to four. There were three different sets of marriage laws for Christians, Hindus, and Muslims. Divorce was easy for Muslim men, impossible for Hindus, and almost impossible for Christians. In lieu of divorce, Christians just separated and remarried without bothering to register, but there was very little of that.

Like most, the chemist's first marriage was an arranged marriage. After he and Asharani got married, he would spend some nights in her apartment and some with his first wife. Although the rani had brought Asharani up like a daughter and loved her dearly, she was extremely angry about this marriage, and refused to have anything more to do with Asharani.

Asharani was a wonderful woman, a devout Hindu, whom I greatly respected because she would treat untouchable women. She would come down to my clinic to see them, but she couldn't have them in her own clinic because then the Brahman women wouldn't come in. Asharani and I became friends over the plight of the poor women we saw in the clinic. Many had 15 or 16 children, and the mothers were exhausted wrecks. Most looked like old women by the time they were 30. Many of those depleted mothers and many of their babies died of malnutrition. So Asharani and I started family planning in Sangli.

When you're in the midst of conditions like that, you realize God has given us information and brains, and he wants us to *use* them. We never advocated abortion, but we were eager to help Indian people learn what Westerners were doing to control the size of their families. It was a great privilege to be able to help these women.

As there came to be more doctors in Sangli, a monthly medical meeting was held. At these meetings, they used to tease Asharani and me because no one else provided family planning. There were the homeopathic doctors and ayurvedic doctors, too, but they were all men, and none would even consider offering family planning to their patients.

So Asharani and I got in touch with the Bombay Family Planning Association. We had women doctors come down and discuss it with us, with the Health Centre nurses, and with the Miraj nurses. When we reported on these classes at the medical meetings, the doctors would laugh and say, "Oh, Asharanibai and Nancybai, you're just meeting to have an excuse for a cup of tea and a chat."

But eventually family planning spread in Sangli, and the government gave every encouragement. We began to see women having just six children, and then just four. Then the government tried to get them down to two children, but it was never forced upon them in our district or in our state.

However, in north India I understand that they were forcing family planning. There the government gave large grants for family planning work, and it became interwoven with the politics of the area. For example, teachers were required to get their students' parents to go to family planning clinics or be sterilized, or the teachers wouldn't receive their monthly pay. There was competition for compliance because municipalities received double the grant if they showed great advances in the work. Indira Gandhi lost the election because of that program in north India, and the whole program had to be stopped.

That was one of the stupidest programs I ever heard of, and I am very grateful that I never had to have anything to do with that. We already had family planning in our health centres when the government wanted to extend family planning into the villages. The municipal doctor in charge asked me if I would go out with their team. They had obtained loop IUDs from America, and they wanted me to teach the women. That loop effort was a failure in our area because there was haemorrhaging. We realized it very soon, and that program was stopped.

Still, we switched to other methods and persevered. I went with them to the villages for a number of years, maybe once or twice a week, because they didn't have lady doctors, so they wanted me to talk to the women. In the villages, they would identify a highly respected woman who wasn't trained in health care, but who could read and write. She would then be taught about family planning so that she could go from home to home, discussing it with the women in the villages. These women didn't give out any contraceptives; they just talked with the women and would go with them when the doctors held clinics in the villages.

Women were encouraged to go to the hospital to give birth. The guideline was that after three children a woman would be encouraged to become sterilized, but there was no force, only incentives. If a woman volunteered to be sterilized after her third child, she was given free hospital treatment, free clothes for the baby, and ten days' wages before she went home.

A man could be sterilized if he had at least three children and requested a vasectomy. The procedures were carefully done under sterile conditions. When the simple procedure was over, the man was given a transistor radio. There was no such thing as TV, and radio was just coming in, so it was a significant incentive. When a man returned for his check-up a month later, he was given 100 rupees, which was quite a lot of money.

All this was done because the need was so desperate. Families were already struggling to feed the children they had, and then another one would come along. They lived in such crowded houses, and worked from morning to night.

My time working in family planning was a wonderful time of getting to know people and of discussing all the ways we could bring better health and better living conditions to the people living in the area. My family planning work was unpaid, but it was a great opportunity for me to work with the government and the private doctors in our neighbourhood to improve people's lives.

Sometimes I am asked how we could keep going in the face of so much poverty and such pervasive need. So often in the health centres we saw babies who died because they were just too tiny. They didn't have enough food, and in the rainy season they were often cold and wet, so many got pneumonia. With a baby, one night with pneumonia is enough; they go very quickly. But we kept going because we could see that we were making a difference there. We started immunizations. We provided antenatal and postnatal care in the clinics, and midwifery and visits in the home. I'd been trained in public health and midwifery, and I used every bit of my training.

***

On 8 September 1962, a border dispute resulted in Chinese troops invading India, crossing the "McMahon line" on India's north-eastern border. All of us were shocked by the Chinese invasion, which occurred during the biggest festival of the year, Divali. When the National Defence

Society was organized in the district, the people of Sangli were quick to join. Naturally, I was on the First Aid Committee. I taught a class in a local doctor's office to 21 women of various faiths. Three of my students were grandmothers. It was a keen class to teach, so eager to understand, so sympathetic to my struggle for the correct Marathi word.

Fortunately, the military action never made it as far as Sangli. I was very proud of both of my countries, the U.K. and the U.S., who helped stop the fighting by threatening to come in if China didn't withdraw, which they did.

***

All too soon, it was time for Lyn's first year at boarding school in Kodai. Although I still had Jody (4½) and Timmy (1½) at home, it was hard to send Lyn, particularly after receiving letters such as this one from Rob, writing of a hike he and some other students took to climb Pillar Rocks with the aid of a rope:

"One slip and you could fall to your death. I nearly had a serious accident for I slipped, but I caught the rope with my hands and held on tight and Steve pulled me up. My hands are all cut with the rope, but that's all." All I could do was remind myself that they were in God's hands.

There was plenty to worry about at home, too. For a year, due to furloughs and whatnot, we Ramers would be the only missionaries in Sangli. In addition, due to drought, there was rationing of sugar, white flour, wheat, semolina, and rice. It was a harder year than most without our fellow missionaries.

***

By 1964, our boys' hostel was larger than ever before, with more than 60 boys. Most were SIS students, but 20 were college students. One evening about 8 p.m., three of our students ran up to our front door, where they shoved a banana leaf into my hand. "We've been poisoned! Look!" When I gingerly examined the leaf, I found a well-cooked, very dead lizard. After 60 boys had eaten their supper, the boys on kitchen duty had found the lizard in the bottom of the pot!

Hard on the heels of the first three boys came groups of others, crying, "We've been poisoned! Help us or we'll die!" On all sides of us, boys were putting their fingers down their throats, and making horrible noises in the hope of being sick. Not long before, ten people had died after a Bombay wedding at which a poisonous lizard had gotten into the curry.

During all this confusion, my mind was racing: What did one do for lizard poisoning? Edinburgh Royal had given no teaching on lizards, but had drummed it into our heads to call a doctor. I ran across the street to Dr. Desai's house but, alas, he was not home. The whole hostel was in uproar. I sent off the three originals with their leaf and the poor wee lizard to Dr. Desai's office. While we awaited their return, Bob got some of the braver boys to go to study hall, and I gave some of the more timid boys sodium bicarbonate, while visions of 60 stomach washouts danced in my head.

In due course, doctor's answer came back: "Non-poisonous lizard. Relax. If hysterical, give sodium bicarb." On being reassured by the outstanding doctor of Sangli, the boys quieted down, though many seemed surprised to find themselves still alive next morning.

***

Like the clinic and the school, church life was busy, too. In November we celebrated Christian Home Week. I visited most of our villages, inspecting the homes of Christians for cleanliness, decorations, Bible, hymn books, etc. Each woman was given a small picture, and the best in the village got a large picture. The visits came at peanut harvest time, and we were showered with peanuts and sugar cane.

By early 1964 Ramchandra Bhandare, the boy once considered lower than buffalo dung, was now Rev. Bhandare, and he had returned to Sangli to take over the district. The Dilleners, too, were back to take over the college hostel, and the Seiberts were expected in July. Our time of responsibility for *all* of the missionary efforts in Sangli was over—until the 70s.

***

For Christmas 1964, I had volunteered to produce the Sunday School Christmas pageant. The pageant was a major Sangli event, drawing 600 to 700 people, including many non-Christians for whom the life of Christ was a new story. As usual, many of our actors failed to turn up for the practices. Nevertheless, on the night of the production, all seemed to be going well until the three wise men were to process from a room at the back of the hall.

"We Three Kings of Orient Are" sounded over the congregation—but no kings appeared! I tore 'round to the room where they were supposed to be, but they weren't there! I ran 'round the outside of our circular hall, but couldn't see them anywhere. I kept asking people where the wise men were. I was directed backstage but found only Herod and his soldiers. Finally, the hymn finished with no wise men in sight, but the program continued with other scenes.

After about 30 minutes or so, the curtain rose to show the cross on the stage, and our women were singing, "Were You There When They Crucified My Lord?" To my horror, I saw the three wise men start to process from the back of the hall! Frantically, I signalled them to turn back, but with eyes downcast they didn't see my signal. Just in the nick of time, an alert member of the audience near the back row grabbed the first wise man, held him back, and saved the day. It turned out that the "wise" men had gone to the wrong back room, and found themselves locked in!

It became a popular joke with the Industrial School boys. Whenever they saw me looking for something, usually my scissors in tailoring class, they would ask, "What are you looking for—another wise man?"

***

As spring approached, we once again made plans to leave Sangli on a working furlough. The children and I had gone to Kodai at the beginning of the hot season, while Bob remained in Sangli for the SIS graduation on the Wednesday before Easter. In our absence, a paediatrician and his family would live in our house while doing language study. Preparing the house for new inhabitants required some fast packing on Bob's part. He later confessed that on the day he left, he pulled his desk drawers out and just dumped them into a trunk!

For the first time in five years, our whole family was together for Easter. Then, by bringing Tim and Jody through Madras to Bombay, we were able to leave on furlough. We travelled on to Calcutta, where we boarded Japan Airlines headed for a year of visiting hospitals and health projects in other countries, then speaking to interested groups, which is called "deputation."

Bob later wrote of this trip, "We have seen people suffering from cultural shock, but our most acute experience of this was in reverse of the usual. When we were whisked aloft from Calcutta in Japan Airlines, we were suddenly in another world. Nor have we yet come down in any place resembling the place we left. Even the refugees in Hong Kong, and the impoverished of Korea, seemed a step ahead of those we knew in India. Yet in most places, the overall standard of living is nearer to that in India than that in the U.S.A. In the airplane we all devoured the more than ample airline meal, and it was so good not to have to think about rationing."

Our first stop was Thailand, from which we took off to tour mission schools, hospitals, and vocational projects in Hong Kong, Korea, and Japan. Old friends from seminary ran some of these projects, so there was a sense of reunion in places utterly new to us. Because I had so longed to go to China, it was a particular joy to visit Hong Kong.

In Japan, we travelled by bullet train, which isn't easy when you're travelling with four children, especially when one of them has a broken arm. Lyn's arm was bound up as the result of a tree swing, which broke only minutes after I had looked it over and pronounced it "safe enough, if you don't go too high." The train stops are very brief; so all six Ramers lined up with our bags, suitcases, cameras, toys, etc., ready to jump off as soon as the train stopped. Each time, the last person had just gotten out the door when the bells rang, and the train tore off to the next destination.

We were able to relax a bit when we got off in Tokyo. This was the train's final station, so we didn't have to hurry. Bob and Rob were at one end of the coach getting the luggage off, while the rest of us got off at the other end. When I saw the train cleaners get on, my Indian habits came to the fore, and I asked Lyn to go back on the train and look under the seats to see if we'd left anything. She no sooner got on the train than bells clanged, lights flashed, and the doors shut! I had visions of Lyn being whipped off to the unknown at 200 kilometres per hour!

I pounded on the door and screamed, but when a cleaner opened the door, there was no sign of Lyn! I couldn't get on and leave little Tim and Jody alone on the platform, so I held open the door and yelled, "Lyn, Lyn!" A crowd gathered to stare at this Herculean woman who was holding up Japan's fastest train!

Bob came back, looked on in astonishment, and calmly asked, "What's wrong?" Just then Lyn got out of the train by another door. By this time Jody and Timmy were screaming, too, and we three fell on Lyn weeping with joy, as if she'd barely escaped the jaws of death! Bob and Rob had no idea of what had happened, so they busied themselves with the luggage and tried to look as if they didn't know us.

We had a wonderful time in Japan, seeing what missionaries were doing to help the people in Hiroshima and visiting industrial schools and hospitals, but eventually it was time to sail to the U.S.A. Bob went to check in with the shipping company and came back to inform us, "Guess what? The engine is in dock in Kobe for repairs, and they may take up to five days."

"Bob," I said, quite alarmed, "we don't have enough money to stay here another five days." I didn't want to be a burden to those who had already hosted us, so I asked Bob to see if we could stay on board the ship while it was being repaired.

The answer was no, but to our delight, the ship's company offered to put us up at their expense in the Sheraton, a very nice hotel in Tokyo. They asked only that we not order the most expensive entrées at every meal. So off we headed for the Sheraton with our bashed-up luggage, a weird hat I'd bought in Thailand, and an assortment of other oddities. After staying six in one room at the YMCA, we were shown to two big bedrooms with a connecting door and a TV in each. The kids ran back and forth between the rooms, "What's on your TV? Guess what's on our TV!"

It was an unprecedented experience to have hotel rooms and all our meals paid for. After settling in, we went downstairs to the restaurant. We looked over the menu, and I asked the kids what they wanted. Tim was very fond of steak, so I asked him, "Do you want steak?" Tim smiled broadly, and to my embarrassment a shocked Rob yelled out, "Do you mean we don't have to have the cheapest thing on the menu here?"

It was such a treat. For our whole trip, we'd existed on "the cheapest thing on the menu." We stayed five days in that luxury hotel, and had just enough money to take a tour to Mt. Fujiyama.

We finally arrived in the U.S., bouncing from Honolulu to Los Angeles, then San Francisco, where we were welcomed by Bob's sister and her family, and Pappy Ramer's identical twin brother. From there it was on to

Vancouver to a wonderful Scottish welcome from my Uncle Jimmie, Aunt Kate, and cousins Nate and Kitty.

Travelling by way of Disneyland and the Grand Canyon, at last we landed in Colorado at the rented house in Westminster that would be our home base. We were so grateful to have a house to go to. In these pre-Internet days, it was no small feat to arrange the one-year rental of a house large enough for six people, especially from India.

Our time in Colorado was intensely busy. In a circular Bob later wrote, "In the first three months as Synod Interpreter in Colorado, I have tried to cover the first two of our four presbyteries and have travelled 7000 miles in Colorado, preaching in 19 morning services, had 27 evening slide programs, six session meetings, five women's and three young people's meetings. Spoken in seven schools and had four radio programs. Nancy has also spoken in more than 12 meetings, and even Robbie has presented his own slide program and the children have all spoken in more than a dozen Sunday Schools."

This deputation was a serious responsibility of missionaries because we needed to let people know what we were doing on the other side of the world. By the end of all those speaking engagements, Bob had travelled more than 20,000 miles in Colorado alone. Then, too, there were conferences, meetings, and courses on refrigeration technology to attend.

*** *** ***

We left Colorado happily anticipating a visit with Dr. Ted and Bunny Stevenson in New Jersey before leaving for Scotland. It was Ted who had come to Sangli and supported the expansion of services that became the Village Health Service.

When Dr. Stevenson met us in New York, he found himself with six Ramers, six suitcases, one air bag, two duffel bags, a record player, a tape recorder, and innumerable shoulder bags to transport. We barely managed to squeeze everyone and everything into Ted's car. The four children balanced on top of the luggage in the back seat, and Bob, Ted, and I sat in the front with our laps full of luggage. After that experience, Ted and Bob decided that when the time came to depart, we would need *two* taxis to take us to Kennedy Airport. When it came time to leave, two long, sleek, black Cadillac limousines with uniformed chauffeurs pulled up in front of the house! We Ramers stood in the Stevensons' baggage-strewn lawn and gaped. Finally Rob managed to ask, "Are those cars for us?" As the chauffeurs looked at us and all our bags, they appeared to be similarly incredulous. But soon both cars were loaded up, and as we drove off, we looked back to see the Stevensons convulsed in laughter as they waved goodbye to this "royal" procession. Without question, it was a stately drive to J.F.K.

After our transatlantic flight, we were happy to arrive in Prestwick, where we were met by—nobody, due to a glitch in communication, but we soon made our way. Once again we rented a camper to use for our Scottish travels, and made our way to the home of my adopted parents, the Forrests.

The kids were eager to try out the camper. Robbie graciously agreed to sleep at the house with me, so the younger kids could spend the first night in the camper. Or maybe he remembered the camper experience from our last sojourn in Scotland.

In a circular, Bob told it this way: "The camper was brand new and everything was stiff and hard to move, but eventually, I got the two younger ones in the uppers [bunks] and myself and Lyn in each of the lowers. Then Tim, our five-year-old, said he was afraid of falling out. So Lyn climbed into the upper, and Tim came down. Then a lot of giggling and after several stern warnings I fell asleep. Then woke to Lyn saying she was cold, so I said, 'Come down and get in with Tim!'

"Then just asleep again when BANG Timmy had fallen out. I got him up. But this had wakened Jody. She was also cold, I said, 'Come down!' She was truly chilled, and so I had her get into the bag with me. … She said it was too "squishy" and she was right, so I decided on another reshuffle, as Timmy was falling out again! So I put Jody and Tim together and gave my lower to Lyn and crawled into the upper. I drifted off to sleep but not for long [as] Timmy needed to go to the bathroom. … Relieved, he went back to his bed, and cold, I climbed back into the upper, and drifted off to sleep. But was soon awake, for I was now COLD on bottom and side. … So I kept turning over and over like a person in front of a fire till I was cold all around! But then mercifully it was beginning to be light. 5:00 a.m. and we had laid down to "sleep" at 11:00 p.m.! You remember the night before this was on the plane, and we lost five hours.

"Then to get up and dressed in clammy clothes, go and buy some bread, cereal, eggs, etc. Try to fold the bunks, set up the table, get the stove started, etc. etc. when one is stiff and sore! But the food restored to us enough strength to get back to Granny Forrest's and find Robbie and Nancy still comfortably in a warm bed with their tea being served to them there! I guess I just don't live right. The next four nights in the camper were much better (thanks to extra blankets from the Forrests) and I almost got over the backaches."

Scotland was a time of family and old friends, missionary teas, and meetings. We spent the last week with my brother, who was now Rector of Offord D'arcy and Offord Cluny. Since last I had seen him, Blair had given up a successful business career, gone to theological college, and become rector of his own churches.

Due to troubles in the Middle East, when we left London on 13 June, it was not to sail the Mediterranean and through the Suez Canal, but to sail all the way around Africa, past Capetown and Durban, and back to India.

Chapter 18: Rajamata in a Chevy Pickup

Soon all the children were going to school in Kodai, and though Bob and I missed them very much, they had each other. Fortunately, we kept in touch by letter. All Kodai students were required to write home every week, and our kids added to our circular letters, too. This was from 1968:

Jody: "At first I was homesick. … Then about two days after Dad left, Ann [Seibert] and I went down to Aunt Agnes's [a teacher's] house and had tea there. Then I didn't get so homesick. The most exciting part of boarding is getting parcels and letters. … I get parcels only on special occasions like Valentine's Day."

Lyn: "You may think that we have nothing to do, not having T.V., but far from it! Especially during hiking season … As Kodai is in the midst of hills and woods, most of the hikes are thru beautiful woods ending in sudden breathtaking views. My favourite hike is to Berijam lake about 13 miles from Kodai. … One of the most memorable hikes was down the Ghat (road down the mountain). Thirty miles in one night! We left at 6:00 p.m. and arrived at 5:00 a.m. We had to wait almost five hours in the heat for the return bus! Upon reaching the dormitory I fell asleep on the floor!"

Tim: "What I like best about Kodai is the horses. We can rent a horse to go round the lake for fifty cents. My favourite pony is Jimmy. … One day the mail man asked our Mom if she would look after a stray kitten … at first Mom said, "No," but then she changed her mind and gave it to me as an Easter present! I call the kitten 'Lion.'"

Rob: "I, Rob, am now in the end of my Sophomore year in Kodai School and that's not such an enviable position. The 10th grade is the year we are initiated into the High School Dorm. We are subjected to "tortures" from burlap undershirts and cold showers, to carrying weights around our neck, and measuring a three mile road with ten foot strings. Then to finish off our initiation week three of us risked life and limb on a mission to a nearby cliff to get orchids for upper classmen's dates."

***

Back in Sangli City, we were informed that Sangli Industrial School was now to be under the authority of the federal government rather than the state. Also, the two-year program was to be condensed into a one-year, 12-month program, which was a challenging transition to make. Except for two five-year stints when Jack Seibert was principal (1960-65 and 1970-75), Bob was principal of SIS from 1954 to 1984, and it seemed they were always trying to train more boys and make the money go further. Along with SIS, Bob was responsible for the boarding school hostel and the property at Kodai and in Sangli. When something unforeseen happened, such as the earthquake at Koyna, about 50 miles away, Bob often became involved in that, too. Though the earthquake left Sangli relatively untouched, SIS people were involved in the emergency relief work of rebuilding the villages.

I continued to chair the Village Health Service committee. The VHS had three clinics in villages in addition to the one in the city of Sangli. Each clinic had a resident nurse and was visited once a week by Dr. Kamle. At this point, Eric Ram, our public health engineer, was off in North Carolina, earning his master's degree in public health education.

***

We had a young raja (or king) in Sangli, and when he was married in Bombay, Bob and I were invited to attend. We didn't go because it was just when the children were coming home from Kodai. However, we did host an American-style wedding reception at our house for the raja and the new rani, complete with American-style wedding cake. It was attended by many of our colleagues as well as the local Peace Corps volunteers. We played games, including "the Ramer game," a complicated "Who would you like to be?" charades game that can be played in any mixture of languages. The handsome groom and beautiful bride looked like an exotic, fairy-tale couple, but the raja was, in fact, quite modern. He had a degree in engineering and taught in a Bombay technical school.

The mother of the young raja was very interested in the village health work, and one day she announced that she wanted to spend a day going to each clinic incognito. I pointed out that she wouldn't remain incognito for very long if we went in her chauffeur-driven car flying the raja's flag. So Her Highness the Rajamata climbed into our battered Chevy truck and came with me to the Sangli Centre. At each village the patil, or headman, entertained us, and the rajamata took a deep interest in the peoples' condition and in what was being done for them. She had a delightful sense of humour, and Dr. Kamle, Mohan (the driver), and I thoroughly enjoyed our day with her. Her Highness also seemed to enjoy her tour immensely, and she was so impressed that she made plans to start a similar centre on the other side of town where there was a great need.

***

Because of my experience establishing health care centres in India, I was invited to speak at a Peace Corps conference at the fancy Bombay hotel, Sun and Sands, which had a private beach and a swimming pool. I was invited for the full three days of the conference, but could only be there for a day and a half because of VHS board meetings. It grieved my Scottish soul to give up free nights at a luxury hotel, but perhaps it was just as well—the rich food kept me up most of the night with diarrhoea and vomiting. I made my public addresses as scheduled, but probably more important were the bull sessions with the young volunteers, answering their questions—practical, moral, and spiritual. These young volunteers weren't always very well prepared to be effective in the vastly different places where they found themselves, but under the long hair and hippie clothes, they were idealistic youngsters who wanted to do something for the world.

***

We were not always in the exalted realms of rajas and the Sun and Sands Hotel. Sangli's little group of people with leprosy, also called Hansen's disease, now numbered more than 100. The old raja had given them an isolated patch of land, which the city had grown to reach and surround. Their huts were quite nice, but the patients and their children were in dreadful physical condition, many having lost fingers or worse.

One evening I took Trixie Mackay to see this group with the idea that a regular clinic might be established for them. Trixie was from Richardson Leprosy Hospital, a mission facility in Miraj. We drove to the leper colony in her new Volkswagen bus, taking with us a social worker and a cobbler, for some friends at home had sent money to pay for sandals to protect the lepers' feet. We parked the car to walk into the settlement of huts, but were suddenly interrupted by a huge man yelling accusations: "You missionaries have put the lepers amongst us so that we'll all get the disease! It is all your fault!"

It seems that this man's wife had developed leprosy. John Londe, the headman of the lepers, signalled to me that the man was drunk, so we ignored him, and he went away. Some minutes later, two girls came crying, "He's stoning your car!" As I ran to see if I could stop him, I caught sight of the utter frustration on John Londe's face. He was desperate to help but saw no way—he had neither hands nor feet.

I found a crowd had gathered around the drunkard, yelling encouragement as he threw stones at the vehicle. I tried to reason with him, but he just bellowed, "You leave here or I'll throw you out!" Saying this, he put a hand on my shoulder, as much to steady himself as anything else. That set the girls to screaming, "He's hitting Sister!"

The crowd cheered, but just then an arm shot out and whirled the drunk aside, and a tall shepherd said, "What do you think you are doing?" Then he turned to the crowd, saying, "These are our nurses; they didn't bring the lepers here. They come to visit and help us—you, too!" and he pointed at a boy who received his injections from us.

The mood of the crowd changed dramatically. When the drunkard started to shout again, the shepherd nodded, and two tall men appeared and marched him away. That was the last I saw of the troublemaker. "Finish your work, Sister," the shepherd said. "I'll watch the car." So I went back to the huts where Trixie and her staff had continued to work.

Soon the two girls were screaming again, this time, "The police are here!" I headed out to the car again in time to see a vanload of police pouring out onto the street and swinging their sticks at the crowd. I was horrified to see them shove the shepherd who had calmed the situation, and I ran to the inspector and implored him to stop.

He glared at me, "Where *were* you? We had a phone call that there was a riot and Mrs. Ramer was being attacked!" I explained the whole story, including how the shepherd had helped, and finally the police left. But when we finished our work and headed back, we found the police van waiting to follow us home. I couldn't help laughing at all the fuss, yet it gave me a warm feeling to know they were concerned. I later learned it was John Londe who had somehow summoned help.

***

In September Bob went to Kodai, so I was in charge of the SIS hostel when a tense situation exploded over vegetables, of all things. A particular kind of Indian spinach was served at noon, and the boys hadn't liked it, so there was a lot left over and it was served again that night. Our boarding master at that time was not experienced in handling teenagers, and a great row resulted, with hot words on all sides. At that point, I was able to act as peacemaker and patch things up, but the boarding master felt he had been insulted. At his request, the moderator of the Church Council ordered me to hand over four boys to the police!

Since we were responsible for all those boys, and I didn't agree with the master's claim that his life was in danger, I refused to involve the police. I won on this point, but the whole situation caused such animosity between the boys, the master, and our executive of the Kolhapur Church Council that I wired Bob to come home quickly. Even with Bob on hand, tensions remained high, so we wrote and asked some of the churches at home for special prayers, and they responded wonderfully.

Meanwhile, members of a dissident group of the Presbytery had declared themselves to be the *true* Kolhapur Church Council and started an anti-missionary campaign in the press. This was, in part, a reaction to the elected Church Council's decision to agree to COEMAR turning over control of their property to the Trust Association of the United Church of North India. COEMAR was the agency of PCUSA (Presbyterian Church U.S.A.) that was in charge of property all over India. Bob was the COEMAR property agent for the Sangli District.

The dissidents in the church wanted to set up a *local* trust, charging that COEMAR would sell the church properties and send the money to the U.S.A., which was ridiculous. The Sangli church pastor sided with the dissidents. It became a long, drawn-out, and painful disagreement resulting in a 12-year court case and a great deal of violence in parts of India, with dissidents taking over schools, churches, and hospitals. Historically, Presbyterians are sticklers about detail, and all the papers were in order, but there was a long, ugly period before the case was finally settled in favour of COEMAR.

At the same time, as chair of the VHS committee, I was facing the possibility of having to close down the clinics due to lack of staff. We were now organized into three efforts: general public health; family planning and maternal care; and child welfare, school health, and nutrition. It all was in jeopardy. Miraculously, just in the nick of time, Dr. Sylvia Marshall, daughter of a former medical superintendent at Miraj, came to do family planning and maternal care, and a paediatrician, Dr. Rao, married cardiac surgeon Dr. Thomas, and joined VHS.

In their own ways, the children were doing their part. Over winter break from school, Lyn and Ann Seibert helped at the Health Centre, combing and doing little girls' hair, and helping mothers bathe their little ones. Meanwhile, in the course of a year, second grader Tim's "Lion" had ten kittens, which he said was "doing our bit to reduce India's rat trouble!"

***

Some years after the Indira committee, my Gujarati friends and I were at Mrs. Deshmukh's house for another committee meeting of some sort. About ten of us were sitting around in her front room, laughing and talking, when somebody said, "Has *he* come in?" meaning Dr. Deshmukh. They would never say his name, just referring to him as "he."

"No," said his wife, "I've got his meal ready for him in the dining room," but all of a sudden he came barging into the front room and saw all these women! Obviously, she had told him to use the back door because we were going to be there, but he had forgotten.

When he saw everyone, he said, "What's this? What's this?"

"Oh, just come away! Come away," his wife said.

But he looked at me and said, "What are *you* doing here?"

"Oh, come, come away," urged his wife, and she persuaded him to go to the back of the house. Everyone was embarrassed because he had said, "Tu kashala ales," "*Why have you come?*" using the language form of address you use with a little child, which is a way to insult someone in Marathi.

After feeding her husband, Mrs. Deshmukh returned, but the room was silent. Then one of the braver women observed, "I smell mutton!" which means beef. They don't use the word "beef." As this was a Hindu home, and eating beef is forbidden in the faith, this was very curious.

"He has to take it—doctor's orders for his health," said Mrs. Deshmukh. "He has to take it to build up his blood."

All the women said, "Ah-ha, yah, ah-ha."

Then one of the bolder women said, "Have you ever tasted *flesh*? Does he let you taste *flesh*?" Flesh is another way of referring to beef.

"He eats mutton for his blood, and doesn't know what's left in the pot," said Mrs. Deshmukh, "so I need mutton for my blood." I often think of that; it was another insight into the lives of the women.

***

All these women called each other by their surnames, not first names, so I was called Ramerbai, and our hostess Deshmukhbai. Other people might call you Mr. or Mrs. I was always Mrs. Ramer with the merchants except for one I frequently patronized. Bob was often called Ramersahib. It wasn't just because he was white. All the Indian men who had any authority would be "sahib." At first, the Christian women would call me "Madamsahib," but I hated that name. When I told them I didn't want to be called that, they started calling me "Madam." When I said that I didn't want to be called "Madam," they asked why.

"Do you know what a madam is in my country?" I asked. "A madam is the head of the prostitutes, and I don't want that title." Then most no longer called me Madam or Madamsahib; I became Ramerbai. Because we became especially close friends, Laxmi and I called each other "Laxmibai" and "Nancybai."

Laxmi was named for the goddess of wealth, but she wasn't wealthy. The shop owned by Laxmibai's husband stood in the centre of the bazaar, and sold everything—matches, soap, sugar, tea, and so on. They and their two sons lived above the shop. Laxmibai and I often ran into each other at the government hospital, where I would be visiting the Christians who were ill, and she'd be visiting Hindu people who were sick.

Every day Laxmibai cooked the main meal for the 30 priests at the Ganapati Peth temple in Sangli. I don't mean she paid for the food to be cooked. She cooked it herself and delivered it to the temple where the young priests served one another. She and her husband were very devout, and this was their way of serving God. She often invited us to the special Hindu festivals and to the children's birthday celebrations in their home. We reciprocated by inviting them to our Christmas.

***

The first Christmas after getting to know all these women, I had invited many of them to our house for a Christmas tea. It wasn't on the actual Christmas day, and I had made sure that it wasn't a holy day for anyone else. I also made sure that the food was entirely vegetarian, being as respectful as I could of my friends' beliefs.

To extend an invitation in those days, you sent somebody around with the written invitation, and people immediately gave their answer, so that's what I did. Every woman signed her name saying she would come, so I was prepared for 40 women that afternoon. Then I waited and waited, but only two women came, Laxmi and Asharani, both very devout Hindu Brahmans and very progressive in their attitudes.

I was terribly disappointed that none of the other women came because I thought I'd gotten to know them. They'd invited me to their homes and I'd gone, and I thought they would come to mine. I asked Laxmibai and at first she wouldn't tell me. Then I asked Asharani, the doctor I'd worked with in family planning, "Why is it?"

"Oh, you know Indian culture," she said. "You have an outcaste as a servant."

"But," I said, "all the stuff we have I purposely bought in an Indian shop, all the sweetmeats and everything, and nothing was made with egg."

"Well, next year do it again, and I'll let the women know that no outcaste will be present in your home at the time."

Bob and I thought for a long time about such a stipulation. We had already gone so far as to bring in all the food, rather than make it at home. The next year I had another tea, and about ten of my good Gujarati friends came. I had refused to say that there would be no outcastes present, but I did serve them myself.

***

Sometimes when I was in the bazaar and had the time, I'd drop in on Laxmibai just for five or ten minutes, or if she were going along the road near us, she would stop in for a cuppa tea. In our house we had two pictures of Christ on the wall, and one day Laxmibai indicated the pictures and said, "That's your guru, your head priest, your leader, your guru."

"Yes, that's my guru." I explained that we didn't really know what God looked like, but that this was a picture of what God might have looked like when he came to earth as Jesus.

"Well," she said thoughtfully, "God made you and me, and we're all on one railway. You're in one carriage and I'm in another. We're all going up the mountain together, but we cannot change carriages."

"Well, that is the way it is in India on the railway," I said, "but in my country, we have corridor trains where you can change carriages."

"Oh, you people!" she said and laughed.

***

When we were in the terrible car accident in Denver in 1960, word got back to India, so everyone knew that my face had been quite smashed up. In the first couple days I was back in Sangli, I had gone into town when Asharani happened to be driving by. When she saw me, she stopped the car, hailed me, and said, "Let me see your face." She looked at my face and said, "I am so grateful to God. I went every day and gave an offering to Shiva to heal you, and God has answered my prayers."

"Thank you," I said, very touched.

When I went on into town, I stopped in to see Laxmibai, and she said, "Ahhh, you look just the same! God has answered my prayer. I gave offerings every day to Ganapati for you to be healed."

"Thank you," I said, once again, thoroughly warmed by the friendship of these two dear friends.

***

Laxmibai and I remained friends throughout our children's growing up years. When her elder son was to be married, she invited us to the wedding. As Christians we knew we should not go to the holiest part of the ceremony, but should arrive a little late for the more reception-like time. But Laxmibai phoned and said, "Ramerbai, I want you and Sahib to be there for the full ceremony."

"Laxmibai, that's all right, we understand. We're used to going to these weddings half an hour late."

But she insisted, and Bob said, "If she asked us, we should honour her." So we went early enough for the holiest part, and people gave us very dirty looks, though no one said anything. For both the ceremony and the meal, men and women were separated. During the meal, few people acknowledged me, so I mostly sat by myself and ate. But Bob was seated in a room with the priests and had an entirely different experience. When we compared notes later, he said, "It was so interesting. I sat next to Laxmibai's husband, and they were all asking me what I really believed. All these priests were sitting there talking together, and it was a wonderful experience."

Years later when Laxmi's husband died, she invited both of us to the cremation. As the raja's son had done when his father died, she invited holy men from each religion to pray before the fire started, and she specifically asked Bob to pray that God receive her husband's soul. That was the kind of friendship we had.

When Laxmi's sons grew up, they became military officers and moved to north India. The shop was closed, and Laxmi moved to live with one of her sons in Lucknow. I never really heard much from them after that. For a while I think we sent them Divali cards, and she sent us Christmas cards, but for about ten years, we lost contact. Then one day one of the Gujarati women stopped me and said, "Have you heard about Mrs. Dixit (Laxmi)?" When I replied that I hadn't heard from her in years, the woman said, "She has cancer and is in hospital very ill in Lucknow."

"I'll pray for her," I said. "Thank you for letting me know." I added Laxmibai to my prayer list, but I heard no more about her until about four years later. One morning about seven o'clock, I was coming to breakfast when one of the Christian nurses from the government hospital came and said, "Mrs. Ramer, do you know Laxmi Dixit?" To my yes, she continued, "She's here in the hospital, the civil hospital."

"Fine, I'll come see her this afternoon."

"No, she wants you to come right away."

"Right away?"

"Yes, she is miserable, Mrs. Ramer, she's dying. She's dying of cancer; she should have died days ago. We've given her all kinds of medicine, but she's in terrible pain and afraid to die. She just cries all day and night. Today she asked me, 'Do you know Ramerbai?'"

"How did she know you knew me?"

"We Christians all wear crosses, so she must have guessed I knew you. Please, she wants you to come right away." With tears in her eyes, she said, "She's suffering so much, please come right away."

I turned to Bob, and said, "What can I say to her, she's dying? Bob, you're the minister, you go."

But he said, "She's asked for you, you'd better go."

"But what'll I say to her?"

"Take the Marathi Bible and say whatever God puts in your heart, and I'll pray for you."

Before 8 a.m. I was in the hospital ward looking around for the stout friend I remembered, but I couldn't see her anywhere. Suddenly, somebody raised a hand and murmured, "Nancybai?" It was Laxmibai. I would never have recognized her; she was just skin and bones. She held out her arms to me, and I knelt down and hugged her. We both cried.

"Nancybai, I'm dying and I'm afraid to die. What will I be when I am born again? I'm a sinful woman."

She was a wonderful, generous woman, so I began to offer reassurance, but she interrupted, "No, I am a sinful person. What can I do? What can I do? I'll die and I'll be reborn as an outcaste and my children and my children's children! I'm so afraid to die."

Then the words of Jesus in John 14 came to my mind, and I said in Marathi, "Let not your heart be anxious. You believe in God, believe also in me."

"Where did you get those words?"

"From the Bible," I said.

"That's what he said to me!"

"Who said to you?"

"Your Jesus, your Jesus came to me last night! I'd been crying for days, and I said, 'If there's any God who can forgive sins, will you come and forgive my sins?' Your Jesus came, and he said those words you just said! 'Well, what can I do?' I asked, and he said, 'Send for Ramerbai.' I didn't even know if you were still in this country! But here you are, and I am so glad to see you. What do I do now?"

"Lord, help me!" I thought, and John 3:16, which I have recited so often, had taught so often, came into my mind, so I said, "God so loved the world that he gave his only begotten son, that whosoever believed in him should not perish." All of a sudden, that word—'perish!' I thought, "This is what she feels, that she's perishing."

"Did your Jesus say this?"

"Yes, and that's what I believe. He's forgiven me, and if you believe in him, he'll forgive you."

"Oh, I believe in him. I saw him, just like that picture in your house! Now tell me more, what more do I do?"

"You can pray, you can talk to God."

"How can I talk to God?"

"You just talk."

"Does he talk Marathi?"

"He talked to you; you said last night he talked Marathi."

"You do it first."

So I prayed and said we were both sinful women coming before him, asking God's forgiveness and accepting his promise. I prayed, "Please help Laxmibai to feel your presence."

Suddenly she said, "I can pray," and she just poured herself out. She was one of the finest women I ever knew, but she knew her good deeds couldn't erase her sins. When she finished, she said, "What do I do now?"

"Just say, 'In Christ's name, Amen.'"

"In Christ's name, Amen."

We were both crying, and she said, "That was beautiful!" She hugged me and kissed me.

When I told her I had to get back, she said, "That's all right, I'm all right now. My family's coming up, and I'll tell my family I'm not afraid to die. Christ is waiting for me, and he will look after them."

At home I told Bob about it. "She said, 'I'll do anything, what do I need to do? Do I need to give money to the church?' I said, 'No, no, you don't need to do anything.' But should she be baptised?"

"You know, if you go in the government hospital," said Bob, "you have to get permission from a judge to give baptism to a Hindu. She's at the end of her life. This would cause a great uproar in the Hindu community against her family. I will go and see her."

So he went to see her and prayed with her and told her, "If you want to be baptised, we can arrange it, but there are a lot of government restrictions that will cause trouble to your family."

"I don't want to cause trouble to my family, but I believe, so I'm just going to tell everybody that I believe. Is that all right?"

"That's all right, that's baptism by the Holy Spirit, to go out and tell good news."

When I went in the evening to see Laxmibai, she said, "I'm so relieved; I feel so at peace."

Her family was all around her, her two sons, their wives, her grandkids, and her son said, "I'm so grateful that you came and prayed with her. You have given her peace. We'll do anything you say we should do. We'll give money, we'll do anything."

"No, that's not necessary. God has talked to her himself." Then Laxmibai put her arm around me and said something I'll never forget. "Nancybai, why didn't you tell me this before?"

I thought of all those times when we'd sat and had cups of tea, but had never really talked of my faith. I went back to Bob in tears, "If I'd told her before, she wouldn't have gone through all this anguish." After visiting Laxmibai in the hospital, I was so shaken and utterly wiped out.

But he said, "Nancy, she wasn't ready to receive it then. When the time was right, God opened up the way."

The next day when I went back to the hospital, I met one of the doctors in the corridor, and he said, "Mrs. Ramer, what did you say to Laxmibai? How did you get her to stop that hysteria? She doesn't want morphine or anything, and she's smiling at people. She doesn't seem to have pain, but she's still dying, you know."

"It was a spiritual renewal, and she accepted Christ," I cautiously answered.

"Oh, yes, hallucinations, hallucinations," he said and walked down the hall. When I reached Laxmibai, she was telling everyone about her experience, including her family and all the nurses. But she did so in such a joyous fashion that people weren't offended, just stunned.

It is awesome, very startling to find that God is at work and uses us at times like that. I can tell you that I had no idea what I was going to say to Laxmi before I went in, but those words just came. That's why John 14 is so very precious to me now.

When Laxmi died, her sons had a funeral. Bob, the Indian pastor, and the Hindu priests all were there. I believe there are many secret Christians in India. I found that many Hindus had a terrific fear of death because reincarnation was a very frightening thing to face. When the soul was reincarnated, you might be punished for a sin. If you came into the world as an outcaste, it meant you had sinned and been cast out by the gods, recreated without a soul. Consequently, many suffered a terrible dread.

Our principal language teacher, who taught us Marathi, was familiar with the gospels, Acts, and Romans because he had to teach us so we could preach those stories in Marathi. He talked a lot about God forgiving his sins. While he felt that God had changed his life, it was very hard in Indian culture to be publicly Christian.

"Who do you pray to?" I once asked him.

"I call him Rama, but he's your God. I pray to him, and I feel him answering my prayer." Part of the trouble is that Christian churches were loath to receive high-caste Hindus into the church because that was the one area where they felt free. We had many a battle with the churches over that, and we finally had to accept it. There are many people Bob used to call "Christian Hindus," who lived wonderful lives, and called God "Rama." We leave any judgment to God.

Rob, Bob, Lyn and Nancy on the Lambretta scooter, "Ramer Transport" for 30 years

Bob was always the photographer, but this time Tim got a photo of him.

Chapter 19: Signs and Wonders

"Tilgul ghya, anni gord bola!" "*Take the tilgul and speak sweetly*!" Tilgul are tiny, sweet pellets with liquorice centres, and the tilgul festival is an Indian women's celebration. With the eating of the tilgul, women committed themselves to another year of friendship and promised to speak sweetly to their friends.

Carts on both sides of the main street held piles of tilgul for sale. Women sewed tiny packets, filled them with tilgul, and attached them to postcards that they sent to friends, much like greeting cards. They also gave tea parties at which they exchanged small gifts. As the guests departed, they were given a few fingersful of tilgul, with the old, old admonition, "Tilgul ghya, anni gord bola!"

It was a joyous occasion, and the merchants made the most of it. This particular day I was in no mood to dawdle, having a long list of things to purchase before lunch. Although January is winter in India, the temperature could still be a dry heat of 32 degrees C (90 F) in the middle of the day. The sky was a vivid blue with fluffy white clouds, but there was no time to admire it. I had to keep my eyes on the crowd, taking care to avoid stepping in animal droppings or human deposits.

But it was the children I was thinking of. Rob had graduated from Kodai and travelled by way of Delhi, Teheran, Istanbul, Geneva, Stockholm, and Scotland to his ultimate destination—Grinnell College in Iowa. Although we were accustomed to sending the children to Kodai, more than 700 miles away, it was still hard to send Rob to the U.S. on his own. When the Kodai school year started in June, we sent Lyn off to her senior year, Jody to seventh grade, and Tim to fourth grade.

Part of the ritual of sending the children back to Kodai after the Christmas holiday was shopping for everything they would need there, and some surprises for along the way to sweeten the parting. As I pushed my way through the goats, cows, donkeys, and waves of people preparing for the tilgul festival, shopkeepers waved to me, calling, "Come in and visit."

The Indian sweet shop was crowded. While I waited, I studied the glass jars. There was shredded, roasted cocoanut with peanuts, and shev, a soft noodle, fine and crunchy. There was the spicy-sweet chewarda, a mixture of puffed wheat, lentils, peanuts, and raisins. There were sweet puffed rice and brown sugar balls—so many things. As I read out my list, the sweet wallah said, "Are you giving a party, too, Mrs. Ramer? This is a lot more than your usual."

"No, I'm not giving a party," I told him. "My children go back to boarding school tomorrow. They need something to eat on the train to help pass the time, and I like to put surprises in their suitcases." Hearing this, the shopkeeper added some special sweetmeat as his gift to them.

Sweets chosen, I hurried out of that shop and hastened through the masses to the general merchant's shop, hoping he had all the things I needed: batteries for the flashlights each child was required to have, bars of nice-smelling soap, talcum powder for the girls, condensed milk for making candy, and bars of chocolate to slip into the suitcase as a token of love to be found as they unpacked.

"Mrs. Ramer, we have the towels you ordered last month. You wanted eight, yes?"

I had already bought others, thinking these were not coming in time. Now I would have to sew nametags on these, too! I bought peanuts, bangles, and balls to play with on the train, and kept looking for some appealing new trifle. Next I hurriedly bought some grapes from the villagers sitting along the road. These were the first of the season's grapes, expensive at this time of year, but the children would love them, and they would miss the height of Sangli's grape harvest.

Finally, I felt I had done as well as possible, so I edged my way over to the three-wheeled motorcycles. The driver helped with my many parcels, and as I settled in, he asked if I had gotten all I needed. "Far more than I needed," I answered. "Just go straight to the mission compound."

As we wove in and out of the traffic, I tried to concentrate on what remained to be done before the children left for school. My heart was heavy. With Rob off to college in the U.S.A. and the remaining three at boarding school, there were times I wished that we lived in America like other people. Then I thought back to when Bob had proposed to me.

We both loved children and wanted to have "four, God willing." At that time, we discussed the reality that, as missionaries, we would have to send the children to boarding school, and I wondered if we would be able to do it. That was when Bob told me of the missionary conference he had attended in New York just before leaving for India, where he had met so many wonderful missionary kids. "Without exception," he had told me, "they were wonderful people. If our children grow up like that, I would be so proud and happy."

Even then I resigned myself, "I guess it really means we put them in God's hands, trusting him not only to protect them, but to help us show our children how much we love them even if they are far away." So, from the very beginning, we parents thought of the years ahead when our children would have to leave us.

***

There was turmoil at home. Our Sangli Church was split down the middle, with neither side having sufficient members to support a pastor. But there were encouraging signs. The Sunday School Christmas service, held in a field outside the school, drew quite a crowd. The children's "white gifts" (Christmas Eve gifts of money, wrapped in white tissue paper) totalled enough to provide each of 75 lepers with a week's ration of two kilos each of milo and wheat, and one kilo of rice. The Kolhapur Church Council had sponsored a four-day spiritual renewal gathering, which brought together 600 people, including people with leprosy, for inspiration and communion.

Although our children were away at school, there were people nearby who became like family. One such person was Sam Power. Sam's father died when he was young, so he and his brother had been brought up by their mother. A bright, hardworking boy, Sam had gone through school on Presbyterian scholarships and became an ordained minister of the Presbyterian Church.

The Presbyterian Church ran a youth centre in Sangli on land donated by the raja. When Sam was about 27, he came to Sangli to be the youth director there. With his vivid personality and smiling face, he was a natural as youth director, and Bob greatly enjoyed working with him. Sam soon had lots of young people coming to the centre.

While at seminary in Bangalore, Sam had met a girl named Kusum from south India. They fell in love and were married, so Kusum came and lived with Sam on our mission campus. Sam became very interested in starting an English language school. Many government and business people were coming to Sangli, and they wanted their children to be educated in the

English medium, so we opened what became Emmanuel English School. The school had a Christian focus, and there was optional prayer before school started. The fact that it existed helped to reduce anti-Christian bias.

Sam and his wife had a daughter, and when she was about three years of age, Kusum gave birth to their second child, a little boy, at Miraj Hospital. The baby boy was fine, but Kusum suffered postpartum haemorrhage, and nearly died. Although they finally stopped the haemorrhage, it was followed by a severe infection that infused her whole body, and she was desperately ill. Because Sam had no family in the area, he asked me to come sit with him at Kusum's side. The Indian chaplain at the hospital, Rev. Ghatge, and his wife were good friends of mine, and he told me, "While you're over here all the time, feel free to come into our house and take a rest whenever you like."

Additional doctors were called in and they tried everything, but no matter what they did, Kusum's pulse raced and her temperature raged. "We have tried all the drugs," they told me. "There's just nothing more we can do for her but pray." I had to run back to Sangli to take care of a few things, but returned to spend the night with Sam because the doctors felt that Kusum would go that night. Sam and I sat on either side of the bed where poor Kusum lay deeply unconscious, a drip going into her veins and drains coming out of her abdomen. It was the middle of the rainy season, and outside the rain drenched everyone and everything.

As I looked at Kusum, I thought of her little girl, her baby boy, and Sam, of their nice, wee home and all the fun we had together. It was a terrible shame. I said to Sam, "Let's pray together," and we held hands with Kusum and with each other, and prayed. As I prayed, I wept, overwhelmed at the thought of Kusum dying at such a young age. As we wept and prayed, I suddenly felt a real power moving through me, and I said, "Oh, God, use this for your glory!"

There was a terrific noise, and when I looked down at Kusum, there was thick yellow pus flowing out of the tube in her abdomen where nothing had flowed before. The pus oozing from the tummy of the unconscious woman filled up the bottle attached to the tube. I ran to the nurse for another bottle, and it, too, quickly filled with pus.

Desperately tired by then, I thought, "I've got to go to bed, but she's going to die, and I don't want to leave Sam. If only somebody could come …"

Just then, in walked Dr. Phansopker, Bob's good friend and a family practitioner who knew Sam very well. It was 3 a.m., and Dr. Phansopker had just walked in from the torrential rain, having taken the bus five miles from Sangli.

"I could not sleep, and I thought I'd come and sit with Sam," he said.

"The pus is just falling out of her," I said without preamble, "but I am so tired, I just have to go."

"Don't worry," he said, "you go and sleep. I'll stay with Sam." I went over to the chaplain's house and found the couch in the sitting room already made up for me. Instantly, I fell into a deep, deep sleep.

Compounds in India are very noisy, but I never heard a thing until I woke up about ten in the morning, still dressed in my wrinkled clothes. I got up and wandered through the dining room, calling out for the chaplain and his wife, but there was nobody there. So I had a bit of a wash and made myself a cup of tea. "She's died," I thought, "and they're all at the chapel." So I walked over to the hospital, where I saw Rev. Ghatge and asked him, "How's Kusum? Has she died?"

"Don't you know?" he said.

"Don't I know what?"

"She's fine."

"What do you mean?"

"She's fine—no temperature; she's in her senses; she's eating. It happened last night after all that pus drained out."

I couldn't believe it, but I went to her room and there she was, sitting up in bed and saying, "Oh, how are you?"

Sam had gone home to have a sleep, so it was just the two of us, and I said to Kusum, "Do you remember anything?"

"No, nothing," she said. "I just woke up about six o'clock this morning, and thought, 'I feel well. I feel completely well.' I told Sam, and he said, 'I knew that was happening, I knew God answered prayer last night.'" Two days later, she was discharged, and she was perfectly fine.

That experience shook me to the core. When the woman in the healing story touched the hem of Christ's garment, he said, "Some power has gone out of me." We are channels only. It wasn't me, it wasn't my faith, but for some unknown reason, I had felt the power go through me, and I was left drained and exhausted.

That has happened each time I've been present at a dramatic healing, but I have no way of knowing that it's going to happen. I have wished that it would happen with loved ones; I would like to be able to do it. I have come to the conclusion that this is what God is showing us. It is never the power of the person, it is God finding a channel that he can work through, someone who will not obstruct him or try to take the glory. I can't explain it any other way.

I think that when we are healed from diseases, whether it's sudden and miraculous, or through God using medicine and doctors, if we're brought through catastrophic times, we are humbled and have to realize that God has put more responsibility on us after that experience. But we are never left on the mountaintop; we are always brought down to the valley. It's at the time of being humbled that we have to cling to God so much, and sometimes that's very hard.

***

Unless you are a church person, it may be difficult to understand the significance of the first meeting of the Church of North India, but to us it was a momentous and very joyous occasion. 29 November 1970, is when the United Church of North India (the Presbyterians and the Congregationalists), the Anglicans, the British Baptists, the British and Australian Methodists, the Church of the Brethren, and the Disciples of Christ joined to become The Church of North India.

The unification process had taken years, and even at the end there were fears and clashing traditions. Would there be a Pope of India? Would we use one chalice or individual little glasses for communion? Would the ministers have to be re-ordained?

One of the great leaders of the church in India was a man who had been a friend of ours for many years, Ramchandra Bhandare. Ramchandra graduated from Bangalore Seminary just about the time Bob and I were married. Upon graduation in the 1950s, he was appointed assistant district superintendent in Islampur, a town about 20 miles from Sangli. He served under the superintendent, Dr. Howard, who was in his late 70s and could no longer drive, so Ramchandra was sent to SIS for three weeks to learn to drive. I insisted that he live with us during that time, and from then on we were very close friends.

As a village boy, Ramchandra had spent his days watching the sheep. When he was about ten years old, an American Presbyterian missionary named Bess Freeman came to know this little boy who was always full of questions. When he told her how desperately he wanted to learn to read, she arranged for him to go to Presbyterian boarding school at Kodoli. These church boarding schools were not for the elite, but for the outcastes. Ramchandra did very well in school, going on to Wilson College in Bombay. The rule was that students were not to become Christians while on scholarship, lest there be a question of conversion being a condition of the scholarship, but somewhere along the line, Ramchandra became a Christian, and went on to seminary.

As was the custom, when he was just a boy, Ramchandra's family had arranged his marriage to a nine-year-old girl named Anandi. Anandi means "joy," and it was the perfect name for her. The marriage was not to be consummated until much later, but as a young girl Anandi came to live with Ramchandra's family. Anandi never graduated from high school, but she did learn to read and write, and her graciousness and sensitivity were great assets in every endeavour she undertook.

The young couple had already been married for 16 years, so there was great joy when Anandibai became pregnant and gave birth to the first of their three children. When Bob left the church position of district superintendent to take over SIS again, he recommended Ramchandra as his replacement, so Ramchandra became the first Indian district superintendent of Sangli. As preparation, the Presbyterian Church arranged for him to go to Princeton University for his master's degree.

As wonderful an opportunity as Princeton was, it would mean leaving Anandibai and their little children for three years. Presbyterian scholarships did not provide for bringing families along, because the more family members they brought to the U.S., the fewer graduate students they could support. It was a difficult situation.

At that time there were three missionary families on the Sangli compound—the Ramers, the Seiberts, and the Dilleners. But to us, the Bhandares were a part of us, and we thought it was horrible that Ramchandra should have to leave his family for three years. He would be immersed in American culture, while she would get no further education despite her importance in their work. So often when a foreign student went to American seminary, the Presbyterians, bless their hearts, would be very hospitable, treating them as honoured guests, and they would return to India quite spoiled. So many of those students returned home and got into trouble.

We three missionary families were convinced that Anandibai ought to go along to the U.S. First, we asked the Mission Board to send her, but they said they didn't have the money. So we three couples banded together to pay the fare for Anandibai to join Ramchandra in Princeton. We wrote to Dr. Robert F. Goheen, the president of Princeton, and a former missionary kid born in Vengurla, asking him if he could find a place for the family to stay. We weren't asking for education for Anandi; we just wanted her to be an ordinary woman in America, doing her own shopping and so on, and having an opportunity to learn English in the process. Goheen thought this was the best idea! He said that one area church had an apartment that was available. A lot of churches used to keep an apartment for when missionaries came to town.

With that agreed, we scraped together the money to send Anandi to Princeton, and it was one of the best things we ever did. They lived on Ramchandra's student allowance, and she learned to go to all the places where things were cheaper. Many people in India thought that Americans had so much money they didn't know what to do with it. Anandi saw the truth and came back to India amazed that the church in America did so much sacrificing to give to the missions.

Periodically, people from the New York headquarters came to India to meet with us to discuss our problems and successes. They stayed about a week and met with teachers, the Session, and so on.

One year the man who came was not our usual regional secretary, but someone from the finance department in New York and he said, "I have to have a talk with all six of you missionaries together. You have broken one of the rules of your commitment to the church in America by financing Anandi Bhandare and the children to come to America. You know that if we have to finance the wives, we can't finance as many students. It has shocked us that you people have made this decision unilaterally, going over our heads and even getting some of the churches in America to send money for Anandi's passage."

We were all adults in our mid-30s by then and unaccustomed to being scolded like children. We just sat and looked at him until I said, "Well, we have broken the law. What are you going to do with us now?" And all six of us laughed.

"Well, well," he sputtered, very embarrassed, "you mustn't do it again!"

"Well, I don't think we will," I told him, "because it was very difficult to raise all that money! But you should be thinking about what comes of dividing families up like that!" We all got quite a kick out of that meeting, and the experience brought us missionaries and the Bhandares very close.

After earning his master's, Ramchandra returned to India and became executive secretary of the Presbytery—and our boss. He went on to become executive secretary of the National Council of Churches for India, working with all different denominations. He was one of the strong national leaders who worked to unite six denominations into one Church of North India.

When, after many years of committees and negotiating, the various denominations finally joined together, a great weeklong celebration was held in Nagpur. Foreign delegations came from countries around the world, and Ramchandra and Anandibai were in charge of all the arrangements for thousands of people. As the huge celebration approached, Ramchandra sent word that he wanted Bob and me to be there. Bob was an elected delegate from our church council, so we wrote back and said Bob was coming. Then Ramchandra and Anandibai wrote and said, "I've got so many arrangements to do, let's just get this settled. Nancy must also come!" And so I was able to go.

***

For years the various Christian denominations in India had been meeting twice a year about unification. The Congregationalists and the Presbyterians were already united as The United Church of North India, UCNI. Although the Congregationalists sent students to the Industrial

School, and we shared staff and so on, each denomination kept its own geographical areas of service. The Congregationalists were next to us in Poona and a bit east. South of us were the Methodists and the Anglicans. Wherever there had been a British military post, there was an Anglican church, so there was an Anglican church in Kolhapur, our headquarters.

Although the finances were separate, there was a great deal of cooperation, so in India no one said, "I am a Presbyterian, and I'll die a Presbyterian," or "I'm a Baptist, and we don't meet with them." You see, denomination was *never* preached in India, not with any of the groups. It was Christ that was preached, so when Indians considered unification, they brought no denominational baggage with them.

Bishop Bhandare was involved in all these discussions and pushed for unification because he could foresee that India would eventually be expelling missionaries, which would bring an end to the flow of foreign funds. The churches needed to band together for strength. Ramchandra was a very good public speaker and a sincere man, and he used his diplomacy a great deal. Finally it came to be that all the UCNI (Presbyterians and Congregationalists), Anglicans, Church of the Brethren, the Disciples of Christ, and the British Baptists agreed to unite. Not all the churches joined. The American Methodists didn't, and the evangelicals formed their own union. As part of unification, the American denominations agreed to give our land, schools, and all over to the Church of North India.

Bishop Bhandare and Bishop Luther, an Anglican leader, said, "We must be an all-Indian Church, and we must support our own churches. For a while we'll need money from abroad because we've been supported from abroad. But as we become independent, we should not make the salaries so high that the Indian Church won't be able to pay them." This became quite an issue. The Presbyterians and the Congregationalists were paid salaries on the local Indian scale, but the Methodists, for example, paid their bishops on the same scale as their American bishops.

Bishop Luther was an Indian, but he was a bishop of the Church of England, and was paid on the English pay scale. Still, he said, "I gladly accept this lowering of my salary because we are an Indian church. If we have foreign salaries, we will have to get foreign money to support them, and we cannot be an independent Indian church." Bishop Luther and

Bishop Bhandare fought very hard to make the church all Indian with Indian grades of salary, financial responsibility, and accountability.

Despite the personal invitation, I still didn't think I could go to the unification ceremony because the children would be home from Kodai, but as soon as she heard, Joan Seibert next door volunteered to take care of the children, so I was free to attend. The contingent from our area included Rev. Ghatge, Sushila Ghatge, Mrs. Gaikwad, Sam Power, Rev. Ranabhise, and Bob and me.

It took two trains and 28 hours to get to Nagpur. On the morning we left, church people came to the Miraj station to sing and praise God. It was such an exciting time to be alive! At Poona, where we had to change trains, we confirmed our tickets and climbed on, but when we boarded, we found other people in our places. As always the train was packed, but in the reserved area no standing was allowed. We talked with the people in our places and with the ticket collector, who told us there had been a mistake, and we would have to get off the train and take a later one.

But taking a later train wasn't an option; we would miss the service. We were all determined that we would not get off and announced, "We will sleep on the floor!" One man gave up his bunk to Mrs. Gaikwad, who was about 55 and a rather prominent person. Then I said to Sushila, "Let's put our bedding rolls down between the bunks and just lie there instead."

So we did, ignoring the conductor, who continued to insist, "You've got to get out!"

We discovered that the men in that car were from Poona and were also going to the unification ceremony. They protested to the conductor, "No, you are not going to put the women out, and you shouldn't be putting the men out!" Bob and the other men from our party ended up going into the next compartment, where they had to stand up all night. When I woke up in the morning, I was so worried about our men. I stuck my head out the window and had enough conversation with the next car to learn that about 6:30 a.m. the men in the bunks had traded places to let our men sleep in the bunks during the day.

During this long train ride, we made various stops, and at one station the inspector found Sushila and me on the floor and told us, "It's against the railway rules; you have to get out!"

"Let's just stay," I said to Sushila.

The men from Poona spoke up, too, "They're all right lying on the floor! You are not going to put them out. It's your mistake, not theirs. They've got tickets and reservations!" There was a great deal of arguing.

At another station further on, in the middle of the night, another inspector came on. I woke up to hear our conductor saying, "There are extra people in that car. They are a bunch of *Christians*, and they refuse to move, but they don't give any trouble, so just leave them alone!"

When we pulled into a larger station, I stuck my head out of the window, and Sam Power stuck his head out the window of his car. "What is happening there?" I asked.

"Oh," he says, "we don't have room to move; we were pressed against the wall all night."

For some reason there wasn't a platform at that stop, so the train was high off the ground. But I wanted to take some food to our men, so I jumped down and started to climb into the car with the men. Just then the train began to move, quickly picking up speed, and I was still hanging on to the carriage door! Sam reached through the window and held onto me! The door opened inward, and with all the people pressed against it, the men couldn't open it. Fortunately, the train travelled only a short ways before it stopped, and Bob yelled, "Get back in your own compartment!"

Finally, we got all of us in the one compartment with the original occupants for the final 12 hours to Nagpur, and we ended up having a wonderful time. One of the men was an engineer, and he became very interested in Bob's work at SIS. Sushila, Mrs. Gaikwad, and I got to talk to some of the other women on the train. When we found that many of us were on our way to the unification service, we started singing hymns. We would sing one, and then someone else would say, "Have you heard this chorus?" Then they'd start on a chorus, and we would all join in.

While it was a most uncomfortable trip physically, it turned out to be a time of great joy and fellowship. We had all brought food, which we shared, and it was just like one big picnic. The train ended up arriving hours late, and we were a mess, but when we got to Nagpur, Ramchandra and people from the church were waiting to take us to the homes of the people who would be putting us up.

The Dilleners (then stationed in Landour), Bob, and I stayed with the Bhandares, who hosted not only us, but also officials from the Presbyterian and Congregationalist Churches. I was so impressed with how Anandi handled it all. Even in the bishop's bungalow, there was no running water, but Anandibai had hot water for all of us. Quietly and graciously, she took care of everyone, and I said, "Oh, Anandibai, you are just the perfect wife for Ramchandra."

"But I'm not educated," she sighed.

"Maybe not, but you have the wisdom and the common sense!"

At one point, I remember, we ran out of towels, and Anandi went to Ramchandra's office and talked with the finance man. "What am I going to do?"

This was no big corporate event; there was no budget for towels, but he said, "I'll get you towels."

This gathering was a great event in Nagpur for Christians and non-Christians alike. A huge tent had been erected for the momentous gathering, and there had been a great deal of publicity. Some of the merchants in town had given loads of rice in celebration of this union. The finance man called up a merchant who sold towels and asked for towels to use until the others could be washed, and the store sent over more than 100 towels. It was a wonderful time of generosity and friendship. We were thrilled that Indira Gandhi sent a telegram to say that she was sorry she couldn't come because she was overseas, adding that, as usual, the Christians were setting an example for all of India in uniting as one.

The unification service itself was so moving. All the pastors marched in wearing the gowns and stoles of their various denominations. The gowns were much the same, but the stoles, the scarf-like pieces that go around the neck and hang down the front, were all a bit different because the stoles signified their denominations. Together, heads of the different denominations reconfirmed the pastors, laying their hands on three at a time, pastors from three different denominations simultaneously confirmed into the Church of North India. As each pastor was reconfirmed, he was handed a new stole, the red stole of the Church of North India with the symbolic cross growing out of the lotus.

There were wonderful speeches. It was euphoric, glorious, everybody singing, "We are one in the Lord; we are one in Christ." I still remember the bishop's message: "If we stand in a circle and face in, we will fight. If we stand in a circle and face out to the world, we will grow and strengthen."

We had hoped when this was all over that Ramchandra would be installed as our bishop, but he remained as bishop of Nagpur. Bishop Luther became bishop of Kolhapur and Bombay, and he was such a blessing! Having been an Anglican bishop, he was accustomed to the royal purple shirts, insignias on his car, and other accoutrements because that was the way they did it. But he came to us and was so humble. He wouldn't even have a driver, saying, "I know how to drive; what do I need a driver for? I don't know the district, but I'll learn it." Taking a pastor who knew the area, he proceeded to visit every village and every institution. "No ceremony, please," became his watchword.

In January, we had our local ceremony, the formal handing over from Kolhapur Church Council to Kolhapur Diocese Council. There was a huge meeting in Kolhapur with representatives from every church and every group—deacons, women's groups, youth, members of sessions. There was a great procession into the church with everyone singing, "We are one in the Spirit; we are one in the Lord." As everyone marched in, one of the missionaries played the trumpet.

But there had been many bumps along the road, and many different customs that clashed. In our case, the subject was communion, which was to complete the service in Kolhapur. The Anglicans have the common cup, and we were going to have the common cup for the symbolism, but some of our old Presbyterians, the Indians, not the missionaries, said, "Oh, that is terrible! We could never do that! We must have the little glasses!" After the ceremony, each church was to continue with its own preferred practices, but for a unified ceremony, there had to be agreement on ways of doing things.

Bob had written a history of the work in our area from the Presbyterian records, and he went to Bishop Luther and told him, "According to the history of the church, this mission was started in the days of the common cup, and the church in New York gave a communion service with the common cup to Kolhapur. It's in the history."

Soon Mrs. Luther called me to say, "Let's see if we can find that cup!" So we hunted everywhere we could think of, and in a dusty old cupboard in the old church offices, we found it—the whole set, from about 1880! It was tarnished, but I assured Bishop Luther that once polished, it would be beautiful. Once it was cleaned, we could read the inscription: "From the Presbytery of New York to the Presbytery of Kolhapur." Neither former Anglicans nor former Presbyterians could argue with using that communion cup.

On the day of the service, Bishop Luther added his own words before the service of communion: "We are the descendants of those who came to this area, and we share with them in the blood of Christ." It was so moving, and I am still moved when I think of it.

Alas, it wasn't long after the euphoria of unification that problems began to surface. The local church council began violently protesting the turning over of all the former Presbyterian property to the larger Church of North India. There was forcible breaking of locks and taking over of schools.

Very often after union there has been trouble in the church. When Presbyterians in the north and the south of the U.S.A. united, we were all so thrilled, but immediately the question arose of where the headquarters would be. Then, who would move to Louisville and who wouldn't? Sometimes I don't know how God puts up with us.

***

We had a ten-month furlough coming up in 1971, and on our last weekend in India we planned to go to Woodstock School in Landour to visit the Dilleners. We went by taxi, and I'm sure none of us will ever forget the trip. We had already been delayed by not one, but two, flat tires when the radiator overheated, and the taxi driver scalded himself trying to deal with it. I rendered first aid by the roadside with the help of some men at a tea stall. I just added "hai" onto all my Marathi words, and the Hindi speakers seemed to understand well enough! A passing taxi took our driver to hospital while Bob changed the tire. With the driver gone, Bob was driving when we had our third flat! On the road again after fixing *that* tire, we drove to the hospital—where there was no driver to be found!

After an hour of searching fruitlessly for a lost driver whose name we didn't know, we piled back into the taxi and Bob drove us up the long, winding mountain road. We were thrilled to see Peg and Peter Dillener were still there. They had waited for us for six hours!

Although our driver had no idea where we were going to stay in Landour, by 10 p.m. that night he had tracked us down. It was a joyful reunion on both sides! After a lovely visit with the Dilleners, we continued on our journey through Moscow, Oslo, Copenhagen, and Brussels, then London with Blair and his family, and on to St. Andrews and Iona, which I had longed to see again. It was a delight to see our families again, and to have another welcome respite from our work.

***

But back home in India, money was tight. Funds from the U.S.A. were being drastically cut, and many of our Christian village schools had closed. Even those that remained open had fewer pupils because many couldn't afford the books or the uniform. It seemed an impossible situation. But through the help of the German Church under an organization called Kindernothilfe (KNH), the hostels for village boys were being run by local Christian leaders under CNI (Church of North India).

Bob and I interviewed each child in order to fill in their case sheets. We listened to their cheerful descriptions of their home life, food, and daily habits, and it was difficult to hold back the tears. The income of most students' parents was the equivalent of about 25 pence (42 cents) a day, and even that couldn't be counted on. We went back to our homes and thanked God for opening our eyes to the terrible needs of his children. Meanwhile, Bob continued to represent COEMAR in the dispute over the ownership of the property, because a few local churches were still trying to get the property back from CNI. (Over the years we had been called missionaries, fraternal workers, and now, collectively, COEMAR, the Commission on Ecumenical Mission and Relations, but the Indian nationals always just referred to us as missionaries.)

On the brighter side, after more than 20 years in India, we finally bought a family car. It was a used car, but still quite a step up from the Lambretta scooter that had been our only personal motorized vehicle for two decades.

The years-long drought had brought India to a situation of even greater need. Thousands of people had no water and no food for themselves or their animals. There was no way for the unskilled to earn money to buy food because there were no crops to be cared for. However, the government developed a magnificent relief organization, and thousands were given work digging wells, breaking rocks for repairing roads, and digging percolation tanks, which collected and controlled rainwater. Just as the government projects came to a close, there was enough moisture to bring back some of the fieldwork, but the need was still great.

I thanked God for churches at home that sent money for cereal to give away. At one particularly dark time, a minister in Pennsylvania wrote asking if his church could help with wells. Our own United Presbyterian Church also sent money for wells and other relief. The bishop and our Indian colleagues planned and directed the relief programs. Fifteen wells were drilled in our diocese, and about 30 feeding centres were opened in the villages and towns, saving so many from otherwise certain starvation.

Both Rob and Lyn were off at college by now, but came back to India to help in the villages when they could. In one of the circulars to our friends, Lyn wrote this: "For two weeks in Kodai I helped mornings at a crèche [daycare] for coolies children. The children there all spoke Tamil of which I know about five words, but we managed to communicate! But those poor little ones. The crèches had very few toys and were sadly understaffed: lack of funds. But we made a few more toys out of old t-shirts, scraps of cloth, single mittens, *anything*. We had to teach the children how to play—some would just sit. Those wee ones really blossomed with a little love and soon their imaginations took over. I brought some old typewriter reels which we showed them how to roll across the floor. One little chap about 3 stuck one on his nose, threw a small scrap of artificial fur over his head and presto a fierce dog.

[Then this, in Sangli.] "The first week of August little Shanti Anandi, "Peaceful Joy," came to stay with us for a fortnight. While we tried to find a place in an orphanage for her, she had been in hospital since April with miasma [severe malnutrition], gastroenteritis, bronchial pneumonia, osteomeilitis and arthritis in her leg. When she was admitted, she was only 2 kg [4.4 lb.] Her mother had gone crazy when Shanti was born. Even now, the mother screams at the sight of a baby. The father is fond of Shanti, but can't care for her as both he and his family have leprosy. Now with the aid of K.N.H. she has a place in a home in Poona. Shanti is really a bright loving baby and only five months old! It was hard to say goodby, but we will keep in touch through the K.N.H. fostership scheme because I am her godmother." As her foster parent, Lyn supported Shanti on her vacation earnings.

We all became so fond of little Shanti. Jody wrote to Bob and me from Kodai, "Hey, don't you think we should adopt Shanti? I mean after you keep her a while it will really hurt to give her up to an orphanage, where she wouldn't have such a good life or get half the love she really needs. Just think when Rob and Lyn leave [again] how lonely it will be unless there is someone else to keep you company. That someone else should be Shanti. … It wouldn't be that hard to adopt her it would be good too for all of us, so please! Love, Jody."

Chapter 20: A Garden of Children

Tatoba Londe had leprosy and got around on a small platform with four iron wheels, drawn by his wife Shantibai, who herself had only one hand. Due to leprosy, the parents had suffered terrible disfigurement, but their children were beautiful. The Londes provided my first real contact with people with leprosy.

One day Tatoba came to ask me to find a place in a boarding school for his eldest son, John. I wrote to all the schools, but none had a place for him. But John's parents refused to give up, and went personally to a school in Poona, travelling in the train's luggage compartment, which was the only way leprosy people could take the train. From the train station, John's mother walked 20 miles, pulling his father on the little cart, to the school in Poona. There they waited at the gate, refusing to leave until the school admitted young John, which they eventually did.

Back in Sangli, Tatoba came one day and implored me to write and tell the school, "Watch John carefully when he's near the canal." The canal that ran near the school had never been a problem, but I wrote nonetheless. But before they even received the letter, a telegram came: "John Londe fallen in canal. Drowned." Tatoba must have had a premonition when he asked me to send that letter.

Some time later, the Londes were on their way to a festival, Shantibai pulling the cart on which Tatoba sat holding their baby, Daniel. Their little girl, Purlabai, was running alongside the family when suddenly a bullock cart raced toward them. Tatoba grabbed for his daughter's clothing, but it was too late. Her dress became caught in the wheel, and the little girl was pulled down to the ground, where the wheel crushed and killed her.

When Tatoba and Shanti came to tell me of the tragedy, I cried and tried to comfort them. Tatoba responded, "One day I will be with her and John in Heaven, and God will give me two good arms and two good legs to ran and hug my children."

Their tragedies seemed endless. When little Daniel was two years old, Tatoba was on a train near Bombay when he was thrown from the train and killed. This happened all too often to people with leprosy. Shantibai and Daniel returned to Sangli, where they begged for a meagre living. One day when he was only three, Daniel rushed into an open house and stole a stainless steel pot. The people in the leprosy colony lectured and beat Daniel because his dishonesty reflected badly on them all and threatened their livelihood as beggars. Still Daniel continued to steal.

Daniel wasn't the only boy who desperately needed help. The leper colony was also home to Suresh, a little boy whose legs were bent under him and useless from polio. The leprosy people begged for help for these two boys, so I went to KNH to ask if there was somewhere, anywhere, they could go. "No," they said. "Why don't you start a place?" So Dr. Samson, Mrs. Kumandini Seelam, Bob, and I developed a plan to establish a children's hostel in Vengurla, and we called it "Balniketan," which means "Garden of Children."

The staff at the mission station in Vengurla was already stretched well beyond what was reasonable. Money was tight. Everyone was on reduced salary, and often they were months behind in getting that. These children weren't our responsibility, or that of the people at Vengurla, but we all just did what we could on our own time. It was 1974 when the first children were transferred by ambulance to Vengurla.

The children were ages three to eight, and I wondered how they would do being away from their parents, whom they had never left before. How would the people in Vengurla manage? We were still on rationing from the drought. We sent what money we could, and one of the merchants in town gave us a 50-kilo sack of rice. I couldn't go because of a board meeting in Miraj, but nurses rode along with the children, and that evening Bob and I got in the car and drove to Vengurla. We were driving over the mountains in the dark, so with a stop for dinner we didn't arrive until eleven o'clock at night. The children were all asleep, and Kumandini put Bob and me up in beds on the veranda protected by mosquito nets. Kumandini was the nursing superintendent at the Vengurla mission hospital, St. Luke's. Because the hospital was not very busy, she took on the care of the children.

In the morning we awoke to children gathered all around the bed, whispering to each other, "Don't waken them, don't waken them." Here were all these little smiling faces just beyond our nets. We told them we were getting up and would join them downstairs. There we saw how gently and compassionately Kumandini welcomed them.

Kumandini had the children all sitting in a circle. Their eyes glowed when they saw her bring out a big pot full of steaming Cream of Wheat. The children all sat cross-legged with a plate in front of them. Kumandini began serving the cereal, and the hungry children began to eat. "No, stop, stop!" she told them. "We are going to wait until the last one is served, and then we are going to thank God for this food."

But some of the children at the end had started the beggar cry, "Mala de! Malay de! Malay de!" "*Give it to me!*"

"You stop," she told them, "and wait until everyone is served. You *never* need to use the beggar cry again. You are going to have three full meals every day, and because of that, we will not eat a spoonful until we have thanked God for the food he is giving us."

The children just looked at her. *No more begging?* Then she told them to shut their eyes and clasp their hands for the blessing. Tears came to my eyes when I saw the joy of those children as they ate up. She said, "If you want more, you just come up to where I'm sitting with the pot and say, 'Please, may I have more?' and you may have more." Seeing them come up shyly, then smile broadly when they got more on their plates, the tears ran down my face.

We also saw Kumandini teaching them to brush their teeth. As we watched from the veranda, Kumandini lined up the children and gave them a neem twig, which in India is used for a toothbrush. She taught them to take the twig and chew it to make a kind of brush at the end of the twig. Then she went around and gave them tooth powder in their hands.

At first she didn't notice what was going on. The children were eating the toothpaste, and commenting to each other, "It's good, it's good." So then she started over and taught them to use the tooth powder to brush their teeth. These little ones had much to learn.

It was already a worry, how the staff would take care of the children when all the grants from America had been cut, and we were bringing in more children to be fed. But there was another serious concern. How would the Christian community react to the presence of 20 children whose parents had leprosy? Would they take them in at a time when things were already going so hard with them? I was never so surprised as when we finished breakfast, and Kumandini said to us all, "Now we'll all go over to the church."

The church was across the street from the hospital, and many people gathered there for morning prayers at 7:45 a.m. every day, so they were already in the church when the children were marched in and seated in the front two pews. Then the minister stood up and said, "God has given us a wonderful gift today. He has sent us children to be looked after, children that are special to God because their parents have a very bad sickness, and God knows these children need help. And so we welcome everyone into our family …," and he called out the name of every child.

As each child came forward, the pastor turned him or her to the congregation with an introduction. "This is Suresh. We're glad to have you, Suresh." Then, "This is Daniel. We're glad to have you, Daniel; you're part of our family," and so on. These little children beamed.

At first, the children stayed at the mostly empty hospital in Vengurla, but the group of children soon grew. The mission owned a lovely 7 ½-acre property on top of a hill where they could live. A former leper colony, it had beautiful mango and cashew trees, but the buildings were in serious disrepair. It was very difficult to get workers to go up there to fix it up, and in the end most of the work was done by volunteers from SIS, with the carpentry master and Bob on the weekends. After two weeks of work, another group from SIS went down and cleaned up the well. Then the children were transferred from the hospital to this lovely site on a hill from which you looked down on lush, green Vengurla.

Bob and I went to Balniketan one weekend a month to see how the children were doing, sometimes bringing new children to stay. When the children moved from the hospital to the hill, we needed more help because Kumandini was still the superintendent at the hospital and couldn't be in both places. So we talked with a woman named Dorothy. She and her husband were both staff nurses at St. Luke's, and with business so slow she was about to be laid off.

Although she had two children of her own, Dorothy Dhanawade was hesitant. "I don't know if I'll be able to look after them all. My husband thinks it might be a good idea, but we don't really know how we'd get on."

"You know," I said, "God wants us to look after these children, and they need somebody to stay there at night, someone to be parents to them." Dorothy agreed to try it, and it turned out that the children just loved her. However, we became concerned about her husband. As work dropped off at the hospital, he wasn't making much money, and he became a heavy drinker. I worried about the children being there when he was drinking, so I talked with some of the leprosy parents about it.

"You know, their own parents drink heavily sometimes," they said philosophically. "It happens in all families, and as long as he doesn't beat our children, we'll just trust God to look after them." I was touched at such trust from parents more than 150 miles away from their children with no way to visit them. As it turned out, Mr. Dhanawade later gave up alcohol altogether.

***

One day I was just back from a trip to Balniketan when one of the most cantankerous people in the Sangli leprosy colony came to the door. He was always complaining, always asking us to do this or that. That day he was there to say, "I want you to take my little boy."

"We've just come back from Vengurla," I told him, "and I don't think I can take any more children now for at least six months until we get everything settled."

The father became so angry. His son was only three, but he desperately wanted him to go. "If I keep him, I have to take him with me to Bombay and have him on the Bombay streets."

"Leave him and his mother in Sangli," I suggested.

"No, we don't have our own little hut in Sangli, but we do have a special place on the street in Bombay where we can sleep and have a roof over our heads for the rainy weather. But I still don't want to take Prakesh." He had saved up and bought Prakesh a little khaki outfit, like a soldier's outfit, and he was so proud of his son. "Please, please take him. I've got to go back to Bombay."

Finally, Bob said he was going down with the carpentry master to make some repairs, so they would take little Prakesh. I went along and all the way to Vengurla, six or eight hours on the road, Prakesh howled his head off. The only thing that would yield a pause in the howling was a sweet.

We arrived just as the children were going in for their evening supper. They all ran to meet us calling, "Mai! Mai!" "*Auntie! Auntie!*" as they called me. When Prakesh got out, here all the children knew him!

"Oh, Prakesh is coming!" Girls and boys gathered around and hugged him. When he saw the other children, he went off with them so happily. He turned out to be a very happy child, full of fun, and he adjusted to Vengurla beautifully.

Six months later, in November, we brought the children home to Sangli for the holiday of Divali—35 children travelling by public bus. We arranged for Christians in Kolhapur to meet them and help them make the change of buses to Sangli. There we picked them up and brought them to the compound where they would meet their parents. Not knowing what to expect, I worried—would their disfigured parents look even more so now that they'd been away? What had I done in taking them away? But when we arrived, the kids could hardly get out of the vehicles fast enough! They'd brought sweets and fruit from Vengurla to their parents, and were eager to sing for them and show them all they had learned.

At worship that Sunday, these 35 kids sang their heads off. They knew all the hymns and could recite Bible verses. Again, I wondered what would happen, as most of the parents were Hindu. When Prakesh's father, back from Bombay, came up to me, I didn't know what to expect, but he said, "Prakesh is looking very good; he's very happy. But you know, when he came home, we sat down to have our food. I started to eat and he said, 'No, you can't eat your food, you have to thank God for it.'

"'Thank God?' I said. 'What has God done for me? Look at me, I'm a beggar; I can't do anything, I've got this horrible leprosy. Why should I thank God? There isn't any God.'

"And Prakesh said, 'Daddy, don't say that. There is a God and he loves you, and he loves me.'"

Then this once very angry man looked at me and said, "We always say thank you to Jesus before we eat now."

I thought there might be a fuss when it was time to go back to Balniketan, but the kids all went back happily; the only tears were those in their parents' eyes. As the children grew older, they went on to our mission school in Vengurla. A local man who helped with the yard work walked them the half-mile to school each day, then went back and walked them home. Amazingly, these children of lepers had no trouble in Vengurla; nobody threw stones at them. The church people at Vengurla treated them as family and, though they were still on half salary, they made sure every birthday was celebrated with birthday sweets and a special dinner, which was far more than these children had ever had.

***

Prakesh had been at Balniketan about two years when we heard he was in hospital, desperately ill with encephalitis. We sent word to his father and mother in Bombay through the leprosy people's network because they could spread the word so fast. We urged them to go directly to Vengurla. Then we got word that Prakesh was much worse. We prayed so hard for that bubbly little boy, the only child of his parents. Then came the sad news that Prakesh had died.

We held a memorial service in the leper colony in their little church, and I felt so bad. About ten days after that, I was in the sitting room with some visitors when I looked up and saw Prakesh's father, mother, and aunt at the door. Expecting a torrent of anger, I excused myself to meet Prakesh's family on the veranda. "I am so very sorry about Prakesh."

The father took my hand, and said, "Prakesh was sent by God to teach us. He told us Jesus was his friend, and that he was going to go to Jesus. We all three want to go to Jesus, too. Can you tell us how we become Christians?" I was so taken aback that I hardly knew what to say.

"I will send the Bible women to teach you." It was a hardship, but for two months Prakesh's father didn't go to Bombay to beg, but remained in Sangli to learn about the Bible. I was very apprehensive about the reaction to lepers wanting to be baptised. There had been instances of Christians refusing communion to lepers.

After completing their studies, Prakesh's parents and aunt came to be examined by the pastor while I waited nervously outside. When the pastor came out, he said, "Nancybai, those people not only know their Bible, the commandments, the Lord's Prayer and the stories of Jesus, but they have been visited by the Holy Spirit!"

It was amazing to us, the wonderful caring of God. These were children of leprosy that I had thought I could do nothing about. We had no place for them, and I thought I couldn't take the responsibility. Vengurla as a mission station seemed about to close. But God picked up these children and gave us all a big shove. I thank God for what Balniketan has done.

I wrote in our 1974 circular about Balniketan:

"This children's hostel was made possible by the help of Kindernothilfe in Germany and each child has a foster parent in Germany who sends their support each month, but the Americans help, too. Gifts came to help us get the many, many things needed to start the hostel. The Gillette Church in Wyoming sent money to set up the hostel and provide the first month of support and to help pay for petrol for the 150-mile journey from Sangli each month over the mountains and through the jungle to Vengurla by the sea. ... But we praise God for the miracles we have seen there and especially to have the good news that Dr. Ron and Edith Seaton have been appointed to Vengurla by the support of three denominations. ...

"The children came home to their parents at Divali time for ten days. I was so relieved not only to get 35 children transported by public bus over the hot dusty miles but to see them all come back on time and their parents all puffed up with pride and joy. I wish you could have seen Daniel's mother's excitement when she received her first letter written in Daniel's own handwriting! Suresh is determinedly wearing boots and braces to straighten his leg. He dislikes them strongly, but he perseveres. What courage he has! He will need it for he has some operations to go before his legs will be right, yet he plods back and forth the half mile to school each day."

Daniel went on into high school. He didn't finish, but he is very clever. He's kept the house on the edge of the leper colony where his family had lived, and he has formed a team and gone into construction. They build small buildings, particularly latrines, a skill he learned at our mission. When he left Vengurla and came back to Sangli, we needed some latrines built by our village centres, and he organized some other men from the colony, and they built them. Latrines were needed all over, and Daniel earned enough to marry and have a family and to provide for his mother.

Suresh, who had poliomyelitis, had a series of operations. By the time he was 18 he wore braces, but could get around quite well. The last I heard he was working as what we would call a bookie. People who want to bet on anything go to him, and he also sells state lottery tickets. I might have preferred that he did something different, but he is working to support his mother and earning the way he can.

***

Many remarkable people were involved in the work at Balniketan. Dr. Probarker Samson used to come every two months to Vengurla to attend to the children. He was a doctor with the leprosy mission, and the husband of a dear friend of mine. He changed Richardson Leprosy Hospital from an ashram to a full-service leprosy hospital, and became the medical superintendent there. He also set up a two-year program to train health visitors to go into the villages to identify tuberculosis, leprosy, and malaria at the early stages. The government so respected this program that they paid for people from all across India to attend.

Dr. Samson earned his master's in public health at Johns Hopkins and became one of the best-known leprologists in India. Then Leprosy Mission International appointed Dr. Samson director of the Leprosy Mission of Southeast Asia. He helped set up hospitals and leprosy treatment centres at the invitation of the governments in Laos, Vietnam, Burma, and China, where missionaries were not permitted to go. His wife Rohini was a nurse with additional administrative training, and they became a very valuable and respected team.

On a trip through Asia I visited the Samsons in Singapore, where I met the director of leprosy work for all of China, a man who was very impressed with Dr. Samson. Dr. Samson had told him how he had been brought up with the help of missions, mission schools, and grants, and the director said he would very much like to meet a missionary, as he had never met one. Growing up under Communism, all his life he'd heard how evil missionaries were, but as he researched leprosy work he'd seen how much the missionaries had done. So the Chinese doctor stayed over an extra day with the Samsons in order to meet me when I arrived.

As I talked with the Samsons and this Chinese doctor, I looked at Probarker, remembering him as a young boy, working with Bob whitewashing and fixing houses during their summer holidays, working to earn his scholarship. Now he was highly respected throughout the world for his commitment to leprosy work and for his strong faith.

***

Our work with the children of lepers was very rewarding, but so was our work with the adults. One day a wizened old woman named Baisibai was found unconscious on the steps of the Sangli train station. People were just stepping around her, doing nothing, but some of the other leprosy beggars saw her, picked her up, and carried her all the way to the leper colony, then came to me for help.

Baisibai's greatest problem was starvation, and with a little food she came around. The lepers took her home to care for her, sharing whatever they had from a day spent begging. When she came around and felt better, Baisibai was one of the most cantankerous people you ever saw. She ranted at the other beggars, "Why did you save me? Why didn't you let me die?" We were giving out rations at that time, and whenever she came for her rations, she always complained about the kind of rice or wheat they got.

The rationing had begun one Christmas. The cover photo of a big national magazine from Bombay showed a leprosy beggar, blind and sitting on a corner. The caption read, "Give us this day our daily bread." That so hurt me that I said to Bob, "All these beggars, can't we at least give them their daily bread?"

There the daily bread is made of milo flour, which is very cheap, so each month we put some money aside to buy grain to give out. When people heard we were doing this, they would give us a bit of money that became a special fund for buying grain. When the grain merchants heard about it, they gave us extra grain for less money, so it was as if Jesus were multiplying the food. On ration day, one person of each family would come at five o'clock, and we were able to give them some wheat as well as milo, and often a little rice, too.

Now Baisibai had only stumps for feet, so one day when she came for her rations I told her, "You don't need to come. I'll send your rations home with the others."

"No," she said, "I don't trust them; they wouldn't give them to me."

Remember "the missionary barrel"? Churches used to gather outgrown clothes and send them to the missions in barrels. We received a whole lot of clothes, which we gave out to those in need. By government regulation we had to make a list of everything we received and to whom each piece had been given, along with their signature or fingerprints. One day we had spent all afternoon giving out these things and were just finishing when I saw Baisibai hobbling over. I said to the nurse, "We don't have anything left for Baisibai; we've got to give her *something*." In the very bottom of the barrel was a beautiful, black woollen dress with satin around the yoke and satin cuffs. "This would make a beautiful jacket," I thought in passing, but when Baisibai came, we said, "Here, this is for you."

She didn't even have a full sari on, just rags, and I thought she would complain as usual, but she immediately removed the rags and put on this black dress. Here was Baisibai with a very twisted face, one eye gone and slipped down on her face, and with only two teeth in the front. Here she stood in this fancy black dress with her scraggy grey hair—smiling. And I understood, "This is what it *means* to have clothes that make you feel good."

Baisibai put her rags on over the dress and went away pleased with herself. It was the rainy season and quite cold, and now she had something that covered her from head to foot. I considered the person who had given that dress, and thought, "I bet they never thought it would go to a beggar," but no one could have appreciated it more.

Another time we were sent 300 blankets through Church World Service. I made up a list to be approved by the collector, then told those who were to receive blankets to come at a certain time to the compound. The collector came to confirm that we were giving these out to people who really needed them.

There had been a big fire among huts in a very poor area of the city, so we were giving blankets to them. About 200 lepers and 100 others came. After the collector's wife gave a speech, she gave a blanket to each person. Because Baisibai couldn't walk up to receive her blanket, the woman gave it to me, and I took it to Baisibai. She had such a smile on her face when she was handed that blanket! She put it up to her cheek, and afterwards when everybody else was gone, I said, "Baisibai, did you hear what the collector's wife said? It is against the law for you to sell this blanket. These are all new woollen blankets, but it is against the law to sell them."

She looked up at me and said, "I know God loves me, now that I have this blanket. You've told us God loves us, but now I know. Because of God, people in America sent this dress and this blanket, and I would not give them up for anything."

From then on, Baisibai took her blanket everywhere. She sat on her blanket in the street begging, and she took it home to her hut at night. She really became a different person, a much more pleasant person because, as she said to me, "I know God loves me now."

After I retired, I went back to Sangli a few times, and when I went back in 1995, I learned that Baisibai had died. Those who cared for her told me, "We buried her in her blanket. It was always so important in her life because it meant somebody had loved her."

***

The spring before we were to go on our next long furlough, Jody was in a play at school, so Bob and I made a special trip to Kodai to see her. After our short visit, we left Tim at Kodai to finish up some things and returned to Sangli with Jody. When we got off the bus, Sugandh said in alarm, "You don't have Tim with you! The police are looking for Tim because Wellenkur (our neighbour who owned a mill) is accusing Tim of shooting his cow!"

"Tim's been in Kodai for the last six months, so he couldn't possibly have shot his cow," I said, "and besides, we don't own a gun." Actually, Tim did have a BB gun, a hand-me-down from Rob. At first he had used it to shoot crows, but when he saw the crows dying, he stopped, and never again shot any living thing. The BB gun was kept in the principal's office at Kodai except when Tim took it out to the woods when they went on hikes. Nevertheless, it was the headline in all the newspapers: "Missionaries' Son Shoots a Cow!"

The SIS caretaker said he'd seen the cow try to jump the fence and get caught on the barbed wire. The veterinarian confirmed that it was a barbed wire-like wound, not a bullet hole that had become infected and killed the cow.

Still, the police insisted on pursuing it and came regularly to our door, asking, "Has Tim come back?" Under the circumstances, I wouldn't let Tim come home from Kodai. He wasn't guilty, but I knew what would happen if the police took him back in their offices. There was a big demonstration at our house, with people railing against missionaries because they had killed a holy cow.

Non-Christians in Sangli, meaning to be kind, said to me, "Mrs. Ramer, we know Tim didn't mean it. It was just an accident."

Over and over, I explained, "Tim wasn't even here, he didn't shoot the cow!" The police in Kodai, 750 miles away, had on record that he had been in Kodai attending classes. As foreigners, we always had to report our whereabouts to the police. There had even been a policeman at the play with us, so he knew Tim was in Kodai at the time of the suspected shooting.

The dispute went on for over a year! The time for our furlough was approaching, but the Sangli police would not release our passports because Tim was on my passport, and they wanted Tim to come back to Sangli. Despite the evidence and the testimony of the caretaker and the vet, Wellenkur wouldn't give up, but finally we persuaded the police to release our passports.

The proud parents surrounded by (L to R) Lyn, Rob, Jody and Tim

The Ramer Band on Tour

Chapter 21: Eve Teasing

For our 1974-75 furlough, we could only get a three-month visa, so our trip to the U.S.A., England and Scotland was a quick one. The trip home by air was quite amazing—only 22 hours from Denver to Bombay by air, with an hour's stop in New York City and two more hours in Frankfort. It was quite a change from the days of travelling by ship. Although we had been gone only a short time, we were welcomed back with garlands of flowers at the train station and garlands in church on Sunday! Garlands at the school and at the Richardson Leprosy Hospital, and even garlands at the Sangli Water Works! We had never had such a wonderful welcome home to Sangli.

***

We had just returned from furlough when the rajamata (the raja's mother) asked us to tea, and said, "Wellenkur's determined to bring a case against your Tim, but if you'll pay 2500 rupees, he'll drop it."

Bob rarely got angry, but when he did, he really spoke his mind: "This finishes it; this is nonsense, I will not pay 2500 rupees. I am going to make a case against Mr. Wellenkur for defamation of character!"

To this, the rajamata said, "No, no, no, I will pay the 2500, don't worry. I'll just pay, and it'll all be dropped."

But Bob refused to accept her offer and went to the collector, who was like a governor, to pursue the suit, but the collector said, "This is all nonsense. Tim didn't do anything, but don't you go to court. I will settle Wellenkur." And apparently he did because that was the last we heard of it.

Wellenkur had always been a cantankerous neighbour. On top of the cow issue, he was writing letters saying that our students were stealing coal from the back of his cloth factory, and that we were using coal for cooking the food for the hostel. "You can come and see the kitchen," we told him. "We don't use coal," but he wouldn't listen.

Then we heard from our hostel housefather, who lived on the other side of the cloth factory, "There are people who come at night. When we're all at dinner and the whole campus is quiet, they come to the fence, and the watchman at the fence gives them basket loads full of coal. They carry the baskets to the gate and fill a cart every night!"

"All right," Bob said, "when they come, you send one little boy to us to tell us they are there. Don't say anything else, and don't make any fuss, but when we yell, bring all the schoolboys out."

That night the little boy came and said, "They're there." Bob got in the car and drove slowly and quietly, with no headlights, down to the fence, and there were several men and women filling baskets with coal. Frightened, they yelled and began to run, but Bob honked the horn and shouted, "Come and get them!" Our 90 boys in the hostel surrounded them and brought them down to our house.

We called Mr. Wellenkur to show him his own employees were stealing his coal, but he wouldn't come. Then I called his wife, and soon he and the police arrived at our house. When they saw all these folks with the baskets of coal at their feet and the cart full of coal at the gate, they couldn't deny it.

Some time later, Wellenkur's nephew came to our house and said, "I have come on my uncle's behalf to apologize for all the trouble that we gave you and your son Tim because we thought you were stealing the coal." It turned out that the whole accusation about shooting the cow was retaliation for stealing the coal. It just didn't make sense to us. Anyway, he apologized through his nephew, and Bob said, "That's all right, it's all done."

About a year later, Wellenkur and his daughter came to our house to ask us if we would please come to the daughter's wedding. Old man Wellenkur was in his 80s, and here was the younger Wellenkur, asking us to please show that we forgave him by coming to the wedding.

Of course, we went to the wedding, where they honoured us by seating Bob with the priests and me with the ladies. After dinner, as was polite, we went in to give our greetings to the patriarch, old man Wellenkur, who had always been so bitterly opposed to the missionaries and Gandhi as well.

When we conveyed our thanks, he took my hand and said, "We have insulted your family very badly, but you have forgiven us. How can you do that? I would never forgive someone who insulted me the way we insulted you. Now that you have eaten with us, we know we are forgiven, but how could you do it?"

"Jesus Christ forgives us our sins," I explained, "so we must forgive others." I don't know if it made sense to him, but it was how we tried to live.

***

We were happy to be back in India in time for Republic Day. Prime Minister Nehru had declared that while independence was important, the day a country could produce a constitution and govern by the law of the people was *more* important. So while independence was celebrated on 15 August, it was Republic Day, January 25, that was really given over to pomp and celebration.

The January weather was usually auspicious for a celebration, with blue skies, sunshine, and temperatures between 21 and 27 degrees (70 to 80 F). Republic Day was usually memorable, but Republic Day 1975 was a particular standout.

All dressed in Indian clothes for the occasion, we Ramers hurried to be at the SIS flagpole by 7 a.m. Because we weren't citizens, we didn't salute at the flag raising, but stood at attention and sang along with the national anthem. A short speech and a prayer were followed by "Jey Hind! Jey Hind! Jey Hind!" "*Victory to India!*" Once dismissed, we hurried to another flag raising with the 700 students of the Emmanuel English School. Then, at our church, a third flag raising included hymns, Bible reading, and prayer. We arrived at the district police parade grounds just in time for a fourth flag raising before settling into our seats to watch the parade.

Marching past were the police band, the volunteer cadets, the National Women's Corps, and selected school bands. Then the police gymnastics team performed acrobatic feats, followed by gymnastics teams from various schools. Next came the legime band, a Maharashtrian dance procession accompanied by drums and the clang of chains. Schoolchildren dressed in costumes demonstrated ethnic dances, and clowns kept the audience laughing. The police were everywhere, giving out sweets and enjoying the fun, but keeping an eye on the crowd. After the two-hour program, we slowly threaded our way back to campus, driving carefully among the crowds of people and vendors selling everything from roasted corncobs to boiled peanuts.

Back at school we joined the village boys at the hostel for a huge dinner of curry, rice, salad, and bananas, sitting on the floor and eating with our fingers as they did. As we ate, the housefather walked over and quietly informed us that two boys were missing—Sudarker and Premanand. We weren't overly concerned; both were 16 years old, and able to take care of themselves—we thought.

After a couple of hours' rest, we rejoined the students for games and races. With 80 SIS students and 100 or so from the village hostel, there was fierce competition for the prizes. When sweets were served about 5 p.m., the housefather reported that the two boys were still missing. Because both boys were athletic and members of the teams, it seemed unlikely that they intentionally missed the games. Then we noticed a policeman talking with Dr. Phansopker, a member of both the school and the police committees. He soon came over to break the news.

"It seems that Sudarker and Premanand have been arrested."

"What did they do?" I asked.

"Eve teasing!" I knew this to be a serious offence, carrying a six-month prison sentence for those found guilty.

Dr. P. said, "I will go and see what I can do!"

After browsing the bazaar with its lights and decorations, we ate and returned to school for the special variety show that the students, staff, and church people had been preparing for weeks. Still, there was no word on Sudarker and Premanand, so Bob skipped out to investigate.

At the police station he heard their story. As the two boys walked back from the police grounds, they had seen three lovely girls walking ahead of them. Sudarker whistled, and when the girls ignored them, the boys called out, "Hi, lovelies, want to walk with us?"

The girls tried to run through the crowd, but the boys caught up with them. One girl warned them, "My father is the captain in the Sangli City police! You'd better go, or he will arrest you!"

Sudarker heard this as a challenge and boasted, "Who's afraid of the police!" Despite the warning, the boys followed the girls—right to the house of the police captain. Then the crazy boys stood outside the gate calling, "Come, and we will buy you ice cream!" In no time, a police sergeant appeared and arrested them.

Thanks to the intervention of Dr. P. and Bob, the boys were not kept in jail, but were released and ordered to leave Sangli and to stay out for six months! That meant going home to their villages and giving up school, but at least they weren't in prison! More than a year later, Sudarker returned to finish school, and he eventually became a bus conductor. Premanand stayed in his village and worked on the land. None of us, I'm sure, ever forgot that Republic Day.

***

Among our small group of missionaries, you often found yourselves acting as colleagues, friends, pastors, and family all at once. Later in the year, after that unforgettable Republic Day, I had planned a trip to Kodaikanal with Ruth Donaldson, a fellow missionary working in Miraj. In the time since her husband, Dr. Jim Donaldson, had died, Ruth had lost a lot of weight and wasn't feeling well. Dr. Archie Fletcher insisted that she have an exhaustive physical check-up before we left for Kodai. A malignant kidney tumour was discovered, and Ruth went immediately to surgery. After the operation, we had only to look at the faces of Archie and his wife Huldah to know what the future held for Ruth and her family.

The circumstances brought us even closer to Ruth and her six children. Four of the kids were grown, and Jamie was just about to graduate from Kodai, but Debbie was only 13. We thanked God that Ruth was well enough to see Jamie graduate and head off to his first year at the College of Wooster.

We had a good holiday with Ruth, Jamie, and Debbie in June. Bob and I spent many hours with Ruth praying and calmly making plans. We shed tears for ourselves and for her children, but felt that God took Ruth's hand and went before her. Sharing with Ruth the bitter news and the assurance of God's love—these experiences became a permanent part of our hearts and lives.

***

But life goes on. It was wonderful to visit Balniketan, the home for destitute children, to talk and play with the children and see them happy and healthy. We often recorded individual students and brought tapes back for their parents to hear. It was a pleasure to see the parents' faces as they heard the voices of their beloved children. Most of the parents had leprosy, and earned a meagre living by begging. With so few pleasures, they fully appreciated those that they had.

In our own family, Jody had entered Edinburgh Royal, my alma mater, in nursing. Lyn graduated from Durham University in sociology and social administration, and joined Jody in nursing school. A widower now, Pappy Ramer, Bob's dad, spent a year with us in India. He then returned to Denver and married Viola, and they came to Sangli together for their honeymoon.

Back at SIS, our tailoring teacher, Mr. D. A. Kale, was desperately ill with typhoid fever for the two months just before the examinations. My sewing skills were so bad that it nearly kept me out of missionary school, so naturally I ended up managing the tailoring department. In addition to preparing for their exams, our tailoring students sewed clothing for four hostels' worth of students, three sets of clothing for each of 280 students every year. They weren't lacking for practice.

***

Our dog Kolkhoz had always been Tim's special dog, and since her death, Tim had shown no interest in having any other. He had looked half-heartedly at dogs in Bangalore, to no avail. Then one day during the Christmas holidays, Sunil, Sugandh's son, called to Tim, "Come see this dog!"

When Tim went out the back door, the cutest, bounciest, liveliest little pup jumped up over his feet. It was the highest he could jump. Tim played with him for a wee while, then turned to leave, but the pup ran along at his heels, yapping and squirming. "It's a stray dog from the leper colony," Sunil said. "They can't really feed him. Do you want him?"

The pup looked up at Tim adoringly. "Oh, all right. He may run away, but I'll keep him for now." Tim brought the pup to show us. Taking one look, Bob said, "He's a mutt if I ever saw one."

"Great!" said Tim. "We'll call him Mutely."

In no time at all the whole campus knew Mutely. He was a fawn colour and not very big, but he had a big bark. Our self-appointed security guard,

Mutely greeted anyone daring to come near our door with angry barks. The students used to say, "When we are called to Sahib's office, it is scary enough, but when we get near the door, Mutely barks us witless!"

Mutley quickly grew from a silly little pup to a dog with a purpose in life—to follow Tim around. When Tim left for boarding school, Mutley was a dog without a cause, so he decided to guard the *master* of the house. From the moment Bob came out of the bedroom for breakfast, Mutley was at his heels. He followed Bob to chapel, sat at his feet on the platform, and kept quiet through the whole 15 minutes—unless another dog happened to wander into the chapel. Then Mutley sprang up with a furious bark and charged down the aisle to chase the "devil" from that holy place!

In India, we did not have special dog food and delicacies for the canine breed. Mutley had cooked hot cereal and milk each morning with titbits of toast from the table. At noon he had chapatti with leftovers from the table, and at night, special large bones from the butcher, boiled to make a soup. Being Indian born and bred, Mutley had a passion for hot curry, so he sometimes sauntered over to the Priti Jyot boarding hostel, where the boys fed him leftover curry and rice—dog heaven!

For a time, two young missionaries from England, Helen and Ann, lived in the bungalow next door. Both trained at a prestigious nanny school in Britain and had come to help at the crèches. In England Helen had a friend named Peter who was an engineer. "Just a friend," she insisted. One day Helen had a letter from him from Iran, where he was working on a project. He proposed to come for a week to visit Helen in Sangli. Helen worried, "Where will he stay?"

"With the Ramers, of course," I offered.

Peter eventually arrived. He was a handsome young man, rather shy, but interested in all that was going on. We gave Helen some days off, and she took him sightseeing. Since Peter was living with us, after a fierce welcome Mutley gave him no trouble, and Peter paid little attention to him. Helen had come to believe Peter might declare his feelings for her, but on his last day Helen told us sorrowfully, "He hasn't said a word, and he leaves tomorrow."

"We're going to a program in the school chapel tonight," I said. "Why don't you invite Peter to dinner? We'll be out, and you can have the house to yourselves."

That all came to pass, and at the end of the show Peter and Helen joined us as we walked back across the playground with Mutley at our heels. Peter took out a hankie to wipe his brow, giving the hankie a shake to unfold it. Mutley, thinking this was fun, jumped to catch the hankie, missed, and bit Peter's hand!

At home, I washed Peter's wound, and applied permanganate and a bandage. The skin was only slightly broken, but it did make for a solemn farewell. Peter left, having said nothing romantic, and Helen was quite depressed.

A few days later the phone rang. "This is Peter."

"Where are you?" I asked.

"In London."

"I'm so sorry, but Helen is in Miraj today."

"Oh, I don't want to talk to Helen. I just want to ask, how is Mutley?"

"Mutley, our dog?" I puzzled.

"Yes, how is he?"

"He is just fine. Why do you ask?"

"I've been to the doctor, and he says I may be in danger of getting rabies."

"Don't worry, Mutley gets anti-rabies shots every six months," I reassured him. "You'll be all right." Immediately, Peter seemed less worried. "I'll tell Helen you called."

"OK. Goodbye."

We were surprised, and Helen was so disappointed, to know he'd only called to talk about Mutley. Nevertheless, despite his Mutley experience, when Helen went back to England, Peter proposed, and they were married.

***

At this time, in the 1970s, Indira Gandhi was urging the opening of crèches, or daycares, and our Bishop Andrews had long been urging me to open one in Sangli. He quoted my own words back to me, about how every time I went to the bazaar I said we *had to* do something for the beggar children. But I had been quite rude to him, telling him I just couldn't do it. There was no place, no money, and no teacher. The bishop talked to KNH in Germany and they agreed to help financially, but I still resisted, insisting we had to have a Montessori teacher.

Then in December two sisters came to my door asking for help. One was quite sick, and the other, a teacher in Poona, wanted to relocate to Sangli to be near her. "What kind of teacher are you?" I asked.

"I trained with Madam Montessori," Mrs. Sironi replied.

Nearly out of objections, I told her to survey the beggars and see if they were interested. The majority of our mothers went house to house, cleaning pots and pans, which earned them about ten rupees (well under a pound) per month plus a meal, and they were glad to get that. Soon Mrs. Sironi was back—trailing 21 little children whose parents were only too grateful for them to have a safe place to go.

So in January 1976, we opened a crèche for children of poor families under a tree in my front yard. In no time, there were 40 children who came daily from 9 a.m. to 5 p.m. It was a joy to see them change from crying, prematurely old people to laughing, loving, confident children.

Eventually we moved our crèche to some old schoolrooms that we rented with the help of KNH. For each child, KNH arranged foster parents who sent money through KNH for that child. A grant from our Presbyterian Church covered the salaries and administration of the crèches, so it was a real partnership. We regularly had visitors from both America and Germany, and they seemed to be very impressed with what was going on.

Around that time our former SIS hostel became Priti Jyot Hostel, which housed 80 village boys, ages 12 to 18, while they attended city schools. Our new assistant housefather, Mr. Pramod Ghatge, had once been one of my babies in the Shantinagar Health Centre! A college graduate now, he took hold of the work very enthusiastically. The boys played all kinds of tricks on him, so I was surprised to see him come back early from his day off and asked him, "Why did you come early?"

"Oh, it is so boring without the boys!" he said, "and I feel God has called me to this."

***

One of the scariest experiences we had in 37 years in India began with a letter from 15-year-old Tim, the only one of our children still at Kodai. Thursday had long been a special day at our house because that was the day we received letters from the kids at Kodai. The students all wrote letters home on Sunday and mailed them on Monday, and we received them on Thursday. I woke up on Thursdays thinking, "Oh, this is the day to get the kids' letters!"

That particular Thursday morning in October 1976, there was the expected letter from Tim, but as I read it, I became very upset because he had written, "I don't know what's wrong with me, I keep dropping things, and just look at my writing, I can't write properly. HELP! Love, Tim."

Poor Tim was 750 miles away, three days' journey by train! I immediately sent a telegram to the principal and to Tim. To the principal I said, "Please have Timothy examined by Dr. Desai," the highly respected doctor in private practice in Kodai. "Let me know report. Should I come?"

To Tim I said, "Trying to come. Please go see Dr. Desai."

The return telegram came on Saturday: "Timothy is all right. Doctor examined. Come if you wish." I had already booked a place on the train. Tuesday was the soonest I could get a seat.

It helped that I knew that Mel Cassady, a consultant to Kodai School, would be returning to Miraj on that Tuesday. I contacted Mel and pressed him to find out about Tim and to get the whole truth out of them. We would meet at the Bangalore station Tuesday morning, me on my way to Kodai, he on his way back.

When I got off my train at Bangalore, there was Mel. He walked toward me with such a look of compassion in his eyes, and he said, "Nancy, let's go to a nearby hotel. We'll have a cup of coffee, and we'll talk about it there."

I stood rooted to the platform and said, "Mel, I can take it. Tell me now. I've got to know now." I was thinking, "Brain tumour? Drugs? What could it be?"

"Well," he said, "Tim has a disease that I've never heard of called chorea minor."

"Chorea!" I said. "Oh, thank God, that's curable!"

Mel looked at me in astonishment. "Do you know about chorea?"

"Oh, yes."

"He can't control his movements."

"I know," I said, "but that's chorea. It's caused by a strep infection probably." I knew Tim had had a sore throat a month previously. It probably hadn't been treated properly, so now he needed penicillin. Chorea is a disease of the central nervous system, related to rheumatic fever.

"They used to call it St. Vitus's dance when I was in nursing in Scotland. We saw a lot of it there." I was so relieved to know that Tim had something we could probably cope with.

Somewhat reassured, I left Mel to catch my train, arriving at Kodai Road about midday. As I got off the bus, I met some Kodai people who told me Tim was staying at the chaplain's house with Gaye and Ginny Johnson. Their son Alan had been Tim's roommate, and they were great friends.

Gaye and Ginny had been watching for me. Of course, I wanted to see Tim right away, but Ginny stopped me. "Wait a minute, Nancy. Do you know he can't control himself? He can't talk properly?"

"Ginny, I know chorea patients can't talk. They don't have control of their voluntary muscles. Their arms and legs move all the time. They can't sleep properly; they can't eat properly. I know all that."

"Well," she said, "you'll get such a shock when you see him."

Poor Tim was throwing his arms and his legs around. He couldn't talk, but made frantic, unintelligible noises. He was so pleased to see me that the tears rolled down his cheeks. After some thought, I came up with the idea to point at letters on a typewriter. When I hit the right one, Tim would smack the bed. In this way we were able to communicate.

I explained to Tim about chorea, how it would improve, and he would be able to walk and talk again. I could see the great relief in his eyes. Of course, I stayed, relieving Alan and some other school friends who had been staying with him.

Ginny told me that when Tim was in hospital, word had gotten around that he was possessed by the devil. Crowds had gathered at the hospital window to see his wild movements, and that's why she had taken him to her home. We'll be eternally grateful for that.

When I went to see Dr. Desai, we pieced together what had happened, and he was furious with the school. When Dr. Desai saw Tim, he thought the school had sent him up by car, but Tim had walked the mile each way. Back at school, Tim told the housemother that he was to stay in bed until the doctor came to check on him again, but the housemother shooed him off to English class.

When Dr. Desai came to check on Tim and found he wasn't in bed, he was enraged and said to the principal, "Why did you not see this coming on? He is an advanced case. You should have recognized it!"

I decided to take Tim to the very good mission hospital in Vellore where I could nurse him properly. So I sent a telegram to Bob saying, "Medicine not working properly. Going to Vellore Sunday morning. Please come if possible." I knew Mel would have told Bob about chorea, and that he would have already looked it up in my medical books.

The school van was at a football meet, so we couldn't leave for Vellore until Saturday night when the team returned. That meant going down the mountain in the dark, but it couldn't be helped. When at last we could depart, there was a terrible storm, one of those tropical storms where the rain comes down in sheets, and the trees sway. I was terrified to go with just Tim and the driver. Tim was six feet tall, and if we got stuck in the water somewhere, I didn't know if we would be able to get him out of the van. Thank goodness, Chris Riber volunteered to come with me. He was a Kodai teacher who had had nurses' training during the Vietnam War.

When we got to the hospital in Vellore, we found our friends Bob and Lou Carmen were there. Bob, a doctor, ordered immediate penicillin injections, but Tim jerked so much we could barely get the needle in. It was also nearly impossible to get any food or fluids into him.

To make it all worse, the hospital nurses wouldn't go near him. Seeing him thrash around, they, too, were convinced he was possessed. So I stayed with him around the clock. I was so glad of my nursing experience, but it was so hard on Tim, hearing the nurses say they wouldn't go near him.

It was our great good luck that the van developed a flat tire in Vellore. This meant that Chris, instead of returning immediately to the school, was there to help me with Tim so I could get some food and his injections into him. I was *so* grateful for that.

By this time, I was utterly exhausted and thinking, "Oh, Lord, if I could just get some regular help," when Lou Carmen came in and said, "Nancy, you look dead beat. You go get some sleep!"

"No," I said, "I just can't leave him."

"Trust me, Nancy, go and have a sleep." Reconsidering, I thought, "Tim knows Lou Carmen," so I went off, set the alarm, and had two hours of very deep sleep.

I'd just gotten up and was conferring with Lou when I heard two voices talking in the hall. I looked at Lou and exclaimed with heartfelt gratitude, "Bob! Bob's here!"

Lou was looking at me in surprise, quite taken aback, when in walked two Bobs—Bob Carmen and Bob Ramer, and such a hug I gave my Bob for being there! As soon as he'd gotten my telegram, he'd hit the road. He didn't have a reservation and he didn't care, he just got himself on the train and came as quickly as he could.

Meanwhile, Lou was laughing. She had heard only *her* husband's voice coming along the corridor, just as I'd heard only *my* husband's voice. When she heard me say with such relief, "Oh, Bob's here!" she'd thought, "Why, does Nancy have a crush on my husband?" That gave us all a hearty and much-needed laugh.

Bob stayed the rest of the week. Pappy Ramer, well into his 70s by then, was visiting in Sangli and doing his best to cover for Bob. Bob and I alternated nights with Tim, getting a good night's sleep every other night. By the time Bob left, Tim was gradually responding to treatment, though he was in hospital in Vellore for ten days before we could go home to Sangli. It was three months before Tim could go back to school.

Some years later, after I retired, I met Bob and Lou Carmen by accident at an airport. Bob said to me, "How about Tim? Is his heart OK?"

"Yes, his heart's fine; he's in excellent health."

Bob looked at me and said, "That's a miracle."

"Nancy, we were so scared you were going to lose Tim," said Lou. "Just the week before Tim came in, another boy came in with chorea, an Indian boy, and he was at the same stage Tim was—he couldn't swallow properly. We couldn't get needles in to give him intravenous, and he died just a few days before you brought Tim in. We were all so afraid that we had gotten to Tim too late."

Chapter 22: The Joy of Four Latrines

I knew I couldn't handle it. You don't start a new school from your sickbed. We had 70 kids at Balniketan and were eager to open a crèche for children under age five whose parents had leprosy. Most of the parents were beggars or worked in our handloom project, weaving bags and other items for sale. When we applied to start a crèche for younger children, Julie Lipp-Nathaniel of KNH, the German agency, said, "Crèches are needed everywhere, but we don't have enough trained people. Why don't you start a crèche nurses training school (CNTS)?"

I had to refuse. From November 1977 to May 1978, I had experienced intermittent, severe attacks of diarrhoea, and much of my time had been spent in bed. Cancer of the colon had been diagnosed, and I was to have surgery, so I wrote to the KNH board in Germany asking them to get someone else to start the CNTS.

Germany wrote back and said, "You start it anyway, and we're going to have prayer." Happily, the distress was found to be due not to cancer, but to "missionary companion amoeba" and other infections. The bowel was rebelling, but it wasn't cancer.

Still resisting, I wrote back to Germany with my conditions: "OK, but I won't start until we have a qualified principal, an accountant, and a good nursery teacher." Expecting this might stall the project indefinitely, I sent out notices for staff. Within a month, the Lord showed me that right at hand were women ready to fill all those positions!

While I was ill, Sulochana Gorde, who had worked at the Health Centre nearly 20 years ago, had come to visit me. Her husband was retiring, and they had bought a house in Miraj. I talked over the possibility of a CNTS with her.

"We need to do something for girls who fail the matriculate exam," I told her. Those who failed at the end of the 10th grade couldn't go on to college and weren't even eligible for many jobs because so often they had failed English and math. "The girls who really like children and home things—we could train them to work at the crèches."

"That's a wonderful idea!" she said.

Later, as I talked with Bob, he asked, "Did you ask her to be the principal of your crèche school? She's working in Poona now, she might come."

"It never occurred to me. She's got a good job, but her husband is retiring, and they're moving to Miraj."

At this point, I didn't even have the grant yet, let alone a salary figure to offer, but I wrote to Sulochana anyway. She replied with a wonderfully enthusiastic letter, saying, "I'm bored with life just now, and this would give me a chance to be nearer my husband. Besides, I've always wanted to do something for girls who failed the matric—it's so unfair! Oh, I'll *do* it!"

On July 6 Bishop and Mrs. Andrews dedicated half of an old missionary bungalow in Sangli as The Crèche Nurses Training School of the KDC/CNI/CCC. The girls, aged 18 to 22, lived at the school, and Sulochana lived with them. The girls studied anatomy, physiology, hygiene, nutrition, child development, child diseases, first aid, crafts, handwork, educational play, cooking, accounting, budgeting, record keeping, home visiting, the Bible, and all areas of maternal and child care. We later added a second year, during which they rotated into the crèches for practical experience.

As it often does, illness had brought our Lord very near. While I was lying in bed, he gave me a vision of a whole new area of service in the Crèche Nurses Training School—and then pushed me into it.

We eventually had crèches in Shantinagar for beggar children, Prakashniketan (*"Garden of Light"*) in Wanlesswadi for children of parents with leprosy, two in the villages, and one at the hospital in Miraj, plus our residence in Vengurla, Balniketan. Prakashniketan was named for Prakash, the little boy in Vengurla who died of encephalitis.

***

Not long after the opening of the CNTS, there was a woman at Richardson hospital who was being treated for leprosy, tuberculosis, and anaemia. She had recently given birth to a tiny baby who weighed only 2½ kilos (about 3.3 lbs.). The mother wasn't well enough to take care of her, and the hospital wouldn't admit the baby, so the mother gave her to me and asked me to find someone to take care of her. First, I took the tiny child to her father in the leper colony, but he had no hands and couldn't care for her. I asked neighbouring families who had no children, but they said, "No, she's too tiny; she's only going to die." In desperation, her parents asked me to please find someone to adopt their little daughter.

Meanwhile, I named the unfortunate little one Asharani, *"Queen of Hope."* When Sulochana heard about her, she said they would take the baby at the Crèche Nurses Training School; it would be good practice for the girls. Soon baby Asharani was known and adored by everyone on the compound. Even after her mother got better, she asked the girls to keep the baby for the time being because it was so hard for her parents, both beggars, to care for her.

Under the supervision of Sulochana, and with the love of all the girls, Asharani grew into a very loving, happy toddler. As she grew older, the question of her future became more pressing. Then one day Tom and Wendy Moore in Littleton, Colorado, a family previously unknown to us, wrote to ask if we knew of a child they could adopt. The Moores knew the Jewett family from their church, and the Jewetts had two adopted daughters from Sangli, so that was the connection.

Tom and Wendy already had two children and were eager to make Asharani a part of their family. The long, slow machinery of adoption began to move. Finally, after a full year dealing with courts, social workers, and U.S. immigration, Asharani was ready to go to the U.S. It was a heartbreak for us all, including her parents, to see her leave India, but she went forth in God's hands.

Tom and Wendy sent us lovely pictures of Asharani with her American parents, sister Erin, and brother Jason. I took these photos of Asharani with her new family to her Indian parents. Because they had no fingers, I had to hold the pictures for them. But as they eagerly studied the photos, Asharani's father looked up with tears in his eyes and said, "I am so happy, so very happy! Truly God planned this for Asharani!"

***

One February Bob's brother Phil called to say that their dad had had a stroke, was paralysed, and couldn't talk or swallow. We had our hands full at home in India, but I encouraged Bob, "You are booked to go to that meeting in Calcutta tomorrow night. Why don't you take the reservation to Bombay, and instead of Calcutta, get on a plane for New York, and go to Pappy?"

Bob had no winter clothes, no ticket, no money, no tax clearance, no inoculations, and no police permission to travel! We prayed about it all day Sunday. After a village church service, we went to Miraj, where Bob borrowed a suit and overcoat from Mel Cassady. By 3 p.m. Monday, Bob had authorization for time off, a ticket, tax clearance, inoculations, and police clearance. Thanks to the help of many friends, by Monday night, Bob was on his way to Denver.

Bob spent 10 days with Pappy in Denver, and he was sure Pappy knew he was there. Like his departure, Bob's return was eventful, and he wrote of it in our circular:

"Having neglected to make a reservation from Bombay in time, I had to take a ticket in unreserved second class. An aggressive coolie helped me procure a space on the luggage rack for the night. Even though I didn't dare move from here, at least I was not liable to be trampled on, nor to have luggage thrown on my lap like those below me! …

"Though cramped, it was fairly comfortable, and I must have got some sleep for just as the Sangli station was coming into view, they woke me up. … Since the floor was a carpet of people all the way to the door, there was no way to get either myself or my luggage out the door. So I threw first my pillow out the window, then my bedcover and chappals [sandals], followed by my duffle bag, and then myself! Cooperative people handed me my suitcase and briefcase and waved a cheery goodbye as I gathered my things together. My only regret is that there was not a cine-camera to record the arrival that morning in Sangli of the Sangli senior missionary!"

Three weeks after Bob's return, we received word that Pappy had entered the Church Triumphant.

***

The late 70s brought many changes, some bad, some good. SIS was in crisis. Although there were many student applicants, two senior masters were retiring, and it was near impossible to fill those positions because salaries in industry were so much higher. SIS was a CNI school now, but CNI wasn't helping very much.

In 1979 Tim graduated from Kodai, the last child on mission support at the school where there had once been 21.

The first class of crèche nurses completed their 18-month course and went out to start other crèches.

***

One day when I went into the bazaar, there was a little old woman sitting on a street corner, and standing beside her was a child of two or three singing songs. A cute little girl, she danced and acted out the songs as she sang, and people gave her grandmother a little money. After that day, I sometimes stopped to talk with the grandmother, and slowly the story of her granddaughter, Lata, came out. Lata's father had deserted her at her birth, and when she was two years old, her mother left, so her grandmother took care of her. For a time, the grandmother had supported them with day labour, but as she got older she could no longer go out to work, so she came to Sangli. Lata shared her name with a famous singer who was often heard in Indian movies and on the radio, and it was *that* Lata's songs she often sang in the bazaar.

One day as we talked, Lata's grandmother asked if there were any place Lata could go to get an education. Soon we took Lata into our daily crèche. There she got her meals, and when her grandmother picked her up, *she* would be slipped a little food, too.

When Lata was four or five, her grandmother asked if Lata could go to Vengurla to live and go to school. Tim, who was a college student at the time, decided that he would send the money to KNH to support Lata through the foster program, so Lata came to Vengurla. With her singing, Lata was a cheerful addition to Balniketan. She went on through high school, passed her matric, and went into nursing at our hospital in Miraj. Tim and his wife Martha supported her through her nursing school.

On a recent trip back to India, Tim, Martha, and their daughters met up with Lata, then a staff nurse in Kolhapur. She told them she sends 500 rupees a month home to support her grandmother, and visits her regularly. These are the kind of stories I love to tell.

***

It must have been 1980 when we went on a very special furlough. For the first time in seven years, the whole family would be together for Christmas. We were arriving in Denver from three different countries, so the logistics were complex, but most challenging of all was finding a house big enough for us all to be together!

When missionaries were home on furlough, the Synod or the Presbytery was to find housing for them, but the truth is that it almost never got done. Usually, however, our friends rallied around us, and someone would find a furnished house we could rent. Notices were put in church bulletins, and friends talked to friends, but this time, despite months of searching—no luck. We were willing to live six months in one place and six months in another, but still—nothing. It was a few months before Christmas, and I was getting *frantic.*

Lyn and Jody were flying in from Britain. Tim was coming down from Macalester College in Minnesota, and Rob was living in Denver. Jamie and Deb Donaldson, children of our late missionary friends Jim and Ruth, would also be joining us for their first Christmas in America. Then Jody wrote and asked to bring her boyfriend. I appealed to her not to bring him, but Bob said, "Let her bring him. Just tell him he might have to sleep in the cellar with the coal!"

Bob and I arrived in New York on December 14 and still had no place to stay! But when I got to the church offices, a woman said, "Oh, there's a woman who has been phoning and phoning from Denver. She wants you to phone her immediately. It's about a house."

"Oh, that'd be wonderful!"

So I phoned up and the woman said, "Yes, we have a big, furnished house in Lakewood, Colorado, on the outskirts of Denver, and we'd be delighted for you to have it. I wondered what I was going to do because my husband and I are going to Florida!" I was so grateful! Their names were Ruth and Bill Price.

We flew to Denver on the 15th and stayed in Pappy's house until the 18th, when the Prices moved out and turned their home over to us. Ruth pointed out her special Christmas china and said to me, "Be sure to use the Christmas dishes."

"Oh, we won't use that; we don't need anything special," I demurred.

"Oh, no, you must use my English china. I wouldn't feel happy if I thought that wasn't being used at Christmas time." That was the kind of generous person she was.

As soon as the exchange took place, we rushed out to buy a whole lot of groceries, then to the airport to pick up Lyn. Jody arrived the next day with her boyfriend, then Jamie and his sister Deb came, and there was plenty of room for everybody! Rob and his wife, who lived in Denver, came over for dinner, so the whole family was all together at Christmas. Not only that, but Bob's brother Phil and his family drove in from Kansas. After Phil preached at his 5:30 p.m. Christmas Eve service, they drove all night to get to us by Christmas Day.

I had the turkey in the oven and everything else on the way when the garbage disposal went on the blink, and the water refused to go down the drain! Bob said, "Oh, I'll get at it," and had just crawled under the sink with his tools when his brother and family arrived! We hadn't seen each other for so long, so there were great hugs and kisses everywhere.

When Bob and Phil got together, they talked non-stop, and you couldn't get them distracted, so I said, "Bob, you've got to get that sink done." Soon, lo and behold, both of them were underneath the sink. They worked on it, then stopped to talk to one another—both of them lying on the floor under the sink. Finally, they gave a last twist to a pipe, and the whole thing came away!

Fortunately, the mess didn't fall right in their faces, but it went all over their clothes, and we had to pull the soaking men out from under the sink. The kids had all gone out somewhere, and by the time they returned, Bob and Phil were in dry clothes and we'd gotten the kitchen all cleaned up. It was a wonderful Christmas dinner with all my grown kids, their guests, the Donaldsons, and Phil, Pat, and their children. We missed Pappy very much, but we had a wonderful time together.

Then it was time for everyone to go back, and for Bob and me to begin a lot of "itineration," travelling around speaking in churches. We had a little Chevy Citation to drive around to churches with our nearly four meters (about 12 ft.) of displays and maps, our slides, etc. We spoke all over the southwest and west, and were to fly back to Denver from Montana the day that Mt. St. Helens erupted. Needless to say, that flight was cancelled; there were inches of volcanic dust all over everything.

We had the Prices' house until Easter, when they would return. It was March, and we still had nowhere to go from there, when I was speaking in a church, and a lady asked where we were living and how we came to stay there. I told the whole story, and we agreed that it was wonderful the way God opened up a place for us.

"What are you going to do now?" she asked.

"I don't know. We're still looking for a place."

"Well, my husband and I are leaving before Easter to go to Maine to buy antiques. We're there all summer, and we bring it all back about October." I said we were due back in India in November. "Well," she said, "we'll stay until you have to go back if you'll take our house." We went to see their house, and it was a big house, too. Once again the Lord had provided for us.

***

Being apart from our loved ones was something we had had to learn to live with. Although we had not *all* been together for seven years, we had seen all the kids during that time. We had been home on short furloughs, visiting Lyn and Jody in Scotland, and Rob and Tim in America. From when I was little, I was used to being away from loved ones, and that helped.

Letters were most important for keeping in communication. Bob and I were separated for the two years that we were engaged. He wrote every day, so I wrote every day, and you're able to say a lot in letters that you wouldn't say in person about your feelings. Then when we had the children and they went to boarding school, they had to write a letter every Sunday, so it became a habit for all of us. It is one of the hardest things, to be separated from our kids, especially when they were little, then again when they had to leave us in India and come to America or Britain for college. That is when we truly put them into God's hands, and he has not failed us.

***

Back home in Sangli, the next push was to construct a new building for the Shantinagar crèche, and it was a challenge. As I wrote in our circular at the time, "It is in a slum area, and not a pleasant place to work, so I'd nearly gone crazy trying to get the contractor and workers to finish the job.

Finally, I lost my Scottish temper at the foreman and contractor! It galvanized them into action like an electric shock! Things began to *move*. I appealed for the help of the children's parents, the CNTS students joined in, everybody pitched in, until at last we were ready for opening on 1 June 1981.

"The Crèche and grounds were packed, even the roofs of surrounding houses were occupied with onlookers. All wanted to share in our joy. A lovely building with four latrines—oh, joy of joys—four latrines! We thought it was a huge building with two large rooms, dining room, kitchen, and baby room. I can have 75 children! What a joy—until we found that even after taking 75 children mostly under three, we still had over 45 scraps of humanity needing to come! How do you say no to a starving and a desperate mother?"

***

One early morning in 1982 the phone rang. The caller was sobbing and almost incoherent, but finally I understood. Smita Huprikar, the daughter of the Wanlesswadi pastor, had fallen into the well and drowned! Not that wonderful, laughing girl—one of our first batch of trained crèche nurses! A lovely girl, she had started the crèche in Nagpada House in Bombay, and the children there loved her! Smita always had a smile on her face and a child in her arms, with two more hanging onto her skirts. Lord, not Smita!

But it was. She was home on vacation when it happened. It had rained during the night, and in the early dawn she had gone to fill the water vessel. To get the water she had to go down a path to the well. She had slipped on the wet path and fallen headfirst into the well! Her father was in the communion service at the opening of the diocesan meeting in Poona when he was called out.

Bob and I rushed to Wanlesswadi and began to see to the arrangements, including the police inquiry and the post-mortem. At her mother's request, I sat beside Smita during the post-mortem, which was a horrible thing to have to do. The post-mortem turned up nothing unusual except a bump on the head and water in all the air passages.

Smita was only 20 when she died, but she had poured out a great deal of love on many people. The Huprikars had six daughters and one son. It fell to me to give the tragic news to Smita's six-year-old sister. Smita's little sister looked at me with serious brown eyes and asked, "Smita is with Jesus?"

"Yes," I answered, "she is with Jesus."

"Then Smita will be happy," she said, matter-of-factly. "I just wish he'd let her come back sometimes! But since she is happy, I will try not to be sad."

No wonder Jesus said, "Ye must have faith as a little child."

The funeral was conducted, as is the custom, at 5:30 p.m. the same night. Bob was dressed in his gown and prepared to do the service, but Rev. Huprikar said, "I have consoled many, buried many, now I must show that I believe what I said." The Lord upheld him in a marvellous way.

It was a terribly hard day. The new grave was covered with a blanket of yellow marigolds, with candles atop the mound in the shape of a cross. I looked at the setting sun and the glowing candles on the bed of flowers, and I thought of Rev. Huprikar's words, "The Lord has given us a beautiful daughter for 20 years. Now he has taken her to himself. The Lord's name be praised." We came home in a state of shock.

***

The Sangli Industrial School had 200 applications for only 32 student openings. There were so many more than we could help, but it was encouraging that two former students in Poona, who had good jobs, sent money each month, enough to pay the way for two current students.

There was continued tumult over the ownership of SIS and the hospitals. Originally, missionary work in our area was all under the Western India Mission, with the senior Presbyterian missionaries in charge. Then the Suwarta Manda was formed, a joint organization, half Indian–half American. That worked well, so in 1955, the mission dissolved, and all work came under the Indian church body called the Kolhapur Church Council (KCC).

With the church unification, all property was turned over to the Church of North India Trust Association under the control of the Kolhapur Diocesan Council (KDC), but dissidents on the KCC wanted to maintain control of the property themselves. Both claimed SIS and the hospitals.

A court case over ownership had been in the works since 1971. Around 1982 the KCC, the dissident group that was fighting COEMAR (PCUSA) and the Church of North India, tried forcibly and illegally to take over Sangli Industrial School. Our days were filled with prayer, tears, and faithful friends. CNI officers, and both Bishop Andrews and Bishop Bhandare, gave personal and powerful support. There was daily tension as outsiders tried to stir up strikes among the students, and many we thought were friends proved unfaithful. Foreigners no longer had the prestige they once had. That part was good.

In April 1983, the local KCC pastor gave Bob a letter saying that he was past 60 and hereby retired, and that S. B. Guikwad would be principal. Guikwad tried to foment a strike. He invaded Bob's office at the house and pulled the phone out of the wall. After intervention by the police and the bishops, Guikwad was ordered to desist. Still the matter went to court in a case that lasted 12 years and affected more than 50 mission stations all over north India. Being under the authority of CNI, Bob was drawn into a long, ugly court battle for more than a decade.

In December 1983, the court decided in COEMAR's (our) favour, so we celebrated with all our SIS and crèche staff and friends. Food for more than 100 people was cooked in the open in our backyard, and there was a palpable sense of relief, as well as a display of fireworks!

Bob wrote of the court case in our circular: "Where, this year, have I heard the purpose of the mission of the Christian Church most clearly proclaimed to non-Christians, especially to the elite and well educated? No, it was not on the radio, not in any evangelistic campaign, nor in a lecture series. It was in the Kolhapur District Court where every lawyer who was free, and even some judges, crowded into the courtroom to listen to our Bombay lawyer (by the way, a Muslim) plead our case. Both he and also the opposing lawyer made much use of the Charter of the Board of Foreign Missions of the Presbyterian Church in the USA and they proclaimed that the purpose of the mission was to Proclaim Jesus Christ and self-supporting, self-propagating and self-governing churches! It was all so clearly set out and was a really good presentation of what mission is all about, as opposed to so many misconceptions that are spread abroad in India, e.g., 'It is only those who are given things who become Christians, so called "rice Christians."' But the manual showed very clearly that mission meant far more than just converting people in name only.

"In the end the verdict came out in our favour, and it is meaningful for the Church of North India, and especially the Kolhapur Diocese for it means that they have the right to use the property formerly used by the Kolhapur Church Council, and even tho' this has been appealed to the high court, this very positive definite clear verdict in our favour will assure positive stewardship of the property, and is not likely to be reversed in the higher court, because it has been so carefully prepared and is so well documented."

***

During the holidays in her second year, Sushima, one of our crèche nursing students, ran away and married her childhood sweetheart. Romantic it may be, but by doing this she had broken her contract of training, so Sushima was suspended for three months, though she eventually finished as a day student.

In due course, Sushima and John had a little girl, a baby who was severely mentally retarded. Sushima was heartbroken, for many told her that this was God's punishment for having made "a loove marriage." I told her that our loving heavenly father was not that kind of god, rather that he had chosen John and Sushima to be the parents of this wee girl because they loved each other and would share this love with her.

Although we held out little hope, the psychiatrist arranged for John and Sushima to take little Jessica to Bombay for tests to see if anything could be done. By this time, Jessica was one year old with a sweet, lovely face, but very limited mental development. After two weary days spent riding crowded buses and trudging through the filthy streets of Bombay, they returned exhausted and discouraged. Sushima came to see me, and I read out the report, essentially "Nothing can be done for Jessica. No reason found in parents' history or physical findings."

Sushima's patience snapped! "You do so much for other children. Why can't you do something for *my* baby? Just let her smile once! Make her know me just once!" Out of her rage came the push for Dr. George (the clinical psychologist) and me to start a crèche for retarded children. Dr. George resigned his hospital job and took up the work of crèche officer for special crèches. Meanwhile, Jessica and Sushima came to our Prakashniketan Crèche, which was for the children of people with leprosy.

Jessica, who became known as "Candy," spent her days on a mattress under the trees. The other children started to bring her flowers and played with her fingers. They would stop to give her a kiss and to talk to her. Sushima's work was to devote all her attention to Candy, to watch her reactions to all sorts of things, no matter how small. Then came the day when Candy smiled as the children sang! And the day of triumph when Sushima phoned to say, "Candy knows me! She keeps looking for me, then smiles when she sees me!"

Finally, we were given seven tiny, rundown cottages, previously part of the TB sanatorium, for our Shalom Crèche. The very first child admitted to the crèche was Jessica. Sushima laid Jessica in Mrs. Andrews' arms as Bishop Andrews declared the crèche open on 17 May 1983. Jessica was not yet two years old when her mummy became "The Special Crèche Nurse!" The crèche began as a day care centre with seven children, but became residential for about half the children, who eventually numbered 16.

About two months after Shalom opened, Jessica had an attack of upper respiratory infection, which was unresponsive to the drugs, and she went to be with the Lord. The crèche was started, and Jessica's work was done.

After the time of mourning, Sushima returned to her work, serene and dedicated. Her husband had a very good job, with house provided, in a town about 80 km (50 miles) away. We feared that Sushima might leave us to spend more time with her husband, as that distance was too far to travel daily, but no. Her husband John said, "We will arrange to be together as much as possible, but God has called us to this work through Jessica. We will not leave it. Sushima will stay here with the children, and I will come every week."

Sushima later gave birth to a strong, active baby boy. They named him Anand, meaning "joy." Beaming with pride, Sushima said, "Anand will learn to love his family in Shalom Crèche."

How tenderly God plans, how rich his joy!

The Crèche Nurses setting off in the minibus

The Crèche Nurses in class

With the children at Vengurla

REV. ROBERT RAMER MEMORIAL
CRECHE TRAINING CENTER K.N.H.
CHURCH OF NORTH INDIA K.D.C.

The Crèche Nurse Training School after it was renamed for Bob

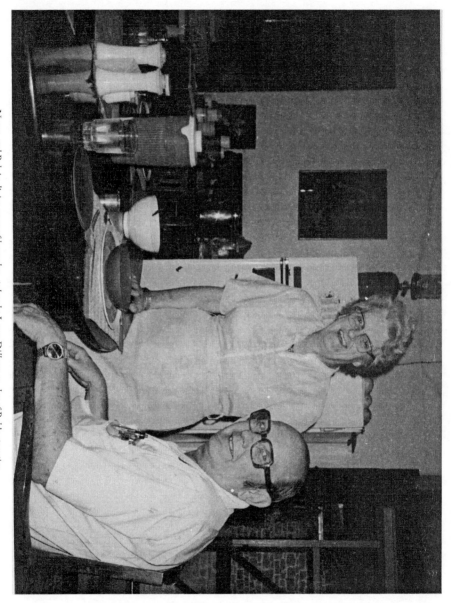

Nancy and Bob in dining room of bungalow, taken by Leroy Dillener on day of Bob's operation

Chapter 23: Farewells

On May 29, 1984, Rev. Leroy and Peg Dillener, former missionary colleagues then living in Pennsylvania, were visiting us at our home in Sangli. Bob had just repaired their camera, and to test it, they took a picture of me serving breakfast to Bob. It was the last picture ever taken of the two of us.

The next day at 4 p.m. Bob went into Miraj Hospital for surgery to repair an inguinal hernia. On the previous Friday he had had an electrocardiogram and complete lab work done, and everything checked out OK. That evening I joined him for dinner, as did our missionary colleagues Dr. Ron Seaton and his wife Edith.

Always the nurse, the next morning I helped with the preoperative preparations. As we waited for the operation to begin, many friends came in to wish Bob well. As they wheeled him into the operating room, Bob looked good and said, "I feel very relaxed and sleepy. I'm not worried at all. I'm surrounded by friends." Three close friends insisted on staying with me during the surgery.

Soon after Bob entered the operating room, I heard the alarm bell go off, but three other operations were going on, so I thought, "Must be someone else." Then the page came for Dr. Thomas, the medical director, and he rushed by. I still wasn't the least bit alarmed until I saw the two doctors in O.R. clothes, both with agony in their eyes.

Dr. Thomas said, "Nancy, Bob is very serious!"

"No! It can't be him!" I said. "What's the pulse?"

"The pulse is there, but no blood pressure." Both doctors, with tears streaming down their faces, hugged me.

"Go back, see if you can't do something!" I said. "Anything!" Then I got down on my knees and prayed, and my friends joined me. I prayed, "Oh, Lord, please bring him back to us," but then I remembered a missionary family who had prayed hard and wouldn't give up on their daughter. She lived, but in a persistent vegetative state for 20 years. So I prayed, "Not my will, but whatever is best for Bob."

The doctors soon returned with the sad news: "Bob is gone."

Soon our family friends Bishop Bhandare and Roy Dillener arrived and rushed to hug me. The bishop said, "I'll call the children."

And Roy, "We'll make all the arrangements."

As is the custom, the funeral was held that same evening at 5:30 p.m. We brought Bob home to Sangli from the hospital, and he lay in the SIS chapel from 11 a.m. until the service. The CNTS students sat on the left side, and the SIS students on the right. All day long they sang alternately, the girls, then the boys, hymn after hymn. It was so beautiful. People poured in to see Bob, and many came just to sit with me. Everyone was so helpful, so supportive, so loving.

At 5:30 over 2000 came to the funeral, which was a beautiful service. At the end, 16 pastors in their white robes shouldered the open coffin covered with flowers and led the procession from the campus to the cemetery. The streets were lined with people, showing their respect and sorrow. They laid him to rest as the sun was setting, Bob's favourite time of day.

On the third day, it is the Indian Christian tradition to have a short graveside service when family and a few close friends come to throw flowers. It is also a time for those who couldn't get to the funeral. For Bob, more than 1000 gathered, and the cemetery was filled—such an outpouring of love from everyone.

During the long, drawn-out court case over the church property, there had been many nasty allegations, but as I looked on the host of people at the funeral, and at the later service, I thought, "These are the true feelings of the people about Bob, no matter what they write in newspapers or say in court." The real respect and love were shown on their faces as they silently watched and wept.

At the funeral, Rev. Dillener said, "Everyone called Rev. R. P. Ramer 'Bob.' Who is Bob? Builder of Boys—he worked as an educator for 36 years at Sangli Industrial School. Builder of Buildings—so many buildings, so much care of property; he was God's steward. Builder of Beginnings for God—new churches, Sunday School work, TAFTEE [The Association for Theological Education by Extension] classes. And lastly, Bringer of Blessings." That was especially true for us, his family, to whom he brought love, laughter, vision, and challenge. Every memory of him is a blessing.

***

I very quickly heard from all our children. Tim and Jody came at once, arriving June 4. Friends had helped them obtain visas and seats on a flight to India in record time. Rob arranged to come when Jody left, then Lyn to come later. Tim made plans to stay with me until at least the end of September.

My plans were very confused. As a PCUSA wife, I was not employed, so would normally return to the U.S., but Bishop Andrews asked me to stay to help finish up things. I awaited the board's decision on this, knowing I would stay until at least the end of October. God had his everlasting arms around us. He sent me so many angels of mercy, and the support of my children meant so much. All our PCUSA officers poured out their concern. I will *always* be thankful for all their support. Half of me was gone, but I felt Bob, as always, saying, "Go on, God's grace is sufficient."

***

The children recalled that time in a later circular letter.

Jody: "Andy and I were awakened with a phone call from Delhi telling us of Dad's sudden death. Shock froze my system and I just functioned. 'Oh, my God, Andy, get Tim!' We still share a house with Tim. The rest of the night was spent weeping, walking and praying. 'How could this happen!' Working with hospice patients and their families, I knew one day this would happen. But the pain was much deeper than anything I had imagined.

"One afternoon [in Sangli] as I was helping Mangala to make lunch, she told me of the death of her sister some years ago. 'I prayed so hard that she would not die and when she died, I felt God had turned away from me. I refused to pray. One day in the middle of the night I awoke and felt I had to pray. As I was praying, God said to me in Marathi, "Dukhat ani Sukhat mazi stuti kar, mug me tumhala anand parat dein." "In sorrow and in joy worship me, and I will give you my joy again."' Along with the knowledge that we will see Dad again, this is of deepest comfort to me."

Tim: "A dear friend of ours, Mel Duncan, told of a dream he had the night of Dad's death. He saw a beautiful cottonwood tree with many trunks. He noticed that one of the main trunks had broken and fallen. In his dream he felt sad about the loss of its strength and beauty. Then he noticed that the rest of the tree was continuing to grow, and that it was still strong and beautiful. We feel this dream is a gift from God. The dream not only shows the deep loss our family feels at my Dad's death, but also gives the assurance that our family will continue to grow strong and beautiful. ... I have decided to delay medical school for a year and to spend extra time in India. This land had always been my home, but suddenly it's taken on a special significance for me, and so I would like to experience as much of it as I can while I have the opportunity."

Rob: "When I was growing up in the tumultuous atmosphere of the late 1960s and 1970s, I often got frustrated with [Dad's] incessant concern for taking care of details. He would spend hours making sure the books balanced or solving the latest staff problem in the Industrial School, but rarely spent hours talking about Vietnam or civil rights. Later I found he took peace and justice issues very seriously and studied them closely. But his method was to work hard at building concrete educational and technical programs, which would help people solve these problems in their own lives. And the way he did it was not with great flash but with the determination and discipline of working hard every day."

Lyn: "It is good to know how many people had loved Dad. Your telegram put it so well, Mum. 'Dad is with his Lord. His victory won.'"

***

Rev. Jack and Joan Seibert, our colleagues for many years in Sangli, volunteered to return for six months, so that I could go on leave. Even more important, Jack could help orient the new SIS principal. What a great relief it was to see Jack and Joan at the station in Sangli! Their joy and enthusiasm were just what we all needed. I poured all the worries onto them, took them around to see all the work, and then handed over our keys and house. I was able to walk out and leave everything to them. How do you say thanks for such a gift?

Bob's brother Phil had come to help, and he, Tim, and two others were with me in Bombay when Indira Gandhi was shot and killed by Sikh members of her security guard. Bombay was stunned, but orderly. The masses loved Indira. It was like what America experienced when John Kennedy was shot. There were many reports of dreadful rioting in north India and in the cities, but few reported the lovely things that were done. Some people in Bombay blocked half the road and made a huge portrait of

Indira out of flowers. Others made them out of coloured sand. They wrote on them, "Indira is immortal." It was in the midst of this grief that our friends saw us off from Bombay on what would be for me a short furlough to be with the children.

At the time, many people said to me, "This will be a sad Christmas," but no! How could it be? For Christmas means God came to earth. Because of Christmas, Bob is with our Lord, and we cherish Christ's promise that we will meet again, never to be parted.

Bob's memory lives on. Memorial gifts in remembrance of him went to Robert P. Ramer Memorial Fund for an endowment for SIS. The Crèche Nurses Training School was renamed for Bob.

When our family members go back to India, they visit my husband's grave, which is right next to the leprosy colony, and the leprosy people come round to meet and talk with them. It is they who take care of Bob's grave, and it is beautifully tended.

At Bob's grave

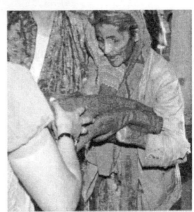

Baisibai receiving her blanket

With Rev. Tatoba Phandare

Chapter 24: One Chicken, to Go

At the end of my brief furlough, I stood in the Minneapolis/St. Paul airport with my three-month-old grandson in my arms and my daughter Jody and my sons Rob and Tim surrounding me. What a privilege it had been to be with Jody when David Robert Ramer Chrastek was born, just six months after Bob died! Now it was time to leave them all and return to Sangli to serve two more years. No longer "a missionary wife," I had been appointed a fraternal worker in my own right. Hugs, kisses, and tears, then I was on the plane.

Jack and Joan Seibert had been living in our house and carrying on Bob's and my work, so it was easy to slip back into the daily routine in Sangli. I was so thankful that I wouldn't be alone; Prakash Rubdy had become part of the family, and he would be staying with me.

When Prakash's father had been appointed director of Kindernothilfe, he moved to Delhi, but Prakash did *not* want to go. So his father, a close friend of Bob's, asked if Prakash could stay with us while he finished high school. I was glad that Prakash had stayed on with the Seiberts until I got back, so when they left, Prakash was still there with me.

An Indian engineer had been appointed as principal of SIS, so I had no responsibility for the school itself or for SIS boarding. The SIS staff asked me to continue teaching the weekly Bible class Bob had taught. The staff decided to meet in the evenings immediately after school, from 5:45 to 6:45 p.m. We were doing a TAFTEE program, which is a study by correspondence. There were discussions, arguments, and a great deal of laughter. We had tea and cookies, and often on those evenings Prakash prepared our evening meal.

God surrounded me with many ministering angels! As I thought back to that time after Bob died, events were hazy, so I searched for my prayer journal from 1985-1986. As I read my thoughts and prayers, I was amazed at the pressures, complications, and emergencies that I poured out to God in my prayers, and more amazed to see how God answered them.

One particular emergency stands out in my memory. College had started, and it was the early rainy season, hot and humid. I had just lain down after lunch for a wee nap when Yeshwant, the gardener, knocked on the door.

"What is it?"

"A man is lying on the veranda." That was not unusual; I assumed he probably wanted medicine.

"Let him lie there. I'll come in half an hour!"

"But madam Sahib, he is *really* sick, he's unconscious, and he's a European!"

Now and again we had had hippies from Europe and the U.S. drop in, stay a few days, and move on, but that was in the '60s and early '70s, not recently, so who could this be? I got up to see and, sure enough, stretched out on our veranda was a tall young man with long, scraggy blond hair and a torn waistcoat exposing chest and tummy. He had a piece of cloth serving as a loincloth. No doubt about it, he was a white person, and he was out cold. I suspected drugs, but where had he come from?

Just then Prakash came home from college, and we gave the guest some water to drink. That revived him enough to try to speak, but his speech was slurred. He kept saying something like "Christian." While I made tea and some eggs for him, Prakash and Yeshwant washed him up a bit and put Tim's pants and shirt on him. We had to hand-feed him, but he swallowed easily. He had no fever, but still couldn't talk, sit up, or walk. We made him comfortable, and I called Dr. Arun Rukedekar, the psychiatrist at our mission hospital in Miraj, who suggested we bring him to his clinic.

One thing we found out—he was speaking German! Dr. Rukedekar was able to understand that his *name* was Christian, and his home was in Austria. Dr. contacted the Austrian ambassador, who requested he be treated. After a few weeks, the Austrian embassy arranged to have two volunteer doctors come to Bombay to take Christian back to Austria. They insisted he must not be left alone, so two of our Sangli staff took him to Bombay, and delivered him to the embassy.

Christian did visit us a few times before going to Bombay, and told us that he had gone to Goa to a party. The next thing he knew, he woke up in a shack, and his belongings, even the clothes he'd worn, were gone. He stumbled out of the shack, and some beggars took him to the train station where he got on the train without a ticket! He had no food and little fluid, and soon passed out on the train. When the conductor found Christian had no ticket, he put him off the train at Sangli. Because he was white, the stationmaster told the rickshaw driver to take him to the missionaries. Seeing no one around, the driver had just dumped him on our veranda.

Incidentally, the Austrian government paid all the hospital bills, his travel costs, and other expenses, and they wrote a nice letter of appreciation to Dr. Rukedekan and to me. I often wonder who he was, and how he is now.

***

As I settled back into life in Sangli, I realised that the industrial school staff were suffering their own grief and shock. The school accountant had a nervous breakdown, and his family turned to me to make decisions for them. I wrote in my prayer journal:

"Dear Father, I need you so much. I need you to guide me. I seem to be in the middle of everything, and both sides turn to me to solve their problems. The Bishop calls so often for he is having trouble with the executive committee, the executive people come and want me to intervene. Property taxes are to be paid, and now Dr. Phansopkar, who volunteered to take charge of property management, has had a stroke. He is in bed and tries to help, but the money that is to come from Delhi isn't here yet. I keep sending telegrams and try to phone Victor. The new principal doesn't get on with his staff at the industrial school—he complains to me, and the staff complain that the principal is dishonest, etc., etc. Pastor Awale wants me to preach every Sunday in the village churches—and I have the 6 crèches, the managing of them, the Crèche Nurses Training School—Lord, how can I cope? Please, take my hand, lead me day to day. Give me your wisdom, and your love. Prakash is grieving deeply for Bob—I spend a lot of time trying to counsel him. Lord, walk with me today."

God so wonderfully upheld me and sent me his ministering angels. The Miraj family were a great support. Drs. Kalindi and Cherian Thomas, Dr. Samson and his wife Rohini, Dr. George and Irene (who didn't use their long last name), Drs. Arun and Mary Rukedekar. The last two were psychiatrists and lovingly reached out to Prakash, by playing chess with and counselling him. The others popped into the house for tea in the late afternoon, or invited us for dinner at night when I could pour out my latest worries.

My colleagues in the Crèche Nurses Training School were so sensitive, seeing to all the little details. Mrs. Nanandekar, the office manager, and Mrs. Indolikar, my secretary, took responsibility for the daily accounts of six crèches and the training school, representing 650 people to be fed and educated. I only needed to check the figures weekly. Mrs. Bhopale, principal of the CNTS, kept the curriculum going and oversaw discipline. Sister Musaji was housemother to the 30 crèche nursing students, lovingly and strictly watching over them. Mrs. Sironi, in charge of the compound crèche with 120 children, watched for my light to go on at bedtime, then slipped over to give me a massage each night.

My family wrote constant letters, and I replied with copies of a detailed letter and a personal note each week. Bob and I had announced to family, the Presbyterian board, and the church in India that we would retire June 1, 1986, when we had both reached 65, but everything had changed now that Bob was gone. Where was I to live? We had no house; all the plans we had made had gone up in smoke! The Church of North India, through the Bishop and executive committee, requested of headquarters in New York that I be allowed to continue. Fred Wilson, director of worldwide missions, said that they would be happy for me to stay on, if I was physically fit and happy, until I was 70! The staff in New York was very supportive, encouraging, and understanding, but counselled me that I should also consider my family.

Ah, there it was. All the family were encouraging me to come home, but where was home? A letter from Rob in late January said, "Come back home. You are needed in the U.S. church, too! Come back this year! It is time to start Phase II!"

But where to go? What about Prakash? The Bishop was adamant: "We need you. Bob is gone, we need your balance. We are your family. At least stay another year!"

Then Jody wrote, "Come home, your grandchildren need you. Stay in our house, send your boxes here. You always put the church first, now put yourself and us first!"

Wow, that shook me! Had I let them think that the church was more important to me than my children? I knew God was first in my life—at least I tried to do that—but not the church. After much prayer, I decided to retire, but when? Our bungalow was packed with audio-visual and film development equipment, and tools, tools, tools. And the books—theology, engineering, education, a mini-library! How could I possibly deal with all that?

Then came a telegram from Rob: "If you leave at the end of April, I will come for two weeks, help you pack, and escort you home!" Who could refuse that? So after more prayer and discussions with Drs. Kalindi and Cherian Thomas, Dr. Probarker Samson, and Dr. J.D.A. Phansopkar, I sent in my notice of retirement effective June 1, 1986, leaving India April 29. I had a month's earned leave, so would spend May in England with Lyn, Giles, and their darling new baby son.

That left two months to pack everything, have a sale, and close up the house. In that time I was expecting half a dozen visitors from Germany and the U.S. From then on my daily prayer was: "Dear Father, please help me to get strength for this day. I need help." And each day God's help was available in many quiet ways.

Rob's daughter Jessica, age nine, came to India in late February 1986, escorted to Delhi by her maternal grandfather. (Her grandparents, the Garwicks, had been Methodist missionaries in north India.) A friend flew with Jessica from Delhi to Bombay, where I met up with her for the 12-hour train trip to Sangli. I didn't know Jessica very well, but my heart went out to this wee lassie as she got off the plane. She looked so lost!

Jessica went to our English medium (language) school on the campus, and was hailed as a celebrity. Her classmates were all eager to play with her, and the crèche nurses took her to the bazaar. She and Prakash had a good amount of sibling rivalry. I tried to be with her at bedtime, meals, and as often as I could in between, but there were four women's retreats to be arranged, and CNTS year-end exams, as well as Holy Week programs to prepare.

The carpentry department made the packing boxes as Bob had taught them, and friends helped to pack and list items. Rob supervised the packing and the sale, and sold the car. Every department held a farewell function and a dinner. The Bishop arranged for the diocesan farewell to be in a mandup, a huge, open-sided, decorative tent that held chairs for 300 to 400, and well-wishers came from all the areas in the Presbytery.

After many speeches, the Bishop put a gold chain and cross around my neck, saying, "With this chain, I dedicate you to go out in God's name.

Scotland and America sent this daughter to serve us for many years. Now we in the Church of North India send you in our name to serve the church in America to the glory of God!"

The children and their mothers from the six crèches also had a gathering. I requested "no presents," but to my surprise two pre-schoolers presented me with a beautiful silk sari embroidered in gold. I gasped and said, "What a beautiful sari, but when will I ever wear it?"

"Wear it when you speak in the church in America, and tell them we all gave a bit to buy it for you because we love you." Everyone laughed, but I had tears to be wiped away!

Many, many people came to talk to me of my leaving, and I remembered them as little children at the Shantinagar Health Centre, or as village boys at the hostel, or as Sangli Industrial School students—even as anxious, young mothers having their first babies. At my last TAFTEE class, after the staff left, as I put the Bibles away, I prayed, "Lord, what will happen to them? Am I leaving forever?"

The Lord answered, "I had to leave my disciples; I had to trust my heavenly father. Let go and let God."

As I left India, so many of my dreams were unfinished, but God's were not. As I looked at the Robert Ramer Crèche Training Centre staff, I saw young women trained and capable of administration. I looked at our young crèche nurses, who had come to us feeling they were failures, and now were mothering the children, confidently organizing menus and budgets, and dreaming up new projects to interest the children. I never dreamt of such a centre—God's dreams are far greater than mine.

When I came to India in 1949, I said, "I will stay three years, no longer!" As I left 37½ years later, I said, "How richly India and God have blessed me! Praise the Lord for his living, loving, on-going plans!"

Just as we were leaving Sangli, already in the van with all our luggage, one of our leprosy patients came panting across the playing field with a live chicken in her hand. We opened the van's door, and she thrust the chicken into Jessica's hands, saying, "This is for you to take to America, or eat it on the way!"

That's my beloved India.

Epilogue

I have returned to India four times since leaving in 1986. On one such trip, I took part in the 100th birthday celebration of the area's oldest Indian pastor, Tatoba Phandare of Digraz. Phandare's memory reached back to the early missionary days at the turn of the century.

During my years in India, Christian missionaries made a commitment never to criticize another religion. Indian children on scholarship were forbidden to change their religion, lest converting to Christianity be seen as a condition of receiving an education. Knowing this, I asked Phandare, who had been born an outcaste, why he became a Christian pastor. Was it for the benefits? The pastor's salary? His reply as recorded in my circular letter of that year:

"A Presbyterian pastor's salary? No, it was very, very low. No, you can't understand what it is like to be told you have no soul, to be taught that because of past sins you have no future; that you cannot be cremated because there is no soul to escape—you are like an animal.

"Then came the missionaries to tell us that we do have a soul! That we are so precious to God that he died so that our sins are forgiven. We are free of karma! When you believe this, then you begin to experience Christ for yourself, and your joy is so great that you have to tell others. That's why I'm a Christian and a pastor!"

Nancy Orr Ramer

At 83 Nancy lives in St. Paul, Minnesota, U.S.A. where she is a frequent speaker at missionary and other church gatherings, a deacon at Macalester Plymouth United Church, a peer counsellor to the blind, and a political activist for the causes of peace and justice.

Jan Shaw-Flamm

Jan Shaw-Flamm is a freelance writer specializing in higher education and the professions. Her work includes profiles, speeches, annual reports, tributes, alumni publications, newsletters, and development materials. Clients have included Macalester College, the Minneapolis College of Art and Design, Carleton College, the University of Minnesota, the Minnesota Private College Council, St. Paul Public Schools, *Minnesota Medicine*, *Twin Cities Business Monthly*, and others. This is both her first book and her first collaborative project. Jan lives in St. Paul, Minnesota with her husband and two daughters.

Author's Acknowledgments

I am a storyteller, not a writer. Being a child of the Great Depression, a teenager nursing in World War II, then a missionary for half my life, I have many true stories to tell. My husband, family, and friends often urged me to write them down and make a book. After grandchildren arrived, I decided for *them* I'd do it, and I started to write a few chapters, but months, then years, would go by before the next chapter was attempted.

Then my friend Jan Shaw-Flamm stopped in to help me type a chapter. Jan volunteered to help "put it together for the family," but it has become much more. Jan is a freelance writer, and it is her skill and patience with my storytelling tapes, our letters, and my scribblings that has produced this book. After two years of hearing about it, Jan's friend Pat Haswell, a freelance editor, volunteered to copyedit the book. While we were pondering publication, my daughter Lyn visited from England, reminded me that as well as having a print company, they had just started Roundtuit Publishing, a joint venture publishing company, and volunteered to print and publish the book. Another friend of Jan's, cartographer Carol Barrett of CRG Digital Design, offered to work with us to develop maps, including one of our campus in Sangli, India, based solely on memory.

I am so grateful to all these wonderful people. How to say thank you is beyond my vocabulary. I must also thank Jan's family for their patience in sparing Jan's time and attention. We had a cheering squad in my family; Rob, Lyn, Jody, and Tim urged us on. Above all, my heartfelt thanks are to my Lord and Guide who has shepherded me throughout my life, allowing me to be one of his ambassadors. My thanks would not be complete without expressing my gratitude to the Presbyterian Church USA, and to the many people throughout the U.S.A. who became our Partners in Mission and supported us with letters, prayers, and friendship. As I remembered the experiences recounted in this book, I thought of the hundreds of times when in my frustration and despair, God surprised me by his wonderful answers to prayer and the "angels of mercy" he put in my way.

I hope you enjoyed reading this book. I pray that you, too, will experience the delightful surprises that God has planned for you.

Nancy Orr Ramer
June 2004

Writer's Acknowledgments

I would like to add my own thanks to Nancy's. Pat Haswell, editor par excellence, gave a wonderful gift of time and talent. Cartographer Carol Barrett dazzled us with her knowledge of maps and her ability to drive intricate software to create them.

Every client for whom I have ever worked has my gratitude, but I must especially thank Jon Halvorsen, whose direction, articulate feedback, and respectful ways make him every writer's dream editor. This is a better book because authors and teachers Susan Perry and Shannon Olson also generously share what they know.

My husband Andy and daughters Alison and Joanna advised and encouraged me, and never once suggested that I should be spending all those hours on work that came with a *paycheck*. Other friends and family, so special, but too numerous to mention, helped birth this book with their untiring interest and enthusiasm.

Nancy's family has been wonderfully supportive. I've profited from their publishing and writing advice, enjoyed generous help with photos, slides, and maps and, at working lunches, eaten food they schlepped up the stairs. It is my hope that they will soon write their own stories of the Sangli years.

Finally, Nancy. It is my extraordinary privilege to know her. Because of this book, I know the child who sailed the Atlantic alone, the young woman who nursed the sick and wounded through World War II, the faithful and hardworking missionary and mother, and the matriarch in her 80s who is more open-minded, informed, and intellectually alive than a whole roomful of younger people.

Jan Shaw-Flamm
June 2004